A SATIRE
OF THE THREE ESTATES

A Satire of The Three Estates

by

SIR DAVID LINDSAY

A play adapted by
Matthew McDiarmid
from the acting text made by
Robert Kemp
for
Tyrone Guthrie's
production at the Edinburgh
Festival 1948 with music by
Cedric Thorpe-Davie

Introduction and Notes by
Matthew McDiarmid

HEINEMANN EDUCATIONAL
BOOKS LTD · LONDON

Heinemann Educational Books Ltd

LONDON EDINBURGH MELBOURNE TORONTO

SINGAPORE JOHANNESBURG AUCKLAND

IBADAN HONG KONG NAIROBI

NEW DELHI

ISBN 0 435 23540 0

This version first published 1967

Reprinted 1970

Published by
Heinemann Educational Books Ltd
48 Charles Street, London W1X 8AH
Printed and bound in Great Britain by
Bookprint Limited, Crawley, Sussex

CONTENTS

INTRODUCTION

The Author

Sir David Lindsay was born in 1486 on his father's estate, the Mount, in Monimail parish, Fife, the county which contained the metropolitan seat of the Scottish Church, St Andrews, and where the movement for ecclesiastical reform was strongest. Where he received his education is not known, but before 1511 a place had been found for him at the court. In that year, the Treasurer's Accounts tell us, he performed in an interlude at Holyrood Abbey, wearing a 'play-coit' of blue and yellow taffeta. After the king's death in the battle of Flodden (1513) he was appointed gentleman-usher to the infant James V, a post which he lost with the coming to power of the Earl of Angus in 1524 and regained with the young king's escape from the earl's tutelage four years later.

It seems to have been his experience in these years of government by a self-seeking faction that made him commence as a poet and satirist, for his first and best poems, *The Dreme*, his *Complaint* and *The Papyngo*, were written at this time and make all the criticisms of the nation's state that were to be voiced more extremely and powerfully in his play.

From 1530 he was one of the king's heralds and about 1542 received his knighthood and appointment as chief herald, Lyon King of Arms, in which capacity he went on various embassies – to the Emperor Charles V at Brussels, to Francis I at Paris, to Henry VIII at London and to the King of Denmark. As a herald he had the opportunity to develop the remarkable sense of dramatic spectacle that is displayed in the *Satire*: one of his duties was to supervise the pageants and other formal entertainments of the court, and he is known to have composed the masque which welcomed the newly arrived queen, Marie de Lorraine, to St Andrews in 1538. It seems likely also that the first version of the

7

Satire, played before the king and queen in Linlithgow Palace on Twelfth Night 1540, was occasioned by James's temporary wish to conciliate England and the Scots party of reform. The daring of its political and ecclesiastical criticisms and their reported acceptableness to the king can hardly be explained otherwise.

James's motives, however, do not reflect any ambiguity in Lindsay's reforming attitude. This was soon displayed in the most partisan way. Provoked by English aggression the government soon reverted to an anti-reform policy , which was not halted by the rout of Solway Moss and the king's consequent death (1542) but intensified under the direction of Cardinal Beaton. When the cardinal was assassinated in 1546 in his castle at St Andrews, where two months earlier he had watched the burning of George Wishart for heresy, Lindsay published his detestation of the dead man in a poetical 'tragedie' and visited the murderers in the seized castle. Only such considerations as his personal prestige and the government's need to temporize in a threatening situation can have allowed him to retain his official post. In 1552 he presented his play in a much expanded and much more trenchant form at the Castle Hill of Cupar in Fife, and in 1554 it was performed at Edinburgh before the Queen-Regent herself. Lindsay died in the following year.

His final theological position, Protestant or Roman Catholic, is still a matter of debate. His contempt for the hierarchy of his day is not. His approach to the issues of reform was indeed not so much that of the theologian as the practical moralist, and his criticism was not aimed only at the Church as such but at 'Covetice' as practised by all three of the governing Estates. His subject was justice in the commonwealth, and it may be said that his moral concern is less with the private than the public relations of men. That he was no Puritan, in the common sense of that term, is evidenced not only by his play but also by the delightfully human account that he wrote, only two years before, of the love affair of a deceased friend, William Meldrum – he had too lively a sense of humour and too realistic an appreciation of the appeal of Lady Sensuality.

A Satire of the Three Estates is known to us from three sources: an eye-witness's detailed report of the Linlithgow version of 6 January 1540; George Bannatyne's transcript of 'only Sertane mirry Interludes thairof', derived from the Cupar play of 7 June 1552; and Robert Charteris's 1602 edition, which reflects its performance on the Greenside at Edinburgh, 12 August 1554. The two texts that concern the editor do not differ significantly where they can be compared. The edition shows lengthening of a few lines and some unimportant verbal changes but no serious attempt at revision – Douglas Hamer's statement that the character of the Prioress has been introduced overlooks the testimony of his own comparative texts (vol. 2, p. 132). It is necessarily Charteris's Quarto that is mainly followed in the present text, but the evident interference of Anglicizing printers in some instances has encouraged the present editor to prefer some of the earlier readings.

What is published here is not everything that Lindsay wrote but, with some additions that will be noted, the inspired selection of lines made by Robert Kemp for Tyrone Guthrie's celebrated Edinburgh Festival production of 1948, which discovered the dramatic merits of this liveliest and most interesting of pre-Elizabethan dramas. Their selection omitted very little in the action or speeches of the *Satire* that was essential to the significance or effect intended by Lindsay. His own Edinburgh production, according to Charteris, lasted nine hours, and though very lengthy intervals are obviously included in this reckoning, the total text represents a duration of entertainment that few modern audiences would find acceptable. Considerable cuts therefore were required, yet it was possible to make them in the way described. The mere repetitiousness and comparative irrelevance of some of the matter that so prolonged a spectacle imposed upon its provider, could be cut without much loss of meaning – thus the unactable obscenity of the Pardoner's devil's ceremony of divorce between a cobbler and his wife (referred to in my note to. l. 1498), that delighted an idling crowd between serious scenes, was left out; as also a somewhat lengthy model sermon, and a recital of proposed Acts of Parliament that had already been implicitly or explicitly recommended in the play; the part of Common Theft; and finally the *sermon joyeux* of Folly, which concluded the performance by farcically rehearsing criticisms already made.

This last excision has been accepted, though it helps to clarify an aspect of Lindsay's conception of the action that should be clear enough elsewhere but has been generally overlooked by critics. The editor has departed, however, from the Festival arrangement in certain instances[1] – in allowing Theft to come on and be hanged, since the Border reiver's farewell speech appeared too significant a part of Lindsay's social panorama to be omitted; in letting Covetice make his momentary but meaningful appearance; in giving something more of the comic interlude of Chastity and the Craftsmen, a little more of the Pardoner's scene, and a few more of the absurdly self-revealing speeches of the members of Spirituality.

The major change has been a scrupulous return to the words of Lindsay – except for the half-dozen cases where 'if' has been substituted for 'gif' and 'to' for 'till'. Since this text is intended, however, for the student of literature and not phonology, the spelling has often been brought nearer to the more familiar one of later Scots poetry, though usually in such a way as to render Lindsay's sounds approximately.

The stage directions of the Festival producers, which reflect Lindsay's intentions and often merely amplify his own, have been retained in italics, as also the two sixteenth-century Scots songs which appropriately supplied the ones missing from the extant texts. Difficult words are glossed for the reader's convenience, while the longer notes will provide the fuller comprehension of the text needed by students.

[1] Lines inserted by the editor are indicated by the initial M in the notes on pages facing the text.

The worthwhile result of this editorial procedure is that Lindsay's masterpiece is presented in an acting version that speaks only his language and gives a just idea of his dramatic intention and achievement.[2]

Commentary

Dunbar and Lindsay both mention the 'farses and plesand plays' enacted at the Scots court but these have not come down to us, and the three lonely descriptions of plays previous to the *Satire* are not of court productions. One is of a Passion play, composed in 1535 by a Friar John Kyllour, for a Perth audience, that is said by John Knox to have sharply criticized the religious hierarchy; the others, with the same intention, are a tragedy of 'John the Baptist' and a comedy of 'Dionysius the Tyrant', written by James Wedderburn and acted about 1540 at the West Port and play-field of Dundee. Their agreement with Lindsay's play in respect of purpose and out-of-doors staging illustrates the peculiarly propagandist and popular turn that Scots drama had taken in these years. The *Satire* is thus very much a play 'of the people and for the people', a fact that accounts for much of its abounding vigour. How much it benefited from this popular address is made clear when it is compared with the very different form that it took at its first production in Linlithgow Palace. The comparison indeed provides the best means of appreciating the peculiar nature and quality of Lindsay's dramatic achievement.

The Twelfth Night interlude of 1540 was more or less correctly so described by its reporter. It was a simple 'morality' piece with conventional comic elements, presenting ten characters – Solace, the merry Prologue; a king flattered by three courtiers, Placebo,

[2] For further study readers are referred to the useful editions of Douglas Hamer, *The Works of Sir David Lindsay* (Scottish Text Society, 4 vols., 1931–6), and James Kinsley, *Ane Satyre of the Thrie Estaits* (Cassell & Co., Ltd., 1954); also to the historic accounts of the Edinburgh production given by Tyrone Guthrie and Robert Kemp in their prefaces to Kemp's version, *The Satire of The Three Estates* (William Heinemann Ltd, 1951). For Kemp's Scots version see *The Scots Review*, 1948.

Pickthank and Flattery; a Poor Man who complained of being beggared by the courtiers, of suffering from the exactions of Church law and custom, of the lechery of priests, and who reminded his royal auditor that 'all erthely kings are but officers'; a learned Doctor, Experience, who confirmed the allegations of Poor Man, exposed the scandalous behaviour of nuns, and discoursed on the true office of a bishop; a Man of Arms, representing the nobility, who combined with a Burgess to support Poor Man against a wrathful Bishop who threatened him with death; the whole discourse being concluded by the apparently hitherto silent king's approving the proposed reforms. This dramatic sermon seems to have been preached with Sir David's characteristic vigour, for the Scots eye-witness asserted that after the performance James threatened to send his bishops to his less tolerant uncle in England if they did not mend their ways. Its limited cast and want of action, however, must have precluded any hint of the panoramic vitality, the range of entertainment and criticism, that was exhibited at the Castle Hill of Cupar to an audience of Fifeshire lairds, farmers, townsmen, and their women-folk. Specifically the reader of the *Satire* will reflect how much better qualified as a Prologue is the herald, Diligence – a rôle possibly taken by Lindsay himself; how slight a part is given to the first play-king; how much life came in with the three Vices; how much more significant a conception is John the Commonweal than Poor Man, who is none the less allowed to stay and make his memorable speech; how comparatively lonely and ineffectual a representative of Spirituality the wrathful Bishop of the first version must have been; and finally, though the reader may not feel that he would greatly have missed the good sisters Chastity and Verity – Chastity's comic plight is another matter – he will certainly welcome the splendid figure of Lady Sensuality.

Also, the later play is not only more various in its characters and scenes; it presents a developing moral action in two Parts or movements, successively set in court and parliament – though there is, of course, only one setting, the stage of Lindsay's imagination, where very uncourtly and very unparliamentary figures

present themselves without any effect of incongruity or interruption.

In Part I young King Humanity, as Diligence has foretold,
sleeps in the arms of Lady Sensuality till Divine Correction rouses
him rudely to his duty of reform. He has been led there by wanton
courtiers, and now it is the opportunity of the three Vices (fools)
Flattery, Deceit and Falset, to introduce misrule. The first of them
is a kind of comic devil who flatters the fool in every man. He sees
to it that grey-bearded Good Counsel does not come near the
king, helps Sensuality to ward off Chastity, and persuades the
Spirituality to accuse Verity (True Religion) of being a heretic.
But now Divine Correction enters and the Vices flee, Flattery
and Sensuality to the protection of Spirituality. They will be
sought out and exposed there by the parliament that is now
summoned.

In Part II Diligence is about to make his proclamation when he
is interrupted by the complaints of Poor Man, beggared by
the seizure of his mare and cows. Flattery, now a friar and
pardoner, tries to sell him remission of his pains in the next world
but what Poor Man wants is his livelihood in this one. Flattery is
chased off but returns with the other Vices when the Three
Estates enter 'gangand backwart'. Spirituality is dismayed by the
king's intention of reform, still more so by the sudden appearance
of John the Commonweal, who identifies the Vices, so that they
are arrested, along with Lady Sensuality and Covetice. Its members have now to listen to John's charges of injustice and corruption. When a counter-charge of heresy fails, they are investigated
and found to be fools. Only the indestructible Flattery escapes
punishment, characteristically by helping to hang his mates. He
ends the play's action with a gleeful remembrance of how

> I beguilet all the Three Estates
> With my hypocrisy.

How inadequate as a description of the play any such outline
of the argument must be, the reader, still more the auditor,
will easily discover. It is the auditor who will soonest learn how

extravagantly vital are these morality characters, or rather caricatures, and how impressively human a spectacle this formal extravaganza presents. He will best appreciate how central are the rôles of Lady Sensuality and Flattery, how much the king of the first part and the Spirituality of the second are their puppets and fools. It is indeed a play of fools. Too much has been made of its religious and propagandist meaning. That it has such a meaning is undeniable, as undeniable as the social and spiritual abuses of which Lindsay complained. In that respect he says only what the orthodox chroniclers, men like John Mair, John Bellenden and the Franciscan, Adam Abel, had already said; it is the vehemence of his anti-clericalism – his Protestantism is arguable – that distinguishes his attack. As has been remarked, he was more the critic of a corrupt commonwealth than of an established religion and, as we shall see, his attitude was not simply that of the indignant moralist.

Beyond the theme of reform is Lindsay's other theme, one traditional to the 'sottie' or fool-play, that the number of fools is infinite and of folly there is no end: Lady Sensuality is always attractive, flattery of the self is endless, and therefore so also are error and injustice; and all these have their unfailing, tragi-comic source in humanity. It is this imaginative awareness of an essentially foolish world that one must yet try to reform into some shape of dignity, that makes Lindsay's play something more than a smart piece of Reformist propaganda. Since it is great folly and not great villainy that he exposes he gives to each object of attack a farcical vitality and human significance that frees the *Satire* from the flat and factual categories of the morality drama. Critical neglect of his real intention and consequent misunderstanding of his achievement, even when Tyrone Guthrie's performance had discovered it so brilliantly, is perhaps due to a mistaken notion that such an interpretation pertained only to the production; yet it is clear enough in Lindsay's text, and particularly in the 'sermon joyeux' of Folly – perhaps unactable nowadays and necessarily omitted in this edition – that he tacked onto his play as a kind of epilogue-commentary.

The problem of making a single story of his panoramic vision of folly gleefully disrupting a divinely ordered society was solved by Lindsay in the way that we have seen. The lively presence on the stage of the Three Estates for the greater part of the action, and the continued activity of Lady Sensuality and especially the three Vices in both Parts, secured the necessary impression of unity. The feeling for the stage that Guthrie discovered everywhere in Lindsay made him keep up a lively alternation of the grave and the gay in his action and talk. Perhaps the most remarkable single evidence of his dramatic flare, however, is the effectiveness of his many verse-forms as a means of expressing his theme. There is a variety of this sort in *Everyman* and indeed in all the moralities and miracle plays, but the *Satire* is a metrical medley. Grave stanzaic patterns, varying with the effect intended, express the aspect of order, as in the opening invocation of Diligence and young King Humanity's prayer for guidance, or parody the anti-order, as in Lady Sensuality's splendid self-advertisement; while several kinds of quick-moving patterns convey the absurdity of Spirituality and the Vices – Flattery bounds onto the stage with a clatter of rhyme and the Prioress declares for freedom and marriage in verse that sounds like a jig. The two main differences of effect are something like that between the stately pavane and the brisk French 'brawl' mentioned in the play.

This technique of various formality gives a very simple but impressive emphasis to the significant contrasts; the serious becomes the ceremoniously serious and the foolery is that of the professional fool. The opposites of Reason and Unreason are thus mutually enhanced. It is these extreme contrasts that create the extraordinary life of the play – as between the fantastic triviality of Flattery's salesmanship as a Pardoner and the distressing matter-of-factness of Poor Man's 'speech of the black verity'. Burns's *Jolly Beggars* achieves its 'life-and-go' by somewhat similar means. A play with such a theme and such a technique is perhaps best appreciated in the terms of paradox; it is one of the most brilliant examples of our serious theatre of the absurd.

MATTHEW P. MCDIARMID

15

DRAMATIS PERSONAE

DILIGENCE, a herald
KING HUMANITY
WANTONNESS ⎫
PLACEBO ⎬ courtiers
SOLACE ⎭
LADY SENSUALITY
HAMELINESS ⎫ her maidens
DANGER ⎭
FUND-JONET, a bawd
GOOD COUNSEL
FLATTERY ⎫
FALSET ⎬ vices
DECEIT ⎭
VERITY True Religion
BISHOP
ABBOT
CHASTITY
PRIORESS

PARSON
LORD
MERCHANT
SOUTAR, cobbler
TAILOR
JENNIE, the Tailor's daughter
SOUTAR'S WIFE
TAILOR'S WIFE
VARLET
DIVINE CORRECTION
POOR MAN
WILKIN, the Pardoner's boy
JOHN THE COMMONWEAL
FIRST SERGEANT
SECOND SERGEANT
COVETICE
SCRIBE
THEFT *or* COMMON THEFT

1–13	Stanzaic arrangement and alliterative cadence are generally characteristic of the introductions to the miracle plays and are here used for formal effect.
4	*bales*, pains.
6	*haily*, holy.
8	*seasit*, seated.
11	*shawn*, shown.
12	'Sovereigns' or 'Sirs' were common modes of addressing the more important, seated members of an audience.
14	*tent*, heed; *coy*, quiet.
14–44	announce the coming of Divine Correction and the summoning of a parliament of reform, though this will not take place till the 'sleepand' years of King Humanity, that occasioned 'misrule', have been illustrated in Part I.
17	*the whilk*, who.
18	*but variance*, truly.
24	*rung*, reigned; *thir*, these.
25	*innocents . . . beirs.* David Straton and Norman Gourlay in 1534 and George Wishart in 1546 had been burned for heresy. In Lindsay's eyes they were not heretics.

PART ONE

There is a fanfare of trumpets and the members of the THREE
ESTATES *of the Realm of Scotland enter. They are the* SPIRITU-
ALITY *or Bishops, the* TEMPORALITY *or Barons and the*
BURGESSES, *who are Merchants. They make their way on to the*
stage through the audience.

DILIGENCE: The Father, founder of faith and felicity,
That your fashion formit to his similitude;
And his Son, your Saviour, shield in necessity,
That bocht you from bales, ransonit on the Rood,
Re-pledgand his prisoners with his heart-blude;
The Haily Gaist, governor and grounder of grace,
Of wisdom and weilfare baith fountain and flude,
Save you all that I see seasit in this place,
   And shield you from sin,
And with His Spreit you inspire   10
Til I have shawn my desire!
Silence, Sovereigns, I require,
   For now I begin!

People, tak tent to me, and hauld you coy!
Here am I sent to you, a messenger,
From a noble and richt redoubtit Roy,
The whilk has been absent this mony a year,
Wha bade me shaw to you, but variance,
That he intends amang you to compear,
With a triumphant awful ordinance,   20
With croun and sword and sceptre in his hand,
Tempert with mercy when penitence appears.
Howbeit that he lang time has been sleepand,
Where-through misrule has rung thir mony years,
And innocents been brocht upon their biers

26   *reporters*, informers.

31   *The Three Estatis.* The ecclesiastical hierarchy, the nobility, the burgh representatives, made a full sitting of the Scots parliament; the burgesses were chiefly consulted on matters of finance and property, but it is less the actual functioning of parliament than the representative classes of the country that Lindsay has in mind, hence the later appearance of John the Commonweal and Poor Man.

37   *famous*, worthy

51   *ane*, one.

By false reporters of this natioun,
Thocht young oppressors at the elder leirs
Be now well sure of reformatioun! (*A fanfare.*)
And here by open proclamatioun,
I warn in name of his magnificence   30
The Three Estatis of this natioun,
That they compear with debtful diligence
And to his Grace mak their obedience.
And first I warn the Sprituality,
And see the Burgess spare not for expense,
But speed them here with Temporality!

As DILIGENCE *names them,* SPIRITUALITY, TEMPORALITY
and the MERCHANTS *take their places.* DILIGENCE *turns to the*
audience again.

Als I beseek you, famous auditors,
Conveent into this congregatioun,
To be patient the space of certain hours,
Till ye have heard our short narratioun.   40
And als we mak you supplicatioun
That no man tak our words into disdain,
Howbeit ye hear by lamentatioun,
The Common-Weal richt piteously complain.
Prudent people, I pray you all,
Tak no man grief in special;
For we sall speak in general,
    For pastime and for play.
Therefore, till all our rhymes be rung,
And our mis-tonit sangs be sung,   50
Let every man keep weill ane tongue,
    And every woman tway!

A Fanfare and March. Young KING HUMANITY *enters with his*
train, chief among whom are two lighthearted courtiers, WANTON-
NESS *and* PLACEBO. *The* ESTATES *sing* 'Salve, rex humanitatis.'
The KING *kneels before his throne.*

KING: O Lord of lords, and King of kingis all,
    Omnipotent of power, Prince but peer,

55   *ringand*, reigning.

57   *heaven . . . clear.* The Ptolemaic cosmography as described in the contemporary *Complaynte of Scotland* included a celestial region or heaven containing the planetary spheres, and an elementary or sublunar one composed of four elements, earth, water, air, fire.

68   *thy pleasure.* The theme of Part I is King Humanity's failure to prefer God's pleasure or will to his own.

70   *gars*, causes; *sic*, such.

74   *ocht*, aught.

75   *ban*, curse.

77   *Placebo*, Latin, 'I will be pleasing'; the name of the flattering friend in Chaucer's *Merchant's Tale*, who encourages the amorous inclinations of old January.

84   *rout*, company.

87   *the Mess*, the Mass

89   *shent*, undone.

Eterne, ringand in gloir celestial,
Unmade Maker, wha havand na matteir,
Made heaven and earth, fire, air and water clear,
Send me thy grace with peace perpetual,
That I may rule my realm to thy pleaseir,
Syne bring my saul to joy angelical.   60
I thee requeist, wha rent was on the Rood,
Me to defend from deedis of defame,
That my people report of me but good,
And be my safeguard baith from sin and shame.
I knaw my days endures but as a dream;
Therefore, O Lord, I heartly thee exhort,
To give me grace to use my diadeam
To thy pleasure and to my great comfort.
The KING *takes his seat on the throne.*

WANTONNESS: My Sovereign Lord and Prince but peer,
What gars you mak sic dreary cheer?   70
Be blithe sa lang as ye are here,
    And pass time with pleasure:
For as lang lives the merry man
As the sorry, for ocht he can.
His banes full sair, sir, sall I ban
    That does you displeasure.
Sa lang as Placebo and I
Remains into your company,
Your grace sall live richt merrily,
    Of this have ye na doubt!   80
Sa lang as ye have us in cure,
Your grace, sir, sall want na pleasure:
Were Solace here, I you assure,
    He wald rejoice this rout!

PLACEBO: Good brother mine, where is Solace,
The mirror of all merriness?
I have great marvel, by the Mess,
    He tarryis sa lang.
Bide he away, we are but shent!

23

90   *ferly*, wonder.

99   *berial*, jewel.
100   *preclair*, loveliest.

104   *fleyit*, frightened.
105   *thrang*, crowd.

111   *quart*, quart-pot.
113   *nippit*, scant.
113–20   M. (see Introduction, page 11).
114   *hippit*, hipped, bodied.

117   *thocht*, though.
118   *preen*, pin.
119   *Peebles On The Green*, a poem sometimes attributed to James I, but in fact dating from no earlier than the close of the fifteenth century. Solace's hope of reward for services is as absurd as the ridiculous events of the rustic celebration at Peebles that the poem describes.
122   *sirs* (see note to 12), addressed to the audience.

I ferly how he fra us went.
I trow he has impediment
   That lettis him nocht gang.
WANTONNESS: I left Solace, that same great loon,
  Drinkand into the borough's toun –
  It will cost him half of a croun
   Althocht he had na mair!
  And als he said he wald gang see
  Fair Lady Sensuality,
  The berial of all beauty
   And portraiture preclair.
Enter SOLACE, *the third Courtier, running.*
PLACEBO: By God, I see him at the last,
  As he were chasit, rinnand richt fast;
  He glowrs, even as he were agast,
   Or fleyit of a gaist.
SOLACE, *drunk, at first addresses the audience.*
SOLACE: Wow! Wha saw ever sic a thrang!
  Methocht some said I had gane wrang.
  Had I help, I wald sing a sang
   With a richt merry noise!
  I have sic pleasure at my heart
  That gars me sing the treble part.
  Wald some good fellow fill the quart,
   That would my heart rejoice!
  Howbeit my coat be short and nippit,
  Thanks be to God I am weill hippit,
  Thocht all my gold may soon be grippit
   Into a penny purse.
  Thocht I a servant lang has been,
  My purchase is nocht worth a preen.
  I may sing Peebles On The Green
   For ocht that I may turse.
  What is my name? Can ye nocht guess?
  Sirs, ken ye nocht Sandy Solace?
  They callit my mother Bonny Bess,

124   *between the Bows.* A sexual *double entendre;* the 'Bows' were the burgh gateways.

125   *swyve,* copulate.

128   *mows,* joke

129   *speir,* ask.

131   *play-fere,* play-fellow.

136   *ring,* reign.

139   *fery-fary,* confusion.

144   *advance,* praise.

157   *what rack (of),* what matters.

That dwellt between the Bows.
Of twelve year auld she learned to swyve;
Thankit be the great god alive,
She made me fathers four or five –
   But doubt, this is na mows!
And if I lie, sirs, ye may speir.
But saw ye nocht the King come here?   130
I am a sporter and play-fere
   To that young King.
He said he wald, within short space,
To pass his time come to this place –
I pray to God to give him grace
   And lang to ring!

KING: My servant Solace, what gart ye tarry?
SOLACE *suddenly sees him.*

SOLACE: I wot not, sir, by sweet Sant Mary;
I have been in a fery-fary
   Or else into a trance!   140
Sir, I have seen, I you assure,
The fairest earthly crëature
That ever was formit by nature
   And maist for to advance.
To look on her is great delight,
With lippis reid and cheikis white.
I wald renunce all this warld quite
   To stand into her grace!
She is wanton and she is wise,
And cled she is in the new guise –   150
It would gar all your flesh uprise
   To look upon her face!
Were I a king, it suld be kend,
I sould not spare on her to spend
And this same nicht for her to send
   For my pleasure!
What rack of your prosperitie,
If ye want Sensuality!

169   *till*, to.

171   *Tanquam tabula rasa*, 'as it were a tablet clear of writing', hence 'Ready for good and ill'.

179–80   *a young ... deil*, they will virtuously help him to sow his wild oats when he is young, since everyone knows 'there's na deil like an auld deil'.

180   *syne*, then, afterwards.

184   *whilk*, which; *lemand*, shining.

187   *Chastity*, the personage who appears later in the play.

I wald nocht give a silly flie
  For your treasure! 160
KING: Forsooth, my friends, I think ye are not wise,
  To counsel me to break commandëment
  Direckit by the Prince of Paradise;
  Considering ye knaw that mine intent
  Is for to be to God obedient,
  Wha does forbid men to be lecherous.
  Do I nocht sa, perchance I sall repent.
  Therefore I think your counsel odious
    The whilk ye gave me till,
  Because I have been to this day 170
  Tanquam tabula rasa,
    Ready for good and ill.
PLACEBO: Believe ye that we will beguile you,
  Or from your vertue we will wile you,
  Or with evil counsel for to file you?
    Baith into good and evil
  To tak your grace's part we grant,
  In all your deeds participant,
  Sa that ye be nocht a young sant
    And syne an auld deil. 180
WANTONNESS: Believe ye, sir, that lechery be sin?
  Na, trow nocht that! This is my reason why:
  First at the Roman Court will ye begin,
  Whilk is the lemand lamp of lechery,
  Where cardinals and bishops generally
  To luve ladies they think a pleasant sport,
  And out of Rome has banist Chastity,
  Wha with our prelates can get na resort.
SOLACE: Sir, while ye get a prudent queen,
  I think your Majesty serene 190
  Sould have a lusty concubene
    To play you withall:
  For I ken, by your quality,
  Ye want the gift of chastity.

in nomine Domini, 'in God's name'. The play's free use of religious oaths reflects common speech but is also meant to illustrate current superstition and ignorance, and here makes a comment on Wantonness's counsel.

207   *the monks of Balmerino*. This monastery was in east Fife. The reason for the special reference is not known.

213   *Kaity*, mistress.

214   *bummilbaty*, fool.

215   *Omnia probate*, 'prove all things', Saint Paul's injunction (1 *Thessalonians*, v. 21) misapplied.

217   *awauk*, awake.

217–37   Hamer, in his edition, describes Sensuality as 'the type of court prostitute', but she does not specially belong to the Court. She is 'the perfite pattern of plesance', as Placebo later describes her, and along with Covetice embodies the practical religion of the governing classes. The 'fiery sphere' is the sun and a reference is intended to the conventional May morning of courtly love poetry.

218   *the natural dochter of Venus*, the true-born daughter of Venus. In Scots Law 'natural' meant 'legitimate'.

222   *mak to Venus observance*, 'perform the rites of love', a phrase common in Chaucer.

223   *chaumer*, chamber

Fall to, *in nomine Domini!*
   For this is my counsel!
I speak, sir, under protestatioun
That nane at me have indignatioun,
For all the prelates of this natioun,
   For the maist part   200
They think na shame to have a hure,
And some has three under their cure –
This to be true I'll you assure
   Ye sall wit efterwart.
Sir, knew ye all the matter through,
   To play ye wald begin.
Speir at the monks of Balmerino
   If lechery be sin!
PLACEBO: Sir, send furth Sandy Solace
   Or else your minion Wantonness,   210
And pray my Lady Prioress
   The sooth to declare,
If it be sin to tak a Kaity,
Or to live like a Bummilbaty.
The book says '*Omnia probate*',
   And nocht for to spare!
Music. LADY SENSUALITY *enters with her attendants,* HAMELI-NESS, DANGER, FUND-JONET. *They take up their position at the end of the stage remote from the* KING *and his courtiers, who do not see them.*
SENSUALITY: Luvers awauk! Behauld the fiery sphere,
Behauld the natural dochter of Venus!
Behauld, luvers, this lusty lady clear,
The fresh fountain of knichtis amorous,   220
Replete with joys, dulce and delicious.
Or wha wald mak to Venus observance
In my mirthful chaumer melodious,

226   *hals*, neck.

228   Contraries suggest each other. Lydgate's 'Testament', Part 5, has a long series of lines with 'Behold', each indicating a torment of Christ.

235   *towart*, kindly.

243   *Danger*. In the allegory of the *Roman de la Rose* Danger, signifying prudent coyness or 'standoffishness', obstructed the lover in his pursuit of the Rose. Lindsay's Danger, asking for the support of Fund-Jonet, only affects coyness; her sister, Hameliness (Familiarity) does not trouble to affect it.

245   *Fund-Jonet*, literally, 'Foundling-Jonet'. Hamer, mis-deriving 'Jonet' from 'gennet', a Spanish horse, describes her as 'a male assistant'. She is the Vekke, or go-between, of the *Roman de la Rose*, now frankly appearing as a bawd. She has taught Danger and Hameliness their business and has the conventional hoarse voice of the profession. Her girls would often be foundlings. Jonet is one of the most common of names among Scotswomen of that time.

248   *hass*, hoarse.

257   *japing*, copulating.

There sall they find all pastime and pleasance.
Behauld my heid, behauld my gay attire,
Behauld my hals, luvesome and lily-white;
Behauld my visage flammand as the fire,
Behauld my paps, of portrature perfite!
To look on me luvers has great delight;
Richt sa has all the kings of Christendom –   230
To them I have done pleasures infinite
And specially unto the Court of Rome.
Ae kiss of me were worth in a morning,
A million of gold to knicht or king.
And yet I am of nature sa towart
I let na luver pass with a sair heart.
Of my name, wald ye wit the verity,
Forsooth they call me Sensuality.
I hauld it best now, or we farther gang,
To Dame Venus let us go sing a sang   240
HAMELINESS: Madame, but tarrying
We sall fall to and sing.
Sister Danger, come near!
DANGER: Sister, sing this sang I may not
Without the help of good Fund-Jonet.
Fund-Jonet, ho! Come tak a part!
FUND-JONET: That sall I do with all my heart!
Sister, howbeit that I am hass,
I am content to beir a bass.
Ye twa sould love me as your life –   250
Ye knaw I learned you baith to swyve
In my chaumer, ye wot weill where.
Sensyne the fiend a man ye spare!
HAMELINESS: Fund-Jonet, fie, ye are to blame!
To speak foul words, think ye na shame?
FUND-JONET: There is a hunder here sittand by
That loves japing as weill as I,
Micht they get it in privity.
But wha begins the sang, let see!

260   *daws*, dawns.

260   The song is supplied here by verses of Alexander Mont-
gomerie (c. 1550–c. 1598), the most prominent Scots poet at
the close of the sixteenth century. His song is for May, the
traditional season of love, and was appropriately introduced
in the Edinburgh Festival production, Lindsay's song not
having been preserved.

262   *shroudes*, put on their (green) clothing; *shaws*, woods.

264   *thrissel-cock*, male thrush.

266   *skailes*, clear.

269   *gowans*, daisies.

270   *lowe*, fire.

271   *roan*, rowan

278   *hiech*, high; *turses*, carry; *tynds*, horns.

280   *hurcheons*, hedge-hogs.

289   *maiks*, loves.

Hey, now the day daws,
The jolly cock craws,
Now shroudes the shaws
   Through Nature anon.
The thrissel-cock cries
On lovers that lies,
Now skailes the skies,
   The nicht is near gone.

The fieldis owerflows
With gowans that grows,
Where lilies like lowe is,
   As reid as the roan;
The turtle that true is,
With notes that renews,
Her party pursues,
   The nicht is near gone.

Now hartis with hinds,
Conform to their kinds,
Hiech turses their tynds
   On ground where they groan,
Now hurcheons, with hares,
Aye passes in pairs,
Whilk duly declares
   The nicht is near gone.

The season excels
Through sweetness that smells;
Now Cupid compels
   Our heartis each one,
On Venus wha wakes,
To muse on our maiks,
Then sing for their sakes
   The nicht is near gone.

304   *lyre*, face.

308-15   M.
310   *lair*, lore.

312   *cokks*, God's.

325   *tithands*, tidings.

During the singing of the song the KING *and his court see* SEN-
SUALITY *and her party.*

KING: Up, Wantonness, thou sleeps too lang!
    Methocht I heard a merry sang.
    I thee command in haste to gang
      See what yon mirth may mean.

WANTONNESS: I trow, sir, by the Trinity,
    Yon same is Sensuality,
    If it be she, soon sall I see
      That sovereign serene!

PLACEBO: Sir, she is mekill to advance,   300
    For she can baith play and dance,
    That perfite pattern of pleasance,
      A pearl of pulchritude!
    Saft as the silk is her white lyre,
    Her hair is like the golden wire,
    My heart burns in a flame of fire!
    I sweir you by the Rood,
    I think that free sa wonder fair,
    I wot weill she has na compair!
    War ye weill lernit at luve's lair,   310
      And syne had her seen,
    I wot, by cokks passioun,
    Ye wald mak supplicatioun,
    And spend on her a millioun,
      Her luve to obtene.

SOLACE: What say ye, sir? Are ye content
    That she come here incontinent?
    What vails your kingdom and your rent
      And all your great treasure,
    Without ye have a merry life,   320
    And cast aside all sturt and strife?
    And sa lang as ye want a wife,
      Sir, tak your pleasure!

KING: Forsooth, I wot not how it stands,
    But since I heard of your tithands

347   *deid*, death.

349   *fary*, busy.

351   M.

355   M. *back or edge*, decided one way or the other, perhaps referring to the 'flat or edge' of a sword.

My body trimmles, feet and hands,
  And whiles is het as fire!
I trow Cupido with his dart
Has woundit me out-through the heart;
My spreit will fra my body part,   330
  Get I nocht my desire!
Pass on, away, with diligence,
And bring her here to my presence!
Spare nocht for travel nor expense,
  I care nocht for na cost!
Pass on your way soon, Wantonness,
And tak with you Sandy Solace,
And bring that Lady to this place,
  Or else I am but lost!
Commend me to that sweetest thing,   340
Present her with this same rich ring,
And say I lie in languishing,
  Except she mak remede!
With siching sair I am but shent
Without she come incontinent,
My heavy langour to relent
  And save me now fra deid!
WANTONNESS: Doubt ye nocht, sir, but we will get her.
  We shall be fary for to fet her.
But, faith, we wald speed all the better,   350
  Had we a bag for wage!
SOLACE: Sir! Let na sorrow in you sink,
  But give us ducats for to drink,
  And we sall never sleep a wink
    Till it be back or edge.
The KING *gives them a purse.*
KING: I pray you, speed you soon again!
WANTONNESS: Yea, of this sang, sir, we are fain!
  We sall neither spare for wind nor rain
    Till our day's wark be done!
  Fareweill, for we are at the flicht!   360

39

378   *forfare*, die.

380   *mou*, mouth.

383   *mak collatioun*, dine.

385   *fra-hand*, forthwith.

390   *band*, vow.

Placebo, rule our Roy at richt.
We sall be here, man, or midnicht
   Thocht we march with the moon!
A gay march. SOLACE *and* WANTONNESS *make a detour of the stage and come to* SENSUALITY *and her court.*
Pastime with pleasance and great prosperity
Be to you, Sovereign Sensuality!

SENSUALITY: Sirs, ye are welcome. Where go ye? East or West?

WANTONNESS: In faith, I trow we be at the farrest!

SENSUALITY: What is your name? I pray you sir, declare!

WANTONNESS: Marry, Wantonness, the King's secretair.

SENSUALITY: What king is that, whilk has so gay a boy? 370

WANTONNESS: Humanity, that richt redoubtit Roy,
  Wha does commend him to you heartfully,
  And sends you here a ring with a ruby,
  In taken that above all crëature
  He has chosen you to be his Paramour:
  He bade me say that he will be but deid,
  Without that ye mak hastily remede.

SENSUALITY: How can I help him, althocht he sould forfare?
  Ye ken richt weill I am na Medciner.

SOLACE: A kiss of your sweet mou, in a morning, 380
  To his sickness micht be great comforting.
  And als he maks you supplicatioun
  This nicht to mak with him collatioun.

SENSUALITY: I thank his grace of his benevolence!
  Good sirs, I sall be ready even fra-hand.
  In me there sall be fund na negligence,
  Baith nicht and day, when his grace will demand.
  Pass ye before, and say I am cumand
  And thinks richt lang to have of him a sicht.
  And I to Venus mak a faithful band, 390
  That in his arms I think to lie all nicht.

WANTONNESS: That sall be done ... but yet or I hame pass,
  Here I protest for Hameliness, your lass.

SENSUALITY: She sall be at command, sir, when ye will:

397   *gamond*, a lively capering dance.

401   *tyst*, entice.

402-3   *The fiend . . . marriage*, 'the devil a penny of dowry he will get by this marriage!'

405   *brank*, prance.
406   *wreistit*, wrested.

410   *speir*, ask.

415   *Him . . . hell*. According to a medieval legend, deriving from the apocryphal gospel of *Nicodemus*, during the days of his burial Christ descended into hell and plundered ('herriet'), i.e. rescued, the souls of the faithful.

422   *perqueir*, by heart.
423   *gin*, tricks.

426   *clap*, fondle.

I traist she sall find you flinging your fill!

WANTONNESS: Now hey for joy and mirth I dance!

Music, which accompanies the speech.

Tak there a gay gamond of France!

Am I nocht worthy to advance

   That am sa good a page,

And that sa speedily can rin   400

To tyst my maister unto sin?

The fiend a penny he will win

   Of this his marriage!

A dance, during which WANTONNESS *and* PLACEBO *skip back
to the* KING. *On the way* WANTONNESS *pretends to hurt his leg.*

(*to audience*): I think this day to win great thank!

Hey, as a bridlit cat I brank!

Alas, I have wreistit my shank . . .

   Yet I gang, by Sant Michael!

Whilk of my legs, sirs, as ye trow,

Was it that I did hurt even now?

But whereto sould I speir at you –   410

   I think they baith are hale!

He turns to the KING. *The music ends.*

Good morrow, Maister, by the Mess!

KING: Welcome, my minion Wantonness!

How has thou sped in thy travail?

WANTONNESS: Richt weill, by Him that herriet hell!

Your errand is weil done!

KING (*transported*): Then, Wantonness, full weill is me!

Thou hast deservit baith meat and fee,

   By Him that made the moon!

(*Anxiously*) There is ae thing that I wald speir . . .   420

What sall I do when she comes here?

For I knaw nocht the craft perqueir

   Of lovers' gin;

Therefore at length ye mon me leir

   How to begin.

WANTONNESS: To kiss her and clap her, sir, be not affeared!

43

429   *tail*, the train or very long skirt then fashionable; *tent weill*, take good care of.

433   *preive*, try.

440   *visie*, visit.

443–9   M.

448   *the cures*, the charge.

455   *lustiness*, pleasure.

She will not shrink, thocht ye kiss her, a span within the beard.
If ye think, that she thinks shame, then hide the bairnis een
With her tail, and tent her weill, ye wot what I mean!
Will ye give me leave, sir, first to go to, 430
And I sall learn you the cues, how ye sall do?

KING: God forbid, Wantonness, that I give you leave!
Thou art ower perilous a page sic practiks to preive!

WANTONNESS *sees* SENSUALITY.

Wantonness: Now, sir, preive as ye please, I see her cumand!
Order you with gravity, and we sall by you stand.

Music. The KING *and his courtiers prepare to welcome* SEN-
SUALITY. *She apart first makes her vow to Venus, accompanied by
music.*

SENSUALITY: O Venus goddess, unto thy celsitude
I give laud, gloir, honour and reverence,
Whilk grantit me sic perfite pulchritude.
I mak a vow, with humill observance,
Richt reverently thy temple to visie 440
With sacrifice unto thy deitie!
To every state I am sa agreabill
That few or nane refuses me at all –
Papes, patriarchs, nor prelates venerabill,
Common people, nor princes temporal,
But subject all to me Dame Sensual!
Sa sall it be ay while the warld endures,
And specially where youthage has the cures.

She turns towards the KING.

And now my way I mon advance
Unto a prince of great puissance, 450
Whom young men has in governance,
    Rolland into his rage.
I am richt glad, I you assure,
That potent prince to get in cure,
Wha is of lustiness the lure
    And greatest of courage.

45

458   *celsitude*, Highness.

462   *lammer*, amber, or rather ambergris, a grey, wax-like substance prized for its perfume.

467   *ye's*, you will.

470   *play cap-out*, empty the 'cap' or drinking-bowl.

471   *len*, lend; *that batty tout*. In the 1552 version 'thy batty towt', in the 1554 one 'that batye tout'. Editors have made no sense of this, but 'batty' means plump, well-bodied, and 'tout' means 'drink', hence 'that lusty drink'.

474   *gotten upon the gumes*, made love; *gumes*, men.

476   *lumes*, instruments.

484   *fling*, dance.

The music ends. A detour brings her at last to the KING.
O potent prince, of pulchritude preclair,
God Cupido preserve your celsitude!
And Dame Venus mot keep your corse from care,
As I wald she sould keep my awn heart blude!   460
KING: Welcome to me, peerless of pulchritude!
  Welcome to me, thou sweeter nor the lammer,
  Whilk has me made of all dolour denude!
  Solace, convoy this lady to my chaumer.
SENSUALITY: I gae this gait with richt good will.
  Sir Wantonness, tarry ye still;
  And Hameliness, the cup ye's fill
    And beir him company!
Music, which continues till the departure of KING *and party.*
HAMELINESS: That sall I do withouten doubt,
  For he and I sall play cap-out!   470
WANTONNESS: Now lady, len me that batty tout.
    Fill in, for I am dry.
  Your dame, by this, truly,
  Has gotten upon the gumes!   ~~lowest humour?~~
  What rack thocht ye and I
  Go join our jousting lumes?
HAMELINESS: Content I am with richt good will,
  Whenever ye are ready,
  All your pleasure to fulfill.
WANTONNESS: Now weill said, by our Lady!   480
  I'll beir my maister company,
    As lang as I endure!
  If he be whiskand wantonly,
    We sall fling on the flure!
The KING *and his party go into the arbour at the top of the stage.*
As they disappear GOOD COUNSEL, *a bearded figure, hobbles in*
and addresses the audience.
GOOD COUNSEL: Consider, my sovereigns, I you beseek,
  The cause maist principal of my coming.
  Princes nor potestates are nocht worth a leek,

47

505-6   *our guiders . . . day.* James III was killed in the rebellion of 1488, James IV at the battle of Flodden, 1513, and James V died after the rout of Solway Moss, 1542.

507   *lichtlyt,* scorned.

522   *traist,* trust; *stylet,* honoured.

Be they not guidit by my good governing.
There was never emperor, conqueror nor king,
Without my wisdom that micht their weal advance.   490
My name is Good Counsel, without feignyeing.
Lords for lack of my law are brocht to mischance,
And so, for conclusioun,
Wha guides them nocht by Good Counsel,
All in vain is their travail,
And finally fortune sall them fail,
And bring them to confusioun.
    And this I understand,
For I have made my residence
With hie princes of great puissance,   500
In England, Italy and France,
    And mony other land.
But out of Scotland, wae alace,
I have been banissit lang space –
That gars our guiders all want grace,
And die before their day!
Because they lichtlyt Good Counsel,
Fortune turnit on them her sail,
Whilk brocht this realm to meikle bale – *mediaeval scheme*
    Wha can the contrair say?   510
My lords, I came nocht here to lie;
Waes me for King Humanity,
Owrrset with Sensuality
    In th'entrie of his ring,
Through vicious counsel insolent!
Sa they may get riches or rent,
To his weilfare they tak na tent,
    Nor what sall be the ending!
For wald the King be guidit yet with reason
And on mis-doers mak punitioun,   520
Howbeit that I lang time has been exilet
I traist in God my name sall yet be stylet.
Sa till I see God send mair of his grace,

49

525   FLATTERY. The chief Vice in the play enters in many-coloured dress with a fool's patter. His Scots audience has known him as the Abbot of Unreason – in England the Lord of Misrule – of the Christmas-tide revels, but all Christendom knows him. Only a true fool, he says, would risk his life at sea – the satiric convention of the ship of fools seems to be invoked here – but he went to get himself a 'new array', and the audience will now see their 'awn fool' foster folly everywhere once again.

527   *begariet*, adorned.

532   *stormsted*, storm-stayed; *sen*, since; *Yule*, Christmas.

540   *Hail*, Haul.

541   *a-luff*, steer close to the wind.

542   *raipes*, ropes; *fleid*, frightened.

543   *Roy*, King. Flattery compares himself to the King of the Bean, the person chosen, by the picking of a bean from a cake, to be master of the revels on Twelfth Day (6th January).

545   *waws*, waves.

550   *yeid*, went.

553   *feill*, know.

554   *cast*, ploy.

555   FALSET. Generally signifies falsehood, but particularly false report, misrepresentation. See his accusation of Verity and his hanging speech at the close of the play.

556   *sair*, harm

I purpose to repose me in this place.

GOOD COUNSEL *draws apart.* FLATTERY, *the first of the Three Vices to appear, rushes in, dressed in motley.*

FLATTERY: Mak room, sirs, ho! that I may rin!
Lo, see how I am new come in,
    Begariet all with sindry hues!
Let be your din till I begin,
    And I sall shaw you of my news!
Throughout all Christendom I have passed   530
And am come here now at the last,
Stormsted by sea ay sen Yule Day,
That we were fain to hew our mast,
Nocht half a mile beyond the May.
But now amang you I will remain,
I purpose never to sail again,
    To put my life in chance of watter!
Was never seen sic wind and rain,
    Nor of shipmen sic clitter-clatter.
Some bade 'Hail!', some bade 'Stand-by!'   540
'On starboard ho!' 'A-luff, fie, fie!'
    While all the raipes began to rattle.
Was never Roy sa fleid as I,
    When all the sails played brittle-brattle!
To see the waws, it was a wonder,
And wind, that rave the sails in sunder!
Now am I scapet fra that affray;
What say ye, sirs, am I nocht gay?
    See ye nocht Flattery, your awn fool,
That yeid to mak this new array?   550
    Was I nocht here with you at Yule?
Yes, by my faith, I think on weill!
Where are my fellows, that wald I feill?
    We sould have come here for a cast!
Ho, Falset, ho!

FALSET *enters.*

FALSET: Wae sair the Deil!

51

562   *limmer*, rascal; *loon*, knave.

566   *thae*, these.

573   *felon*, great; *fray*, fear.

578   *That . . . mare*, 'Your purpose is the same as mine' (*samin*, same).
579   *sen*, since.

587   *steir him*, take action

590   *confusioun*, ruin

Wha's that that cries for me sa fast?

FLATTERY: Why, Falset, brother, knawis thou not me?
 I am thy brother, Flattery!

FALSET: Now let me brace thee in my arms!
 When freindis meetis, heartis warms!   560
 They embrace.

FLATTERY: Where is Deceit, that limmer loon?

FALSET: I left him drinkand in the toun.
 He will be here incontinent.

FLATTERY: Now by the Haily Sacrament,
 Thae tidings comforts all my heart!
 He is richt crafty as ye ken,
 And counsellor to the Merchant-men!
 Enter DECEIT.

DECEIT: *Bon jour*, brother, with all my heart,
 Here am I come to tak your part   570
  Baith into good and evil!
 I met Good Counsel by the way,
 Wha pat me in a felon fray –
  I give him to the Deil!
 How came ye here, I pray you tell me.

FALSET: Marry, to seek King Humanity!

DECEIT: Now, by the good lady that me bare,
 That samin horse is my awn mare!
 Sen we three seeks yon noble King,
 Let us devise some subtle thing!   580
 Also I pray you as your brother,
 That we, ilk ane, be true to other.
 I pray to God, nor I be hangit,
 But I sall die or ye be wrangit!

FALSET: What is thy counsel that we do?

DECEIT: Marry, sirs, this is my counsel, lo!
 Fra time the King begin to steir him,
 Marry! Good Counsel I dread come near him,
 And be we knawin with Correctioun,
 It will be our confusioun.   590

596   *clerkis claithing*. Flattery disguises himself as a friar, Falsehood
        as a Doctor in his gown and hood, Deceit as a priest, in which
        capacity he performs the mock baptisms.
598   *new come out of France*, learned men lately returned from studies
        in France.

614   'What does it matter if I can flatter and cajole?'

619–25 M.

Therefore, my dear brether, devise
To find some toy of the new guise.
FLATTERY: Marry, I shall find a thousand wiles.
We mon turn our claiths, and change our styles
And disaguise us, that na man ken us.
Has na man clerkis claithing to len us?
And let us keep grave countenance,
As we were new come out of France!

againstelf dend.

DECEIT: Now, by my saul, that is weill deviset!
Ye sall see me soon disaguiset.   600
FALSET: And sa sall I, man, by the Rood!
Now, some good fellow, len me a hood!
The THREE VICES *disguise themselves in clothes from a bundle*
which DECEIT *has brought on.*
DECEIT: Now am I buskit, and wha can spy?
The Deil stick me, if this be I!
If this be I, or nocht, I cannot weil say,
Or has the Fiend or Fairy-folk borne me away?
FALSET: What says thou of my gay garmoun?
DECEIT: I say thou looks even like a loon.
Now, brother Flattery, what do ye?
What kind of man shape ye to be?   610
FLATTERY: Now, by my faith, my brother dear,
I will ga counterfeit a freir!
DECEIT: A freir? Whereto? Ye cannot preach.
FLATTERY: What rack but I can flatter and fleech?
Perchance I'll come to that honour,
To be the Kingis confessour!
Poor freirs are free at any feast
And marshallt ay amang the best!
Good wives will nevir let freiris want.
For why, they are their confessours,   620
Their prudent heavenly counselours.
Therefore wives plainly taks their parts
And shaws the secrets of their hearts
To freirs, with better will I trow

627 *a cowl of Tullilum.* There was a Carmelite monastery at this place, on the west side of Perth.
628 *porteous,* breviary.

639 *godbairn,* baptismal.

644 *ance,* once.

650 *lurdan,* lazy.

656 *crack and clatter,* lie and chatter.

Nor they do to their bedfellow!
DECEIT *has fetched a monk's cowl.*

DECEIT: Here is thy gaining, all and some.
That is a cowl of Tullilum!

FLATTERY: Wha has a porteous to len me?
The fiend a saul, I trow, will ken me!
The BISHOP *tosses down a breviary.*   *contempt for sacraments*

FALSET: We mon do mair yet, by Sant James!   630
For we mon all three change our names.
Christen me and I sall baptise thee.
There follows a mock ceremony.

DECEIT: By God and thereabout may it be!
How will thou call me, I pray thee tell!

FALSET: I wot not how to call mysell!

DECEIT: But yet ance name the bairnis name!

FALSET: Discretioun, Discretioun in God's name!

DECEIT: I need not now to care for thrift,
But what sall be my Godbairn gift?

FALSET: I give you all the deils of hell!   640

DECEIT: Na, brother, hauld that to yoursell!
Now, sit doun! Let me baptise thee!
I wot not what thy name sould be.

FALSET: But yet ance name the bairnis name!

DECEIT: Sapience, Sapience, in God's name!

FLATTERY: Brother, Deceit, come baptise me!   *Revival*

DECEIT: Then sit doun lawly on thy knee!

FLATTERY: Now, brother, name the bairnis name.

DECEIT: Devotioun in the devil's name!
He splashes FLATTERY *with water.*

FLATTERY: The deil resaive thee, lurdan loon!   650
Thou has wet all my new shaven croun!

DECEIT: Devotioun, Sapience, and Discretioun –
We three may rule this regioun.
We sall find mony crafty things
For to beguile a hunder kings!
For thou can richt weill crack and clatter,

667 *learand,* learning.

676 *bent,* field.

686 *the clippit croun,* the friar's tonsure.

And I sall feignye and (*to* FLATTERY) thou sall flatter.
FLATTERY: But I wald have, or we departit,
  A drink to mak us better heartit.
DECEIT: Weil said, by Him that herriet hell,   660
  I was even thinkand that mysell!
  While the THREE VICES *are drinking, the* KING *appears leading*
  SENSUALITY *from the arbour.*
KING: Now where is Placebo and Solace?
  Where is my minion Wantonness?
  Wantonness, ho! Come to me soon!
  WANTONNESS *and* HAMELINESS *appear.*
WANTONNESS: Why cried ye, sir, till I had done?
KING: What was thou doand, tell me that?
WANTONNESS: Marry, learand how my father me gat!
  I wot not how it stands, but doubt
  Methinks the warld rins round about!
KING: And sa think I, man, by my thrift!   670
  I see fifteen moons in the lift.
  SOLACE, PLACEBO *and* DANGER *appear.*
SOLACE: Now shaw me, sir, I you exhort,
  How are ye of your love content?
  Think ye not this a merry sport?
KING: Yea, that I do in verament!
  The KING *spies the* THREE VICES.
  What bairns are yon upon the bent?
  I did not see them all this day.
WANTONNESS: They will be here incontinent.
  Stand still and hear what they will say.
  The THREE VICES *come forward and salute the* KING.
VICES: Laud, honour, gloir, triumph and victory,   680
  Be to your maist excellent Majesty!
KING: Ye are welcome, good friends, by the Rood!
  Appearandly ye seem some men of good.
  What are your names, tell me without delay.
DECEIT: Discretioun, sir, is my name perfay.
KING: What is your name, sir, with the clippit croun?

688   *Sant Jame*. The brother of John the Evangelist, his body was said to be at Compostella in Spain.

695–699   *they call me Thin-Drink*. Lindsay's pun on 'Sapience' does not seem to have been noted. To Falsehood 'Sapience' sounds the same as 'Sypiens' or 'Sypins', the oozings or dregs of a cask.

697   *plat*, blow.

708–9   M.

703   *heich*, high.

717   *thesaurar*, treasurer.

720   *Sant Ann*, the mother of the Virgin Mary.

FLATTERY: But doubt my name is callit Devotioun.
KING: Welcome, Devotioun, by Sant Jame!
  Now, sirrah, tell what is your name?
FALSET: Marry, sir, they call me . . what call they me?   690
  (*Aside*) I wot not well, but if I lie!
KING: Can thou nocht tell what is thy name?
FALSET: I kend it when I cam fra hame!
KING: What ails thou cannot shaw it now?
FALSET (*confused*): Marry, they call me Thin-Drink, I trow.
KING: Thin-Drink, what kind of name is that?
DECEIT: Sapience, thou serves to bear a plat!
  Methinks thou shaws thee not weil-wittit.
FALSET: Sypiens, sir, Sypiens, marry, now ye hit it!
  FLATTERY *brushes* FALSET *aside*.
FLATTERY: Sir, if ye please to let me say,   700
  That same is Sapientia!
FALSET: That same is it, by Sant Michael!
KING: Why could thou not tell it thysell?
FALSET: I pray your grace to pardon me.
  And I sall shaw the verity –
  I am sa full of Sapience
  That sometime I will tak a trance.
  My spreit was reft fra my body,
  Now heich aboon the Trinity.
KING: Sapience sould be a man of good.   710
FALSET: Sir, ye may knaw that by my hood!
KING: Now have I Sapience and Discretioun,
  How can I fail to rule this regioun?
  And Devotioun to be my Confessour!
  Thir three came in a happy hour.
  to FALSEHOOD) Here I mak thee my secretar!
  (*to* DECEIT) And thou sall be my thesaurar!
  (*to* FLATTERY) And thou sall be my counsellour
  In spritual things, and confessour.
FLATTERY: I sweir to you, sir, by Sant Ann,   720
  Ye met never with a wiser man,

724   *feill*, knowledge.

726   *astronomy*. Astrology seems to be indicated by the collocation with the pseudo-sciences of alchemy, physiognomy, palmestry.

729   *quelling of the quintessence*, extracting the fifth essence, the substance of which the heavily bodies were imagined to consist, in order to transmute metals into gold.

732   *To mak multiplicatioun*, to transmute into gold.

735   *loons*, rascals.

737–43   The comic juxtaposition of foreign conquests and Scots place-names parodies the list of King Arthur's conquests as given in romance and chronicle. See the alliterative *Morte Arthur* (ll. 26–47) and Andrew Wyntoun's chronicle (ed. Amours, Scottish Text Society, vol. 4, p. 19). 'Danskin' is Danzig; 'Almane' is Germany; 'Spitalfield' is probably the village of this name in Perthshire; 'Ruglen' is Rutherglen beside Glasgow; Corstorphine was then a village on the west side of Edinburgh.

745   *A-per-se*, an incomparable person, like one of the Nine Nobles or Worthies (first celebrated in *The Roman d'Alexandre*), of whom the three Christian ones were Arthur, Charlemagne, Godfrey of Boulogne.

748   *loof*, palm.

755   *sa white a face*, considered a sign of noble lineage.

For mony a craft, sir, do I can,
  Were they weill knawn.
I have na feill of flattery,
But fosterit with philosophy,
A strang man in astronomy,
Whilk sall be soon shawn!

FALSET: And I have great intelligence
In quelling of the quintessence,
But to preive my experience,   730
  Sir, len me forty crouns
To mak multiplicatioun;
And tak my obligatioun,
If we mak false narratioun,
  Hald us for very loons!

DECEIT: Sir, I ken by your physnomy,
Ye sall conqueis, or else I lie,
Danskin, Denmark and all Almane,
Spitalfield and the Realm of Spain.
Ye sall have at your governance   740
Renfrew, and the Realm of France,
Yea, Ruglen and the Toun of Rome,
Corstorphine and all Christendom.
Whereto, sir, by the Trinity
Ye are a very A-per-se!

FLATTERY: Sir, when I dwelt in Italy,
I leirit the craft of palmistry.
Shaw me the loof, sir, of your hand,
And I sall mak you understand
If your grace be infortunate   750
Or if ye be predestinate.
The KING shows his hand.
I see ye will have fifteen queens
And fifteen score of concubenes!
The Virgin Mary save your grace,
Saw ever man sa white a face,
Sa great an arm, sa fair a hand!

63

759   *dang*, struck.

767   *carl*, rogue.

777   *lyart*, grey.

785   *swith*, quick; *unsel*, wretch.

789   *devoid*, leave.

There's nocht sic a leg in all this land!
Were ye in arms, I think na wonder,
Howbeit ye dang doun fifteen hunder.

KING: Ye are richt welcome, by the Rood,   760
Ye seem to be three men of good.

GOOD COUNSEL takes up a more prominent position.
But wha is yon that stands so still?
Go spy and speir what is his will.
And if he yearnis my presence,
Bring him to me with diligence.

The THREE VICES quickly confer.
FLATTERY: I dreid full sair by God himsel,
That yon old carl be Good Counsel!
Get he ance to the King's presence,
We three will get na audience!

DECEIT: That matter I sall tak on hand,   770
And say it is the King's command,
That he anon devoid this place
And come not near the Kingis grace,
And that under the pain of treason!

FLATTERY: Brother, I hald your counsel reason.
Now let us hear what he will say.

He addresses GOOD COUNSEL.
Auld lyart beard, good day, good day!

GOOD COUNSEL: Good day again, sirs, by the Rood.
I pray God mak you men of good.

DECEIT: Pray not for us to Lord nor Lady,   780
For we are men of good already!
Sir, shaw to us what is your name.

GOOD COUNSEL: Good Counsel they call me at hame.

FALSET: What says thou, carl, are thou Good Counsel?
Swith, pack thee hence, unhappy unsel!

GOOD COUNSEL: I pray you, sirs, give me licence,
To come ance to the King's presence
To speak but twa words to his grace.

FLATTERY: Swith, hureson carl, devoid this place!

791   *mak it teuch*, swagger.

804   *bousteous*, rough.

806   *laithly*, loathsome; *lurdan*, good-for-nothing.

809   *the Thievis Hole*, the stocks.

811   *pastance*, pleasure.

813   *hurley-hacket*, sledging.
814   *corses*, bodies.

GOOD COUNSEL: Brother, I ken you weill eneuch,   790
  Howbeit ye mak it never sa teuch –
  Flattery, Deceit and False-Report,
  That will not suffer to resort
  Good Counsel to the King's presence.
DECEIT: Swith, hureson carl, ga pack thee hence!
  If ever thou come this gait again,
  I vow to God thou sall be slain!
  They set upon GOOD COUNSEL *and push him from the stage.*
GOOD COUNSEL: Sen at this time I can get na presence,
  Is na remede but tak in patience.
  But when youth-heid has blawn his wanton blast,   800
  Then sall Good Counsel rule him at the last!
  GOOD COUNSEL *is chased out. The* THREE VICES *return to the*
  KING.
KING: What gart you bide sa lang fra my presence?
  I think it lang since ye departit thence.
  What man was yon, with a great bousteous beard?
  Methocht he made you all three very feared!
DECEIT: It was a laithly lurdan loon,
  Come to break booths into this toun!
  We have gart bind him with a pole
  And send him to the Thievis Hole.
KING: Let him sit there with a mischance!   810
  And let us go to our pastance!
WANTONNESS: Better go revel at the racket,
  Or else go to the hurley-hacket,
  Or then to shaw our courtly corses
  Ga see wha best can rin their horses.
  As they make to move SOLACE *stops them.*
SOLACE: Na, Sovereign, or we farther gang,
  Gar Sensuality sing a sang.

818 The excellent song by Alexander Scott (*floruit* c. 1540–70) used in the Edinburgh Festival production has been retained here, Lindsay's song not having been recorded. Scott is best known for his love poems.

820 *sa hie has set her*, has made her so disdainful.

823 *may*, maid.

825 *plet*, fold.

828 *glaikit*, stupid.

838 *Diligite . . . terram*, is translated by the following line and is from the apocryphal *Book of Wisdom*, l.1.

839–51 M.

(They sing.)

To luve unluvet it is a pain,
For she that is my sovereign
   Some wanton man sa hie has set her   820
That I can get na luve again,
   But breks my heart, and nocht the better!

When that I went with that sweet may,
To dance, to sing, to sport and play,
   And ofttimes in my armis plet her,
I do now murn baith nicht and day
   And breaks my heart, and nocht the better!

Whatten a glaikit fool am I,
To slay mysell with melancholy,
   Sen weill I ken I may nocht get her!   830
Or what sould be the cause and why
   To brek my heart, and nocht the better!

My heart, sen thou may nocht her please,
Adieu! As good luve comes as gaes!
   Go choose another and forget her!
God give him dolour and disease
   That breks their heart, and nocht the better!

As the music ends, VERITY *enters, a Puritan maid holding a Bible.*
She stands apart, but FLATTERY *goes out to peer at her as she speaks.*
VERITY: *Diligite Justitiam qui judicatis terram.*
Love Justice, ye wha has a Judge's cure
In earth, and dreid the awful Judgëment   840
Of Him that sall come judge baith rich and poor
Richt terribly, with bluidy woundis rent.
That dreidfull day into your hearts imprent,
Believand weill how and what manner ye
Use justice here to others, there at length

69

860   *novells*, news.

862   *by books and bells*, more fully, 'with bell, book and candle'.
        In the form of excommunication a book is closed, a candle
        put out and a bell rung. Flattery fears that he and his fellows
        will be wholly excluded from the king's company.

866   *Sant Bride*, see note to 1.1527.

874   *beirand the New Testament*. Only English versions were avail-
        able in print, the first authorised printing of a vernacular New
        Testament being at London in 1536.
875   M.
876–79 Kemp's text gives this speech to the Bishop.

That day but doubt sa sall ye judgit be.
And if ye wald your subjects were weill given,
Then vertuously begin the dance yoursell,
Going before, then they anon, I ween,
Sall follow you, either to heaven or hell. 850
If men of me wald have intelligence,
Or knaw my name, they call me Verity.
Of Christis law I have experience,
And has owrsailit mony stormy sea.
Now am I seekand King Humanity,
For of his grace I have good esperance.
Fra time that he acquaintit be with me,
His honour and heich gloir I sall advance.

As FLATTERY *returns* DECEIT *greets him.*

DECEIT: Good day, Father, where have you been?
    Declare to us of your novells. 860
FLATTERY: There is now lichtit on the green,
    Dame Verity, by books and bells!
    But come she to the King's presence,
    There is na boot for us to bide!
    Therefore I rede us, all go hence!
FALSET: That will we nocht yet, by Sant Bride!
    But we sall either gang or ride
    To Lords of Sprituality,
    And gar them trow yon bag of pride
    Has spoken manifest heresy! 870

Here the THREE VICES *go to the* SPIRITUAL ESTATE.

FLATTERY: O reverent fathers of the Spritual State,
    We counsel you be wise and vigilant!
    Dame Verity has lichtit now of late,
    And in her hand beirand the New Testament!

The SPIRITUAL ESTATE *confer in undertones for a moment.*

BISHOP: What is your counsel, brether, now let see.
ABBOT: I hauld it best that we incontinent
    Gar hauld her fast into captivity
    Unto the thrid day of the Parliament

880–3   M.

890   *dulce*, sweet.

894   *forfare*, suffer.

901–2   M.

And then accuse her of her heresy.
BISHOP: Sir Parson, ye sall be my commissair,   880
    And ye, Sir Freir, because ye can declare
    The haill process, pass with him in commissioun.
    Pass all together with my braid benisoun!
    The THREE VICES *approach* VERITY.
FLATTERY: What book is that, harlot, in thy hand?
    He looks at it.
    Out! Wallaway! This is the New Testament!
    In Inglis tongue, and prentit in Ingland!
    Heresy, heresy! Fire, fire, incontinent!
VERITY: Forsooth, my friend, ye have a wrang judgment,
    For in this Book there is na heresy,
    But our Christ's word, richt dulce and redolent,   890
    A springing well of sincere verity!
DECEIT: Come on your way, for all your yellow locks!
    Your wanton words but doubt ye sall repent!
    This nicht ye sall forfare a pair of stocks,
    And syne, the morn, be brocht to thole judgment.
    VERITY *falls on her knees, not to the* VICES *but to Heaven.*
VERITY: Get up, thou sleepis all too lang, O Lord,
    And mak some reasonable reformatioun
    On them that does tramp doun Thy gracious Word,
    And has a deidly indignatioun
    At them wha maks maist true narratioun!   900
    Now, lords, do as ye list.
    I have na mair to say.
FLATTERY: Sit doun and tak you rest
    All nicht till it be day!
    They put VERITY *in the stocks, and return to* SPIRITUALITY.
DECEIT: My lord, we have with diligence,
    Bucklet up weill yon blethran bard!
BISHOP: I think ye serve good recompense.
    Tak thir ten crowns for your reward!
    CHASTITY *enters intoning to herself a Latin Hymn.*
CHASTITY: How lang sall this inconstant warld endure?

912   *harbryless,* shelterless.

940   *uncouth shire,* strange land.

That I sould banist be sa lang, alas! 910
Few crëatures, or nane, taks of me cure,
Whilk gars me mony nicht lie harbryless!
DILIGENCE: Lady, I pray you shaw to me your name.
It does me noy, your lamentatioun!
CHASTITY: My freind, thereof I need nocht to think shame,
Dame Chastity, banist from toun to toun.
DILIGENCE: Then pass to ladies of religioun,
Whilk maks their vow to observe chastity.
Lo, where there sits a Prioress of renoun
Amang the rest of Sprituality. 920
DILIGENCE *points out the* PRIORESS, *who is one of the* SPIRITUAL
ESTATE.
CHASTITY: I grant yon lady has vowit chastity,
For her professioun thereto sould accord.
She made that vow for an abbessy,
But nocht for Christ Jesus our Lord.
I sall observe your counsel if I may.
Come on and hear what yon lady will say.
DILIGENCE *and* CHASTITY *approach the* PRIORESS.
My prudent, lusty Lady Prioress,
Remember how ye did vow chastity;
Madame, I pray you of your gentleness
That ye wald please to have of me pity 930
And this ae nicht to give me harboury!
PRIORESS: Pass hence, Madame, by Christ ye come nocht here!
Ye are contrair to my complexioun!
Gang seek ludging at some auld monk or freir,
Perchance they will be your protectioun.
Or to prelates mak your progressioun,
Whilk are obleist to you as weill as I!
Dame Sensual has given directioun
You to exclude out of my company!
CHASTITY *now addresses the* CHURCHMEN.
CHASTITY: Lords, I have past through mony uncouth shire, 940
But in this land I can get na ludging!

75

944   *bening*, benign.

953   *the Queen of Fairy*, Hecate, the mistress of spirits, goblins, etc.

956   *traist*, trust.

959   *dortour*, dormitory; *dang*, beat.

975   *on steir*, astir. A *soutar* is a shoemaker.
976   *rin arear*, run off.

Of my name if ye wald have knawledging,
Forsooth, my lords, they call me Chastity.
I you beseek, of your graces bening,
Give me ludging this nicht for charity.

BISHOP: Pass on, Madame, we knaw you nocht!
Or by Him that the warld has wrocht,
Your coming sall be richt dear bocht,
  If ye mak langer tarry!

ABBOT: But doubt we will baith live and die   950
  With our love Sensuality.
We will have na mair deal with thee
  Then with the Queen of Fairy!

PARSON: Pass hame amang the Nuns and dwell,
  Whilk are of chastity the well.
I traist they will with book and bell
  Resaive you in their closter!

CHASTITY: Sir, when I was the Nuns amang,
Out of their dortour they me dang,
And wald nocht let me bide sa lang   960
  To say my Paternoster.
I see na grace there for to get.
I hald it best, or it be late,
For to go prove the temporal state
  If they will me resaive.

CHASTITY *crosses to the* TEMPORAL ESTATE.

Good day, my lord Temporality,
And you, Merchant of gravity;
Full fain wald I have harboury,
  To ludge amang the lave.

LORD: Forsooth, we wald be weill content   970
To harbour you with good intent,
Were nocht we have impediment –
  For-why we twa are marriet!

MERCHANT: But wist our wives that ye were here,
They wald mak all this toun on steir,
Therefore we rede you, rin arear,

977   *miscarryt*, ill treated.

978   *ingine*, skill; *men of craft*, craftsmen, men belonging to the Crafts.

978   *S.D.* JENNIE does not appear in Kemp's version.

978–1034 As Hamer notes, Lindsay here exploits two comic traditions, the alleged want of virility in cobblers and tailors, which makes them peculiarly sympathetic to Chastity, and the supposedly natural infidelity of women. There is also the Wife of Bath's favourite theme of female mastery.

979   *pine*, pain.

982–5   M.

990   M; *forthink*, are sorry for.

994–1003 M.

994   *minnie*, mother.

1003   *shapes*, means.

1005–7 Spoken by TAILOR'S WIFE in Kemp's version.

In dreid ye be miscarryt!

CHASTITY *now goes to the end of the stage where the* COMMON PEOPLE *are watching. She approaches* SOUTAR *and* TAILOR, *near whom are* SOUTAR'S WIFE, TAILOR'S WIFE, *and* JENNIE, *the tailor's daughter.*

CHASTITY: Ye men of craft, of great ingine,
Give me harbry for Christis pine,
And win God's benison, and mine,   980
And help my hungry heart!

SOUTAR: Welcome, by Him that made the moon,
To dwell with us till it be June.
We sall mend baith your hose and shoon,
And plainly tak your part.

TAILOR: Is this fair Lady Chastity?
Now welcome by the Trinity!
I think it were a great pity
That thou sould lie thereout!
Your great displeasure we forthink.   990
Sit doun, Madame, and tak a drink,
And let na sorrow in you sink,
But let us play cap-out.

They entertain CHASTITY.

JENNIE: Ho! Minnie, minnie, minnie!

TAILOR'S WIFE: What wald thou, my dear dochter, Jennie?
Jennie, my joy, where is thy daddy?

JENNIE: Marry, drinkand with a lusty lady,
A fair young maiden cled in white,
Of whom my daddy taks delight.
She has the fairest form of face,   1000
Furnisht with all kind of grace.
I traist, if I can reckon richt,
She shapes to ludge with him all nicht!

SOUTAR'S WIFE: What does the Soutar, my goodman?

JENNIE: Marry, fills the cup and tooms the can.
Or ye come hame, by God, I trow
He will be drucken like a sow!

1009 *cow-clink*, whore.

1011 *cummer*, gossip.

1011–15 First speech given to Soutar's Wife, second to Taylor's Wife, in Kemp.

1012 *ding*, beat.

1014 *smaiks*, wretches.

1015 *paiks*, punishment.

1017 *but*, without.

1019 *rock*, distaff.

1020 *dudron*, slut.

1021 *Sant Blaise*, a Cappadocian bishop, after a hermit's life martyred by Diocletian.

1022–3 Spoken by Soutar's wife in Kemp.

1024–5 M.

1026 *Sant Crispinane*. Saint Crispin was the patron saint of cobblers.

1027 *gane*, mouth.

1031 *harn-pan*, skull.

TAILOR'S WIFE: This is a great despite, I think,
  For to resaive sic a cow-clink.
  What is your counsel that we do?   1010
SOUTAR'S WIFE: Cummer, this is my counsel, lo:
  Ding ye the tane, and I the other.
TAILOR'S WIFE: I am content, by God's Mother!
  I think for me, thae hureson smaiks,
  They serve richt weill to get their paiks!
  They drive CHASTITY *away.*
TAILOR'S WIFE: Go hence, harlot, how durst thou be sa bauld
  To ludge with our goodmen but our licence?
  I mak a vow by Him that Judas sauld,
  This rock of mine shall be thy recompence!
  Shaw me thy name, dudron, with diligence!   1020
CHASTITY: Marry, Chastity is my name, by Sant Blaise.
TAILOR'S WIFE: I pray God may He work on thee vengeance,
  For I luvit never chastity all my days!
  She pursues CHASTITY *with her distaff, then the* WIVES *turn on their husbands.*
SOUTAR'S WIFE: But my goodman, the truth I say thee till,
  Gars me keep chastity, sair agains my will.
  I mak a vow to Sant Crispinane
  I'se be revengit on that graceless gane.
  And to begin the play, tak there a platt!
  She strikes the SOUTAR.
SOUTAR: The fiend resaive the hands that gave me that!
SOUTAR'S WIFE: What now, hureson, begins thou for to ban?
  Tak there another upon thy peeled harn-pan!   1031
  (to TAILOR'S WIFE*)* What now, cummer, will thou nocht
  tak a part?
TAILOR'S WIFE: That sall I do, cummer, with all my heart.
  As the WIVES *chase their husbands off,* SOLACE *catches sight of* CHASTITY *and speaks to the* KING.
SOLACE: Sovereign, get up and see a heavenly sicht,
  A fair lady in white abilyement!
  She may be peer unto a king or knicht,

81

1052   *dispone*, dispose of.

1055   *flemit*, banished.

1058   *duleful*, painful.

Maist like an angel by my judgëment!
The KING *rises from among the ladies.*
KING: I sall gang see that sicht incontinent,
  (*to* SENSUALITY) Madame, behauld if ye have knawledging
  Of yon lady, or what is her intent.   1041
  Thereefter we sall turn but tarrying.
SENSUALITY: Sir, let me see what yon matter may mean –
  Perchance that I may knaw her by her face.
  She looks more closely at CHASTITY.
  But doubt this is Dame Chastity, I ween!
  Sir, I and she cannot bide in ane place!
  But if it be the pleasure of your grace,
  That I remain into your company,
  This woman richt hastily gar chase,
  That she na mair be seen in this country!   1050
KING: As ever ye please, sweetheart, sa sall it be!
  Dispone her as ye think expedient.
  Even as ye list to let her live or die,
  I will refer to you that judgëment.
SENSUALITY: I will that she be flemit incontinent,
  And never to come again in this country;
  And if she does, but doubt she sall repent,
  As als perchance a duleful deid sall die!
  Pass on, Sir Sapience and Discretioun,
  And banis her out of the King's presence!   1060
DECEIT: That sall we do, Madame, by God's passioun!
  We sall do your command with diligence,
  And at your hand serve goodly recompense.
  Dame Chastity, come on, be not aghast!
  We sall richt soon, upon your awn expense,
  Into the stocks your bonny foot mak fast!
  The VICES *place* CHASTITY *in the stocks beside* VERITY.
CHASTITY: Sister, alas, this is a care-full case,
  That we with princes sould be sa abhorred!
VERITY: Be blithe, sister, I trust within short space,
  That we sall be richt honourably restored,   1070

1077   *dress*, prepare.

1093   *mangit*, mad.

And with the King we sall be at concord,
For I hear tell Divine Correctioun
Is new landit, thankit be Christ our Lord!
I wot he will be our protectioun!
A fanfare. Enter CORRECTION'S VARLET.
VARLET: Sirs, stand back and hauld you coy.
  I am the King Correctioun's boy,
    Come here to dress his place!
  See that ye mak obedience
  Unto his noble excellence
    Fra time ye see his face!   1080
  For he maks reformatiouns
  Out-through all Christian natiouns,
    Where he finds great debates.
  And sa far as I understand,
  He sall reform into this land
    Even all the Three Estates.
  For silence I protest
    Baith of Lord, Laird and Leddy!
  Now will I rin but rest
    And tell that all is reddy!   1090
Another fanfare. Exit CORRECTION'S VARLET. *The* THREE
VICES *go into conference.*
DECEIT: Brother, hear ye yon proclamatioun?
  I dreid full sair of reformatioun.
    Yon message maks me mangit!
  What is your counsel, to me tell.
  Remain we here, by God himsell,
    We will be all three hangit!
FLATTERY: I'll gang to Sprituality
  And preach out-through his diocie,
    Where I will be unknawn,
  Or keep me close into some closter   1100
  With mony piteous Paternoster,
    Till all thir blasts be blawn.
DECEIT: I'll be weill treatit, as ye ken,

1115   Deceit, it will be remembered, had been made the King's
Treasurer.

1124   *landwart*, country.

With my maisters, the Merchant men,
   Whilk can mak small debate;
Ye ken richt few of them that thrives
Or can beguile the landwart wives,
   But me their man Deceit.
Now, Falset, what sall be thy shift?

FALSET: Na, care thou not, man, for my thrift!   1110
   Trows thou that I be daft?
Na, I will live a lusty life,
Withouten ony sturt or strife,
   Amang the men of craft.

DECEIT: Falset, I wald we made a band –
Now, while the King is yet sleepand
   What rack to steal his box?

FALSET: Now, weill said by the Sacrament!
I sall it steal incontinent,
   Thocht it had twenty locks!   1120

FALSET *steals the* KING'S *box.*

Lo, here the box! Now let us ga,
This may suffice for our rewairds!

DECEIT: Yea, that it may, man, by this day!
It may weill mak us landwart lairds!
Now let us cast away our clais,
In dreid some follow on the chase!

FALSET: Richt weill devisit, by Sant Blaise.
Wald God we were out of this place!
Here they cast away their disguises.

DECEIT: Now, sen there is na man to wrang us,
I pray you, brother, with my heart,   1130
Let us ga part this pelf amang us,
Syne hastily we sall depart!

FALSET: Trows thou to get as mekle as I?
That sall thou not! I stall the box!
Thou did nathing but lookit by,
Ay lurkand like a wily fox!

1138   *craig*, neck.

1139–41   *Rex . . . gloriae*, 'O King of fearful majesty, O strict judge of vengeance, Omnipotent King of glory'. The Latin lines are from the hymn, 'Dies irae, dies illa'.

1152   *weir*, war.
1153   *bud*, bribe; *owrsile*, deceive.

1157   *cankert*, corrupt.

DECEIT *and* FALSET *fight.*

FALSET: Alas for ever my eye is out!

DECEIT: Upon thy craig tak there a clout!

    FLATTERY *has meantime stolen the box and runs out pursued by*
    DECEIT *and* FALSEHOOD. *Their flight is hastened by the fanfare*
    and stately march to which enter DIVINE CORRECTION *and his*
    train. The ESTATES *sing.*

    Rex tremendae majestatis,
    Juste judex ultionis,   1140
    Rex omnipotens gloriae.

CORRECTION: I am callit Divine Correctioun.
    Where I am nocht is na tranquillity.
    By me traitors and tyrants are put doun,
    Wha thinks na shame of their iniquity.
    What is a King? Nocht but an officer,
    To cause his lieges live in equity,
    And under God to be a punisher
    Of trespassers against His Majesty.
    I am a judge, richt potent and seveir,   1150
    Come to do justice mony thousand mile.
    I am sa constant, baith in peace and weir,
    Na bud nor favour may my sicht owrsile.

    GOOD COUNSEL *enters and runs to greet his master.*

GOOD COUNSEL: Welcome, my lord, welcome ten thousand
        times
    To all faithful and true men of this regioun!
    Welcome for to correct all faults and crimes
    Amang this cankert congregatioun!
    Loose Chastity, I mak supplicatioun,
    Put to freedom fair Lady Verity,
    Wha by unfaithful folk of this natioun   1160
    Lies bound full fast into captivity!

CORRECTION: I marvel, Good Counsel, how that may be –
    Are ye nocht with the King familiar?

GOOD COUNSEL: That am I nocht, my lord, full wae is me,
    But like a beggar am haulden at the bar.

1167   *disguisit,* transformed.

1169   *supprisit,* oppressed.

1173   *do but mocks,* only make game.

1181   M.

1185   *stand ford,* warrant.

1195   *eneuch,* enough.

CORRECTION: Where lies yon ladies in captivity?
He turns to VERITY *and* CHASTITY *in the stocks.*
How now, sisters, wha has you sa disguisit?
VERITY: Unfaithful members of iniquity
Despitefully, my lord, has us supprisit.
CORRECTION: Ga, put yon ladies to their liberty   1170
Incontinent, and break doun all the stocks!
But doubt, they are full dear welcome to me!
Mak diligence! Methinks ye do but mocks!
Speed hand, and spare not for to break the locks,
And tenderly tak them up by the hand!
Had I them here, these knaves sould ken my knocks,
That them oppresst and banist of this land!
Members of CORRECTION'S *retinue release* VERITY *and* CHAS-
TITY. *The* COURTIERS *spy* CORRECTION.
WANTONNESS: Solace, knaws thou not what I see?
A knicht, or else a king thinks me.
Brother, what may this mean?   1180
I understand not by this day
Wheder that he be freind or fae!
Stand still and hear what he will say.
Sic ane I have not seen!
SOLACE: Yon is a stranger I stand ford.
He seems to be a lusty lord.
PLACEBO: I rede us, put upon the King,
And wauken him of his sleeping!
He rouses the KING *from the arms of* SENSUALITY.
Sir, rise and see an uncouth thing!
Get up, ye lie too lang!   1190
SENSUALITY: Put on your hood, John-fool! Ye rave!
How dare you be so pert, Sir Knave,
To touch the King? Sa Christ me save,
False hureson, thou sall hang!
CORRECTION *approaches the* KING.
CORRECTION: Get up, Sir King, ye have sleepit eneuch
Into the arms of Lady Sensual!

1197–8   M.

1199   *Noy*, Noah.

1211   *doun-thring*, throw down.

1218   *dilatioun*, delay.

1228   *air*, early.

The KING *rises and faces him.*
Be sure that mair belangis to the pleuch,
As efterwart, perchance, rehearse I sall.
Remember how, into the time of Noy
For the foul stink and sin of lechery,   1200
God by my wand did all the warld destroy.
Sodom and Gomore richt sa full rigorously
For that vile sin were brunt maist cruelly.
Therefore I thee command incontinent,
Banish from thee that hure, Sensuality,
Or else but doubt rudely thou sall repent!
KING: By whom have ye sa great authority?
Wha does presume for to correct a King?
Knaw ye nocht me, great King Humanity,
That in my regioun royally does ring?   1210
CORRECTION: I have power great princes to doun-thring
That lives contrair the Majesty Divine,
Against the truth whilk plainly does maling;
Repent they nocht, I put them to ruine.
I will begin at thee, whilk is the heid,
And mak on thee first reformatioun,
Thy lieges than will follow thee but pleid!
Swith, harlot, hence without dilatioun!
SENSUALITY: My lord, I mak you supplicatioun,
Give me licence to pass again to Rome!   1220
Amang the princes of that natioun,
I let you wit my fresh beauty will bloom!
Adieu, Sir King, I may na langer tarry!
I care nocht that. As good luve comes as gaes!
I recommend you to the Queen of Faerie.
I see ye will be guidit by my faes!
SENSUALITY *and her retinue pass to the* ESTATE SPIRITUAL.
My lordis of the Spritual State,
Venus preserve you air and late!
For I can mak na mair debate,
    I am partit with your king,   1230

1238   Lindsay's stage direction reads, 'Heir sal the Bishops, Abbots and Persons kis the Ladies'.

1262   *dress*, settle.

And am banist this regioun,
By council of Correctioun.
Be ye nocht my protectioun,
    I may seek my ludging!

BISHOP: Welcome, our days' darling!
Welcome with all our heart!
We all but feignyeing
Sall plainly tak your part!

BISHOP, ABBOT *and* PARSON *kiss the ladies, who then take their places with them.* CORRECTION *returns to the* KING.

CORRECTION: Sen ye are quit of Sensuality,
Resave into your service Good Counsel,   1240
And richt sa this fair Lady Chastity
Till ye marry some Queen of blood royal.
Observe then chastity matrimonial.
Richt sa resave Verity by the hand.
Use their counsel, your fame sall never fall.
With them therefore, mak a perpetual band!

The KING *receives* GOOD COUNSEL, CHASTITY *and* VERITY.

Now, sir, tak tent what I will say,
Observe thir same baith nicht and day,
And let them never part you fra,
    Or else withouten doubt,   1250
Turn ye to Sensuality,
To vicious life and ribaldry,
Out of your realm richt shamefully
    Ye sall be rootit out!

KING: I am content to your counsel t'incline.
At your command sall be all that is mine.

Solemn music. He embraces CORRECTION.

CORRECTION: I counsel you incontinent
To gar proclaim a Parliament
    Of all the Three Estates,
That they be here with diligence   1260
To mak to you obedience
    And syne dress all debates!

1269   *compeir*, appear when summoned.

1273   *underlie*, suffer.

1279   *denier*, penny.

1285   *the teind . . . Mire*. The texts read 'Ferry Mire.' Hamer identifies the allusion to Ferny Mire – place-names in this area are also spelled 'Ferry' – a bog beside Lindsay's estate at Mount Hill in Monimail Parish, Fife. The jest lies in the non-existence of the said mussels. Lindsay, like Diligence, was a herald. Compare the complaint of SOLACE at ll. 115–21, and the Scribe's sudden interruption of the dialogue at l. 2077 to complain of unpaid services.

1289   *the coal-pots of Tranent*, the coal-pits of Tranent in Haddington-shire.

1291   *drouth*, thirst.

1293   *ocht*, aught.

KING: That sall be done, but mair demand.
  Ho, Diligence, come here fra-hand
    And tak your informatioun.
  Go, warn the Sprituality,
  Richt sa the Temporality,
    By open proclamatioun,
  In goodly haste for to compeir
  In their most honourable maneir   1270
    To give us their counsails!
  Wha that beis absent, to them shaw
  That they sall underlie the Law
    And punist be that fails!
DILIGENCE: Sir, I sall baith in borough and land,
  With diligence do your command,
    Upon my awn expense.
  Sir, I have servit you all this year,
  But I gat never a denier
    Yet for my recompense!   1280
KING: Pass on, and thou sall be regairdit
  And for thy service weill rewairdit,
    For-why, with my consent,
  Thou sall have yearly for thy hire
  The teind mussels of the Ferry Mire
    Confirmt in Parliament.
DILIGENCE: I will get riches through that rent
    Efter the day of Doom,
  When in the coal-pots of Tranent
    Butter will grow on broom!   1290
  All nicht I had sa meikle drouth,
    I micht not sleep a wink.
  Or I proclaim ocht with my mouth,
    But doubt I mon have drink!
  While DILIGENCE *refreshes himself* DIVINE CORRECTION
  tackles the COURTIERS.
CORRECTION: Come here, Placebo and Solace,
  With your companion Wantonness,

1308   *remissioun*, pardon.

1310   *tables*, backgammon.

1327–8   M.
1328   *waur*, worse.

1331   *whilk*, that.

I knaw weill your conditioun.
For ticeting King Humanity
To resave Sensuality
Ye mon suffer punitioun!   1300

WANTONNESS: We grant, my Lord, we have done ill;
Therefore we put us in your will,
But we have been abusit!

PLACEBO: For in good faith, sir, we believit
That lechery had na man grievit
Because it is sa usit!

SOLACE: Sir, we sall mend our conditioun
Sa ye give us remissioun.
But give us leave to sing,
To dance, to play at chess and tables,   1310
To read stories and merry fables
For pleasure of our King!

CORRECTION: Sa that ye do na other crime,
Ye sall be pardont at this time,
For-why, as I suppose,
Princes may sometime seek solace
With mirth and lawful merriness,
Their spirits to rejose.
And richt sa hawking and hunting
Are honest pastimes for a king,   1320
Into the time of peace;
And learn to rin a heavy spear,
That he into the time of weir
May follow at the chase.

KING: Where is Sapience and Discretioun?
And why comes not Devotioun near?

VERITY: Sapience, sir, was a very loon,
And Devotioun was nine times waur.

CHASTITY: They three were Flattery and Deceit,
And Falset, that unhappy loon,   1330
Against us three whilk made debate
And banist us fra toun to toun.

1333   *soun,* swoon.

1338   *Sant Fillane,* an eighth-century Scots saint after whom Strath-
        fillan is named. He had the special prayers of Bruce before
        Bannockburn.

1339   *paiks,* punishment.

1340   *playit me the glaiks,* made a fool of me.

They gart us twa fall into soun,
When they us lockit in the stocks.
That dastart knave, Discretioun,
Full theftuously did steal your box!

KING: The Deil tak them, sen they are gane!
I mak a vow to sweet Sant Fillane,
Get I them they sall beir their paiks.
I see they have playit me the glaiks!   1340
Good Counsel, now shaw me the best.
How sall I keep my realm in rest?

GOOD COUNSEL: The principal point, sir, of a king's office,
Is for to do to every man justice,
And for to mix his justice with mercy,
But rigour, favour or partiality.
Wha guides them weill, they win immortal fame;
Wha the contrair, they get perpetual shame.
The Chronicles to knaw, I you exhort;
There sall ye find baith good and evil report;   1350
For every prince efter his quality,
Thocht he be deid his deeds sall never die!
Sir, if ye please for to use my counsel,
Your fame and name sall be perpetual.
A fanfare.

DILIGENCE: Hoyez, hoyez, hoyez!
At the command of King Humanity,
I warn and charge all members of Parliament,
Baith Spiritual State and Temporality,
That to his grace they be obedient
And speed them to the court, incontinent,   1360
In good order, arrayit royally.
Wha beis absent or inobedient,
The King's displeasure they sall underlie!
To the audience.
And als I mak you exhortatioun,
Sen ye have heard the first part of our play,
Go, tak a drink, and mak collatioun;

1371   *ingine,* mind.

Ilk man drink to his marrow, I you pray.
Tarry nocht lang, it is late in the day.
Let some drink ale, and some drink claret wine;
By great doctors of physic I hear say   1370
That michty drink comforts the dull ingine!
Music, a march. All go off.

END OF PART ONE

1372	The interlude of the Poor Man and the Pardoner is to be considered integral to the play for its illustration of one aspect of the corrupting influence of Flattery on the Church. As a friar he has not only encouraged the hierarchy to leave the duty of preaching to him, but here destroys its credit with his unscrupulous exploitation of selfishly motivated superstitions. In the 1554 Quarto the interlude is preceded by the statement: 'thair is to cum, I say you / The best pairt of our Play. / The END of the first part of the SATYRE. / Now sall the pepill mak Collatioun, then beginnis the Interlude, the Kings, Bischops and principall players being out of their seats'. The principal players have not left because the interlude is mere pastime but because they must soon re-enter at its close, 'gangand backwart'.
1375	*wiss*, direct
1378–9	M.
1378	*faillies*, faults.
1379	*Provost and Baillies*. These officials (English equivalent mayor and aldermen) would be in the audience.
1383	*brunt shins*, able limbs. The shin is the forepart of the leg between knee and ankle; in this context 'brunt' seems to have meant 'forward', 'active'. John mimics the kind of oath that courtiers affected.
1388	*crookit*, lame.
1389	*meikle*, great.

PART TWO

Fanfare. DILIGENCE *comes on to the empty stage as if to make a proclamation. Before he can do so, the* POOR MAN *enters, addressing the audience.*

POOR MAN: Of your almous, good folks, for God's love of
    heaven,
  For I have motherless bairnis either sax or seven!
  If ye will give na good, for luve of sweet Jesus,
  Wiss me the richt way to Sant Andrews.

DILIGENCE: Where have we gotten this goodly companion?
  Swith! Furth of the field, thou false, raggit loon!
  Fie on you officers that mends not thir faillies!
  I give you all to the Deil, baith Provost and Baillies.
  Without ye come and chase this carl away   1380
  The deil a word ye's get mair of our play!

The POOR MAN *climbs on to the* KING'S *throne.*

  Come doun, or by God's croun, false loon I sall slay thee!

POOR MAN: Now sweir by thy brunt shins, the Deil ding them
    fra thee!

DILIGENCE: Swith! Beggar bogle, haste thee away,
  Thou art over pert to spoil our play!

POOR MAN: I will not give for all your play worth a sow's fart,
  For there is richt little play at my hungry heart!

DILIGENCE: What deil ails this crookit carl?

POOR MAN: Marry, meikle sorrow!
  I cannot get, thocht I gasp, to beg nor to borrow.   1390

DILIGENCE: Where, deil, is this thou dwells, or what is thine
    intent?

POOR MAN: I dwell into Lothian, a mile fra Tranent.

DILIGENCE: Where wald thou be, carl? The sooth to me shaw!

POOR MAN: Sir, even to Sant Andrews, for to seek law.

DILIGENCE: For to seek law, in Edinburgh is the nearest way.

POOR MAN: Sir, I socht law there this mony dear day;

1397   *Session.* The College of Justice, the supreme civil court, was only instituted in 1532, but similar courts had functioned since the reign of James I.

         Senyie. A consistory or diocesan court had jurisdiction over such causes as tithes, testaments, matrimonial and heretical affairs. The Poor Man has been unsuccessful in his plea to the inferior consistory at Edinburgh and now wishes to appeal to the senior diocesan court at St Andrews. The priest's funerary exactions of the '*corspresent*' of a cow, or clothing, like the landlord's 'herild' (i.e. 'lord's due') of a horse or cow, was not exceptional but customary practice. Lindsay's play doubtless influenced the decision of a Church Council in 1559 to mitigate such exactions in the case of the very poor.

1407   *meir*, mare.

1409   *fat*, well fleshed.

1410   *tidier*, plumper.

1412   *mane*, lament.

1415   *baitand*, grazing.

1416   *hereild* (see note to l. 1397).

1424   *cleikit*, seized.

1425   *umest clais*, 'uppermost clothing', i.e. the bed covering?

         rapploch, homespun

But I could get nane at Session or Senyie,
Therefore the meikle dumb deil droun all that menyie!
DILIGENCE Shaw me thy matter, man, with all the circumstance,
How thou has happent this unhappy chance.   1400
POOR MAN: Good man, will ye give me of your charity
And I sall declare you the black verity.
My father was an auld man and a hair
And was of age four score of years and mair,
And Maud my mother was four score and fiftein;
And with my labour I did them baith sustein.
We had a meir that carriet salt and coal,
And everilk year she brocht us hame a foal.
We had three kye that was baith fat and fair,
Nane tidier into the toun of Ayr.   1410
My father was sa weak of bluid and bane,
That he deit, wherefore my mother made great mane.
Then she deit within a day or two,
And there began my poverty and woe.
Our good grey meir was baitand on the field
And our land's laird took her for his hereild.
Our vicar took the best cow by the heid
Incontinent, when my father was deid.
And when the vicar heard tell how that my mother
Was deid, fra-hand he took fra me another.   1420
Then Meg my wife did murn baith even and morrow
Till at the last she deit for very sorrow.
And when the vicar heard tell my wife was deid,
The thrid cow he cleikit by the heid.
Their umest clais, that were of rapploch grey,
The vicar gart his clerk beir them away.
When all was gane I micht mak na debate,
But with my bairns passed for to beg my meat.
Now I have tauld you the black verity
How I am brocht into this misery.   1430

1431   *the Parson.* The vicar held his benefice *in cure* for a religious house, abbey or nunnery; the parson was responsible for the whole parish'.

1432   *teind*, tithe.

1434   *Pace*, Easter.

1436   *Inglis groat*, also known as the 'silver penny'.

1452   *Rome-raker*, anyone travelling to Rome for religious reasons, but here one who goes there for motives of greed, to obtain a benefice or pardoner's license. Lindsay makes fun of the title, 'Sir', that gave priests the comic description of 'Pope's Knights' (see 1450).

1456   *privilege*, license.

DILIGENCE: How did the Parson? Was he not thy good freind?

POOR MAN: The Deil stick him! He curst me for my teind
And haulds me yet under that same process,
That gart me want the Sacrament at Pace.
In good faith, sir, thocht ye wald cut my throat,
I have na gear except ane Inglis groat
Whilk I purpose to give a man of law.

DILIGENCE: Thou art the daftest fool that ever I saw!
Trows thou, man, by the law to get remeid
Of men of Kirk? Na, never till thou be deid!   1440
Be sure of priests thou will get na support.

POOR MAN: If that be true, the fiend resave the sort!
Sa, sen I see I get na other grace,
I will lie down and rest me in this place.
He does so. Enter PARDONER, *who is* FLATTERY *in his disguise.*

PARDONER: *Bona dies, bona dies!*
Devote people, good day I say you,
Now tarry a little while I pray you
    Till I be with you knawn!
Wot ye weill how I am namit?
A noble man and undefamit,   1450
    If all the sooth were shawn.
I am Sir Robert Rome-raker,
A perfite public pardoner
    Admittit by the Paip.
Sirs, I sall shaw you, for my wage,
My pardons and my privilege,
    Whilk ye sall see and graip.
I give to the Deil with good intent
This waeful wickit New Testament,
    With them that it translatit!   1460
Since laymen knew the verity,
Pardoners gets na charity
    Without that they debate it.
Deil fell the brain that has it wrocht,
Sa fall them that the Book hame brocht!

1468   *Black Bullenger and Melancthoun.* Heinrich Bullinger (1504–75), the Swiss Reformer; Philip Melancthon (1497–1560), the German Reformer, who assisted Luther in his translation of the New Testament.

1469   *smoored*, smothered; *cude*, baptismal face-cloth.

1471   *Sant Paul* is cursed because his Epistles were a favourite authority of the Reformers for their criticisms of the Church.

1474   *into the mirk.* in the dark, i.e. secretly.

1477   *Cam of Tartary*, the Khan of Tartary, a comic name for the Devil.

1478   *oyster-shells.* The cockle or scallop shell was the badge of a pilgrim.

1483   *Finn Macoul.* A hero of Irish legend credited with giant strength.

1483   *chaft-blade*, cheek-bone.

1486–7   *Mac Connels corn . . . Bawhidder.* The allusion has not been identified. Balquhidder is a village in West Perthshire.

1489   *Johnnie Armistrang*, John Armstrong, a celebrated Border reiver hanged by James V. See the ballad of Johnnie Armstrang.

1491   *Stand ford*, stand for it, guarantee.

Als I pray to the Rood,
That Martin Luther, that false loon,
Black Bullenger and Melancthoun,
   Had been smoored in their cude!
By him that bure the croun of thorn   1470
I wald Sant Paul had never been born,
   And als I wald his books
Were never read into the Kirk,
But amang freirs into the mirk,
   Or riven amang the rooks!
My patent pardons ye may see,
Come from the Cam of Tartary
   Weill sealt with oyster shells.
Thocht ye have na contritioun
Ye sall have full remissioun   1480
   With help of books and bells.
Here is a relic, lang and braid,
Of Finn Macoul the richt chaft-blade,
   With teeth and all together.
Of Colin's cow here is a horn,
For eating of MacConnel's corn
   Was slain into Bawhidder.
Here is a cord baith great and lang,
Whilk hangit Johnnie Armistrang,
   Of good hemp saft and sound.   1490
Good haily people, I stand ford,
Whaever beis hangit with this cord
   Needs never to be dround!
Come win the pardon, now let see,
For meal, for malt or for money,
   For cock, hen, goose, or grice!
Of relics here I have a hunder.
Why come ye not? This is a wonder.

1499   NOTE: part of the interlude is omitted here; the Pardoner acts as a devil's priest in an obscenely performed ceremony of divorce between a cobbler and his wife. He claims that his 'pardon' can save them from the hell of unhappy marriage. *S.D.* Wilkin does not appear in Kemp's version.

1500–23   M.

1501   *Widdiefow*. The surname means 'gallows-bird'.

1513–1518 *Christian Anderson . . . Bawburd*, a reference to whores.

1515   *limmer*, rascal.

1524   *crack*, brag.

1526   *sain*, bless.

1527   *Sant Bride . . . again!* Saint Bridget, the Irish saint, is remembered here particularly for the legend of her recovery of some stolen cattle.

     I trow ye be not wise!
The PARDONER'S BOY, WILKIN *is heard calling.*
WILKIN: Ho, maister, ho, where are ye now?   1500
PARDONER: I am here, Wilkin Widdiefow.
WILKIN: Sir, I have done your bidding,
   For I have fund a great horse-bane,
   A fairer saw ye never nane,
   Upon Tom Flesher's midden.
   Sir, ye may gar the wifeis trow
   It is a bane of Sant Bride's cow,
     Good for the fever quartane.
   Sir, will ye rule this relic weill,
   All haill the wives will kiss and kneel,   1510
     Betwix this and Dumbartane.
PARDONER: Where sall I ludge into the toun?
WILKIN: With good kind Christian Andersoun,
     Where ye will be weill treatit.
   If ony limmer you demands,
   She will defend you with her hands
     And womanly debate it.
   Bawburd says, by the Trinity,
   That she sall beir you company,
     Howbeit ye bide a year.   1520
PARDONER: Thou has done weill, by God's mother!
   Tak ye the tane and I the tother,
     Sa sall we mak great cheer.
The POOR MAN *wakes up.*
POOR MAN: What thing was yon that I heard crack and cry?
   I have been dreamand and drivelland of my kye!
   With my richt hand my haill body I sain,
   Sant Bride, Sant Bride, send me my kye again!
He sees the PARDONER.
   I see standand yonder a haily man.
   To mak me help, let me see if he can!
   Haily maister, God speed you and good morn.   1530

1531   *at the horn*, outlawed. Outlawry was proclaimed by horn or trumpet at the market-cross of the head burgh of the outlaw's district.

1537   *fra-hand*, forthwith.
1538   *lost*, damned.

1543   *ripe*, search.

1551   *pleid*, plea.

1561   *but weir*, doubtless.

PARDONER: Welcome to me thocht thou were at the horn.
Come win the pardon, and then I sall thee sain!
POOR MAN: Will that pardon get me my kye again?
PARDONER: Carl, of thy kye I have nathing ado.
Come win my pardon, and kiss my relics too.
He blesses him with his relics.
Now loose thy purse, and lay doun thy offrand,
And thou sall have my pardon even fra-hand.
Now win the pardon, limmer, or thou art lost!
POOR MAN: My haily father, what will that pardon cost?
PARDONER: Let see what money thou beiris in thy bag.   1540
POOR MAN: I have ae groat here bund into a rag.
PARDONER: Hast thou na other siller but a groat?
POOR MAN: If I have mair, sir, come and ripe my coat!
PARDONER: Give me that groat, man, if thou has na mair.
POOR MAN: With all my heart, maister, lo, tak it, there!
Now let me see your pardon, with your leave.
PARDONER: A thousand year of pardons I thee give!
POOR MAN: A thousand year? I will not live sa lang.
Deliver me it, maister, and let me gang!
PARDONER: A thousand year I lay upon thy heid,   1550
With *totiens quotiens;* now mak me na mair pleid.
Thou hast resavit thy pardon now already.
POOR MAN: But I can see nathing, sir, by our Lady!
PARDONER: What craves the carl? Methinks thou art not wise!
POOR MAN: I crave my groat, or else my merchandise!
PARDONER: I gave thee pardon for a thousand year!
POOR MAN: How sall I get that pardon? Let me hear!
PARDONER: Stand still, and I sall tell thee the haill story!
When thou art deid and gaes to Purgatory,
Being condemnt to pain a thousand year,   1560
Then sall thy pardon thee relieve but weir!
Now be content! Ye are a mervellous man!
POOR MAN: Sall I get nathing for my groat till then?
PARDONER: That sall thou not! I mak it to you plain!

1568   *steid*, place.

1576–9   M. *abet*, abate, lessen.
1577   *het*, heat.
1578   *blind lambs*, unseen lambs, 'a pig in a poke'.
1579   *dryte*, make dirt; *gambs*, tricks.
1580   *mangit*, mad.

1583   *rout*, blow.

1594   *by adulatioun*, without flattery; 'without any' is a frequent
        sense of 'by'.

The poor man is now very angry.

POOR MAN: Na? Then, gossip, give me my groat again!
　　What say ye, maisters? Call ye this good reason,
　　That he sould promise me a good pardon,
　　And here resave my money in this steid,
　　Syne mak me na payment till I be deid?
　　When I am deid, I wot full sickerly　　　　　　　　1570
　　My silly saul will pass to Purgatory.
　　Declare me this! Now God nor Belial bind thee,
　　When I am there, curst carl, where sall I find thee?
　　Not into heaven, but rather into hell!
　　When thou art there, thou cannot help thysell!
　　When will thou come my dolours to abet?
　　Or I thee find my hips will get a het!
　　Trows thou, butcher, that I will buy blind lambs?
　　Give me my groat! The Deil dryte on thy gambs!
PARDONER: Swith! Stand aback! I trow this man be　　1580
　　mangit!
　　Thou gets not this, carl, thocht thou sould be hangit!
POOR MAN: Give me my groat, weill bund into a clout!
　　Or by God's breid, Robin sall beir a rout!
　　He sets upon the PARDONER, *scatters his relics and chases him off.*
DILIGENCE: What kind of daffing is this all day?
　　Swith, smaiks, out of the field, away!
　　Into a prison put them soon,
　　Syne hang them when the play is done!
　　A fanfare and a march. Enter the KING, *his* COURTIERS, DIVINE
　　CORRECTION, *the* VIRTUES. *The music continues with the speech.*
　　Famous people, tak tent, and ye sall see
　　The Three Estatis of this natioun,
　　Come to the court with a strange gravity.　　　　　　1590
　　Therefore I mak you supplicatioun,
　　Till ye have heard our haill narratioun
　　To keep silence and be patient I pray you.
　　Howbeit we speak by adulatioun

1595   As appears from ll. 1708–23, the spiritual Estate is led by the figures of Covetice and Sensuality, the temporal Estate by that of Public Oppression, and the Burgesses by those of Falset and Deceit. Flattery, though first identified with the Court and now protected by Spirituality, belongs everywhere.

1606   *mon*, must.

1625   *heids*, leaders.

We sall say nathing but the sooth, I say you!

THE THREE ESTATES *enter, led by their* VICES. *They are walking backwards,* SPIRITUALITY *led by* FLATTERY, COVETICE *and* SENSUALITY, TEMPORALITY *by* PUBLIC OPPRESSION, *and* BURGESSES *by* FALSET *and* DECEIT.

WANTONNESS: Now, braid benedicite!
What thing is yon that I see?
   Look, Solace, my heart!

SOLACE: Brother Wantonness, what thinks thou?
Yon are the Three Estates, I trow,   1600
Gangand backwart!

WANTONNESS: Backwart? Backwart? Out wallaway!
It is great shame for them, I say,
   Backwart to gang.
I trow the King Correctioun
Mon mak a reformatioun
   Or it be lang!
Now let us go and tell the King!
Sir, we have seen a mervellous thing,
   By our judgment!   1610
The Three Estates of this regioun
Are cumand backwart through this toun,
   To the Parliament!

KING: Backwart, backwart, how may that be?
Gar speed them hastily to me,
   In dreid that they ga wrong!

PLACEBO: Sir, I see them yonder cumand.
They will be here even fra-hand,
   As fast as they may gang!

GOOD COUNSEL: Sir, hauld you still and scare them not, 1620
Till you persave what be their thocht,
   And see what men them leids.
And let the King Correctioun
Mak a sharp inquisition,
   And mark them by the heids!

119

1642   *lands*, properties.

1646   *leil*, loyal.

1648   *Ye … heid*, perhaps the most common of medieval and Renaissance analogies to express the inter-dependence of governor and governed. Lindsay had read the late fifteenth century *Three Tales of The Three Priests of Peebles*, in which a reforming Scots king summons the Three Estates and addresses the Lords thus (ll. 105-8):

        Ane heid dow not on body stand allane
        Forout members to be of micht and mane,
        For to uphald the bodie and the heid,
        And sickerlie to gar it stand in steid.

THE ESTATES *are singing a chorus made up from words from the*
following verses:

SPIRITUALITY: Gloir, honour, laud, triumph and victory,
Be to your michty prudent excellence.
Here are we come, all the Estatis Three,
Ready to mak our due obedience,
At your command with humble observance,   1630
As may pertein to Sprituality,
With counsel of the Temporality.

TEMPORALITY: Sir, we with michty courage, at command
Of your super-excellent Majesty,
Sall mak service, baith with our heart and hand,
And sall not dreid in thy defence to die.
We are content, but doubt, that we may see
That noble, heavenly King Correctioun,
Sa he with mercy mak punitioun.

BURGESSES: Sir, we are here your Burgesses and Merchants.
Thanks be to God that we may see your face,   1641
Traistand we may now into divers lands
Convoy our gear with support of your grace;
For now, I traist, we sall get rest and peace.
When mis-doers are with your sword owrthrawn,
Then may leil merchants live upon their awn.
The singing ends.

KING: Welcome to me, my prudent lordis all,
Ye are my members, suppose I be your heid.
Sit doun that we may with your just counsel
Agains mis-doers find sovereign remeid.   1650

CORRECTION: My tender freinds, I pray you with my heart,
Declare to me the thing that I wald speir.
What is the cause that ye gang all backwart?
The verity thereof fain wald I hear.

BISHOP: Sovereign, we have gane sa this mony a year.
Howbeit ye think we go undecently,
We think we go richt wonder pleasantly.

DILIGENCE: Sit doun, my lords, into your proper places,

1660   *Dempster*, the officer who pronounced the 'doom' or sentence of the court.

1661   *fence the Court*, formally declare in session. The form of words in a baron court began, 'I defend and biddis in our leige Lord the King's behalfe of Scotland . . . that na man distrouble this court unlawfullie.' (*Habakkuk Bisset's Rolment of Courtis*, Scottish Text Society, note to vol. i, p. 248, l. 10).

1666   *doun-thring*, oppress.

1676   *for-why*, because.

1681   *applyable*, submissive.

1684–5   M.

Syne let the King consider all sic cases.
Sit doun, Sir Scribe, and sit doun Dempster too,   1660
And fence the Court as ye were wont to do.
Music as THE ESTATES *take their places and all present dispose*
themselves for a court of enquiry.

KING: My prudent lordis of the Three Estates,
It is our will, above all other thing,
For to reform all them that maks debates,
Contrair the richt whilk daily does maling,
And they that does the Common-Weal doun-thring.
With help and counsel of King Correctioun,
It is our will for to mak punishing,
And plain oppressors put to subjectioun.

BISHOP: What thing is this, sir, that ye have deviset?   1670
Sirs, ye have need for to be weill adviset.
Be nocht hasty into your executioun,
And be not owr extreme in your punitioun.
And if ye please to do, sir, as we say,
Postpone this Parliament to another day,
For-why the people of this regioun
May nocht endure extreme correctioun!

CORRECTION: Is this the part, my lords, that ye will tak
To mak us supportatioun to correct?
It does appear that ye are culpable,   1680
That are not to correctioun applyable!
Swith, Diligence, ga shaw it is our will,
That everilk man opprest give in his bill.

DILIGENCE(*proclaims*): All manner of men I warn that be opprest,
Come and complain and they sall be redrest,
For-why it is the noble Prince's will
That ilk complainer sall give in his bill.

1688   JOHN THE COMMONWEAL, had appeared in Lindsay's early poem, *The Dreme*, and is here particularly representative of the commons, the classes not represented in the Convention of the Three Estates, but also more generally of the Scots people as distinct from their governors.

1695   *new-made King*. The 1554 Quarto reads 'new-cumde King', which should refer to King Correction, but King Humanity is intended. He is 'new-crowned', or 'new-made' spiritually.

1702   *crookit*, lame.
1703   *owrlookit*, neglected.

1706   On the Vices that lead the respective Estates see note to l. 1595.
1706   *limmers*, rascals.
1707   *canker colours*, corrupt pretences; *heids*, leaders.

1712–13   M.

1719   *clais*, clothes.

JOHN THE COMMON-WEAL, *a sturdy figure, in rags, rushes in. He is seen to be lame.*

JOHN: Out of my gait! For God's sake let me ga!
Tell me again, good maister, what ye say.

DILIGENCE: I warn all that be wrangously offendit, 1690
Come and complain and they sall be amendit.
What is thy name, fellow? That wald I feel.

JOHN: Forsooth, they call me John the Common-Weal.
Good maister, I wald ask at you ane thing –
Where traist ye I sall find yon new-made King?

DILIGENCE: Come owr, and I sall shaw thee to his Grace.
He leads JOHN *to the* KING.

JOHN: God's benison licht on that lucky face!

KING: Shaw me thy name, good man, I thee command.

JOHN: Marry, John the Common-Weal of fair Scotland.
The KING *surveys* JOHN'S *rags*

KING: The Common-Weal has been amang his faes! 1700

JOHN: Yea, sir, that gars the Common-Weal want clais!

KING: What is the cause the Common-Weal is crookit?

JOHN: Because the Common-Weal has been owr-lookit.

KING: What gars thee look sa with a dreary heart?

JOHN: Because the Three Estates gangs all backwart.

KING: Sir Common-Weal, knaw ye the limmers that them leids?

JOHN: Their canker colours, I ken them by the heids:
As for our reverent fathers of Sprituality,
They are led by Covetice, this carl, and Sensuality,
And as ye see, Temporality has need of correctioun, 1710
Whilk has lang time been led by Public Oppressioun.
Lo, where the loon lies lurkand at his back.
Get up! I think to see thy craig gar a raip crack!
Lo, here is Falset and Deceit weill I ken,
Leaders of the Merchants and silly craftsmen.
What mervel thocht the Three Estates backwart gang,
When sic a vile company dwells them amang,
Whilk has rulit this rout mony dear days,
Whilk gars John the Common-Weal want his warm clais?

1720–21   M.

1721   i.e. John would have to become a Border reiver.

1725   *truckers*, rogues.

1728   *pelours*, thieves.

1734   *sweir*, reluctant.

1738   *stewats*, filthy fellows; *brocks*, badgers.

1744–54   The parting speeches of Covetice and Sensuality, along with the Bishop's replies, show what slight expectations Lindsay had of their being separated from the Spiritual Estate.

1744–9   M. Covetice not in Kemp's version.

1748   *Sant Maven*, a Welsh saint who founded the abbey of Saint Meen in Brittany.

1749   *we are twa natural men*, see note to l. 218; they have the same parentage, presumably the Devil.

1752   *dule*, grief.

Sir, call them before you and put them in order,   1720
Or else John the Common-Weal mon beg on the Border!
Thou feignyit Flattery, the fiend fart in thy face!
When ye was guider of the court we gat little grace!
My sovereign Lord Correctioun, I mak you supplicatioun,
Put thir tried truckers from Christ's congregatioun!
CORRECTION: As ye have deviset, but doubt it sall be done!
Come here, my sergeants, and do your debt soon!
Put thir three pelours into prison strang,
Howbeit ye sould hang them, ye do them na wrang!
FIRST SERGEANT: Sovereign lord, we sall obey your commands.
Brother, upon thir limmers lay on your hands!   1731
SECOND SERGEANT: Come here, gossip, come here, come here!
Your reckless life ye sall repent.
When was ye wont to be sa sweir?
Stand still and be obedient!
The SERGEANTS *hustle the* THREE VICES *to the stocks.*
Put in your legs into the stocks,
For ye had never a meeter hose!
Thir stewats stinks as they were brocks!
Now are ye siccar, I suppose!
They go to CORRECTION.
My lord, we have done your commands.   1740
Sall we put Covetice in captivity?
CORRECTION: Yea, heartly lay on them your hands,
Richt sa upon Sensuality!
COVETICE: My reverent fathers tak in patience.
I sall nocht lang remain from your presence.
Thocht for a while I mon from you depart,
I wot my spreit sall remain in your heart.
BISHOP: Adieu, by Sant Maven,
Pass where ye will, we are twa natural men!
SENSUALITY: Adieu, my lord!   1750
BISHOP: Adieu, my awn sweet heart!
Now dule fell me that we twa mon part!
SENSUALITY: My lord, howbeit this parting does me pain,

127

1754   M.

1758   *priset*, approved.

1770   *slaik*, quench; *murmell*, complaint.

1779   *sickerly*, certainly.

I traist in God we sall meet soon again.

THE SERGEANTS *chase* SENSUALITY *and her retinue away to a*
place among the POOR PEOPLE *at the foot of the stage.*

LORD: My lords, ye knaw the Three Estates
For Common-Weal sould mak debates.
Let now amang us be deviset
Sic Acts as with good men be priset;
And for to save us fra murmell,
Soon, Diligence, fetch us Good Counsel,   1760
For-why he is a man that knaws
Baith the Canon and Civil Laws.

DILIGENCE *passes to* GOOD COUNSEL.

DILIGENCE: Father, ye mon incontinent
Pass to the Lords of Parliament;
For-why they are determint all
To do nathing but your counsel.

GOOD COUNSEL: My lords, God glad the company!
What is the cause ye send for me?

MERCHANT: Sit doun and give us your counsel,
How we sall slaik the great murmell   1770
Of poor people, that is weill knawn
And as the Common-Weal has shawn.
And als we knaw it is the Kingis will
That good remede be put there-till.
Sir Common-Weal, keep ye the bar.
Let nane except yoursell come near!

JOHN *lays his hand on the* POOR MAN.

JOHN: Ye mon let this poor crëature
Support me for to keep the door.
I knaw his name full sickerly.
He will complain as weill as I.   1780

GOOD COUNSEL: My worthy lords, sen ye have tane on hand
Some reformatioun to mak into this land,
And als ye knaw it is the Kingis mind,
Wha to the Common-Weal has aye been kind,
Thocht reive and thift were stanchit weill eneuch,

1793   *tint*, lost.

1799–1802 M.
1799   *hichtit*, raised; *mail*, rent.
1800   *watter kail*, cabbage soup.

1802   *harlt*, dragged.

1804   *God's breid*, the sacramental bread of Communion.
1805   *nowt*, cattle.

1811   *our ... thieves*, Border reivers, protected by powerful families,
            raided equally in England and Scotland.
1812   *leil*, loyal.

1821–4   M.

Yet something mair belangis to the pleuch.
Now into peace ye sould provide for weirs,
And be sure of how mony thousand spears
The King may be when he has ocht ado,
For-why, my lords, this is my reason, lo,   1790
The husbandmen and commons they were wont
Go in the battle foremost in the front.
But I have tint all my experience,
Without ye mak some better diligence
The Common-Weal mon other ways be stylet,
Or by my faith the King will be beguilet!
Thir poor commons daily as ye may see
Declinis doun to extreme poverty,
For some are hichtit sa into their mail
Their winning will nocht find them watter kail.   1800
Thus mon they pay great rent or leave the steid,
And some are plainly harlt out by the heid
And are destroyt, without God on them rue!
POOR MAN: Sir, by God's breid, that tale is very true!
It is weill kend I had baith nowt and horse.
Now all my gear ye see upon my corse.
CORRECTION: Or I depart I think to mak an order!
JOHN: I pray you, sir, begin first at the Border,
For how can we fend us agains England,
When we can not, within our native land,   1810
Destroy our awn Scots, common traitor thieves,
Wha to leil labourers daily does mischieves?
Were I a king, my lord, by Godis wounds,
Wha-e'er held common thieves within their bounds,
Where-through that daily leil men micht be wrangt,
Without remede their chieftains sould be hangt!
LORD: What other enemies has thou, let us ken.
JOHN: Sir, I complain upon the idle men,
For-why, sir, it is God's awn bidding
All Christian men to work for their living.   1820
Sant Paul, that piller of the Kirk,

131

1823   *Qui . . . manducet*, from 2 Thessalonians, iii. 10, is translated in the following line.

1827   *couchers*, wasters.

1828   *quintessencers*, see note to l. 729.

1829   *bable-beirers . . . bards*, fools (with their jester's bauble) and minstrels. They were among the classes discriminated against by the Vagrancy Acts.

1830   *swingeours*, scoundrels.

1831–2   M.

1834   *Augustines, Carmelites and Cordeliers*, monks of the Augustinian, Carmelite and Franciscan Orders.

1848   *Justice ayrs*, assizes.

1849   *pickand, pegrel*, light-fingered, petty.

1853   *buds*, bribes.

1854   *compositors*, persons appointed to settle legal disputes.

Says to the wretches that will not work,
Qui non laborat non manducet,
Wha labours nocht he sall not eat.
This been against the strang beggars,
Fiddlers, pipers, and pardoners,
Thir jugglers, jesters and idle couchers,
Thir carriers and thir quintessencers,
Thir bable-beirers and thir bards,
Thir sweir swingeours with lords and lairds,   1830
Mair than their rentis may sustein
Or to their profit needfull been.
This been against thir great fat freirs,
Augustines, Carmelites and Cordeleirs,
And all others that in cowls been cled,
Whilk labours not and been weill fed –
I mean, nocht labourand spiritually,
Nor for their living corporally,
Lyand in dens like idle dogs.
I them compare to weill fed hogs!   1840
I think they do themselves abuse,
Seeing that they the warld refuse;
Having professed sic poverty,
Syne flees fast fra necessity!
CORRECTION: Whom upon mair will ye complain?
JOHN: Marry, on mair and mair again!
For the poor people cries with cares
The misusing of Justice ayrs.
Sic pickand, pegrel thieves are hangt,
But he that all the warld has wrangt,   1850
A cruel tyran, a strang transgressor,
A common public plain oppressor –
By buds may he obtein favours
Of treasurers and compositors,
And through laws, consistorial,
Prolix, corrupt and perpetuall,
The common people are put sa under,

1869–78   M.

1879   *pley*, plea.

1885   *give . . . remissioun.* The 'twa' are the Lords and Burgesses, the
           Prelates feeling no need for pardon.

Thocht they be poor, it is na wonder!

CORRECTION: Good John, I grant all that is true.
Your infortoun full sair I rue! 1860
Sa, my lord Temporality,
I you command in time that ye
Expel Oppressioun aff your lands.
And als I say to you merchands,
If ever I find, by land or sea,
Deceit be in your company,
Whilk are to Common-weal contrair,
I vow to God I sall not spare!
Mairover, my Lord Temporality,
In goodly haste I will that ye 1870
Set into feu your temporal lands
To men that labours with their hands,
Where-through the policy may incress.

LORD: I am content, sir, by the Mess.

CORRECTION: My Spritual Lords, are ye content?

BISHOP: Na, we mon tak advisëment.

CORRECTION: Conclude ye not with the Common-Weal,
Ye sall be punisht, by Sant Geil!
My lords, what say ye to this pley?

LORD: My sovereign lords, we will obey, 1880
And tak your part with heart and hand,
Whatever ye please us to command.
But we beseek you, sovereign,
Of all our crimes that are by-gane
To give us twa a full remissioun,
And here we mak to you conditioun,
The Common-Weal for to defend
From henceforth to our lives end!

CORRECTION: On that conditioun I am content
To pardon you. Sen ye repent, 1890
The Common-Weal tak by the hand
And mak with him perpetual band!

1896   *plain*, complain; *bourd*, joke.

1909   *cleeks*, grasps.
1910   *raploch*, homespun.

1919   *rokets*, surplices.

The LORDS *and the* BURGESSES *receive* JOHN THE COMMON-
WEAL.

John, have you ony mair debates
Against my lords, the Spritual Estates?
JOHN: Na, sir, I dare nocht speak a word.
To plain on priests, it is na bourd!
BISHOP: Flyte on thy fill, fool, I defy thee,
Sa that thou shaw but the verity!
JOHN: Gramercy, then I sall not spare.
First to complain on our vicar –   1900
The poor cottar being like to die,
Havand small bairnis twa or three,
And has twa kye withouten mae,
The vicar must have ane of thae,
With the grey coat that haps the bed,
Howbeit the wife be poorly cled!
And if the wife die on the morn,
Thocht all the bairns sould be forlorn,
The other cow he cleeks away,
With the poor coat of raploch grey.   1910
Wald God this custom were put doun,
Whilk never was foundit by reasoun!
LORD: Are all thae tales true that thou tells?
POOR MAN: True, sir, the Deil stick me else!
For, by the Haily Trinity,
The same was practisit on me!
JOHN *singles out the* PARSON.
JOHN: Our parson here, he taks na other pine
But to resave his teinds and spend them syne!
POOR MAN: Our bishops, with their lusty rokets white,
They flow in riches royally and delight;   1920
Like paradise been their palaces and places,
And wants na pleasure of the fairest faces!
But doubt I wald think it a pleasant life,
Ay on, when I list, to part with my wife,
Syne tak another of far greater beauty!

1928   *like ramis . . . rage.* Allowing for poetic licence Lindsay does
        not exaggerate. Adam Abel, a Franciscan monk, roundly
        asserts in his unpublished *Rota Temporis* (in the National
        Library), written about 1535, that there is not one priest in
        Scotland fitted by his private life to preach a sermon on
        chastity.

1929   *unpizzlet,* rampant.

1929–30 M.

1934   *chafts,* cheeks.

1950   *thae,* these.

1959   *weir,* war.

But ever alas, my lords, that may not be,
For I am bund, alas, in marriage,
But they like ramis rudely in their rage
Unpizzlet rins amang the silly ewes,
Sa lang as kind of nature in them grows.   1930
PARSON: Thou lies, false hureson raggit loon!
   There is na priests in all this toun
   That ever uset sic vicious crafts!
JOHN: The feind resave thae flattrand chafts!
BISHOP (*to* TEMPORALITY): My lords, why do ye tholc that
      lurdan loon
   Of Kirk-men to speak sic detractioun?
   Yon villain puts me out of charity!
LORD: Why, my lord, says he ocht but verity?
   Ye can nocht stop a poor man for to plain!
BISHOP: I will not suffer sic words of yon villain!   1940
POOR MAN: Then gar give me my three fat kye again!
BISHOP: False carl, to speak to me stands thou not awe?
POOR MAN: The fiend resave them that first deviset that law!
   Within an hour efter my dad was deid
   The vicar had my cow hard by the heid!
PARSON: False hureson carl, I say that law is good,
   Because it has been lang our consuetude!
POOR MAN: When I am Pape, that law I sall put doun!
   It is a sair law for the poor commoun!
BISHOP: I mak a vow thae words thou sall repent! \   1950
GOOD COUNSEL: I you require, my lords, be patient!
   We came nocht here for disputatiouns:
   We came to mak good reformatiouns!
MERCHANT: My Lords, conclude that all the temporal lands
   Be set in feu to labourers with their hands,
   With sic restrictions as sall be deviset,
   That they may live and nocht to be suppriset;
   And when they hear a proclamation,
   That the King's Grace does mak him for the weir,
   That they be ready with harness, bow and spear.   1960

1962   *corse-present* (see note to l. 1397).

1964   *kirtle*, skirt, woman; *grice*, pig.
1965   *decern*, decree.

1970   *notar*, notary.
1970   *tak an instrument*. The Scribe, who is a notary, is to record the
            Bishop's protest or counter-assertion of his rights.

1974   *Et . . . tota*. The whole assembly goes along with the opinion
            of the majority.
1976–88   The practice of obtaining or confirming appointment to
            benefices by personal and often corrupt canvassing at Rome
            had steadily increased. One alleged effect of this costly travel-
            ling was the diminution of the already small amount of
            currency in this country. See note to ll. 2033–6.

1985–6   M.

1987   *Sir Simony*, presentation to a benefice in return for a material
            reward, money or some other gift.

1993   *cavell*, blockhead.

1995   *colourt crack*, lying tale.

GOOD COUNSEL: Sa say we all, your reason is sa good!
JOHN: What do ye of the corse-present and cow?
BISHOP: We will want nathing that we have in use,
Kirtle nor cow, teind lamb, teind grice nor goose!
LORD: We will decern here that the Kingis grace
Sall write unto the Papeis Haliness.
With his consent, by proclamatioun,
Baith corse-present and cow we sall cry doun!
BISHOP: To that, my lords, we plainly disassent!
Notar, thereof I tak an instrument!   1970
LORD: My lord, by Him that all the warld has wrocht,
We set nocht by wheder ye consent or nocht!
Ye are but ane Estate and we are twa!
Et ubi maior pars ibi tota!
JOHN: My lords, ye have richt prudently concludit!
Tak tent now how the land is clean denudit
Of gold and siller, whilk daily gaes to Rome
For buds, mair than the rest of Christendom.
Never a penny sould go to Rome at all,
Na mair than did to Peter nor to Paul!   1980
MERCHANT: We merchants, weill I wot, within our bounds
Has furnisht priests ten hunder thousand pounds
For their finance; nane knaws sa weill as we!
Therefore, my lords, devise some remedy!
For through their pleys and their promotioun,
Mair for deniers nor for devotioun,
Sir Simony has made with them a band.
The gold of weicht they lead out of the land!
GOOD COUNSEL: It is short time sen ony benefice
Was sped in Rome, except great bishopries.   1990
But now for an unworthy vicarage
A priest will rin to Rome in pilgramage.
A cavell whilk was never at the school
Will rin to Rome and keep a bishop's mule,
And syne come hame with mony colourt crack,
With a burden of benefices on his back –

2013–14   M.
2013   *parochoun*, parish.
2014   *leir*, teach.

2016   *Look . . . Timothy*. Lindsay cites 1 *Timothy* iii. 1–3: 'This is a true saying, if a man desire the office of a bishop, he desireth a good work. A bishop then must be blameless, the husband of one wife, vigilant, sober, of good behaviour, given to hospitality, apt to teach; not given to wine, no striker, not greedy of filthy lucre, but patient, not a brawler, not covetous.'

2019–22   M.

2026   *teinds*, tithes.

2028   *clayis*, clothes

Whilk been against the law, ae man alane
For to possess mair benefices than ane.
Sa I conclude, my lords, and says for me
Ye sould annul all this plurality!   2000
Advise, my lords, what think ye to conclude?
LORD: Sir, by my faith, I think it very good
   That fra hencefurth na priests sall pass to Rome,
   Because our substance they do still consume.
   And als I think it best by my advice
   That ilk priest sall have but ane benefice.
GOOD COUNSEL: Mark weill, my lords, there is na benefice
   Given to a man, but for a good office!
   Wha taks office and syne they cannot use it,
   Giver and taker, I say, are baith abusit.   2010
   A bishop's office is for to be a preacher
   And of the Law of God a public teacher.
   Richt sa the Parson unto his parochoun
   Of the Evangel sould leir them a lessoun.
BISHOP: Freind, where find ye that we sould preachers be?
GOOD COUNSEL: Look what Saint Paul writes unto Timothy.
   Tak there the Book; let see if ye can spell!
   He hands Bible to BISHOP.
BISHOP: I never read that, therefore read it yoursell!
   BISHOP *casts it away*.
   Na, sir, by him that our Lord Jesus sauld,
   I read never the New Testament nor Auld,   2020
   Nor ever thinks to do sir, by the Rood!
   I hear Freirs say that reading does na good.
MERCHANT: Then before God, how can ye be excusit,
   To have an office and wots not how to use it?
   Wherefore were given you all the temporal lands,
   And all thir teinds ye have amang your hands?
   They were given you for other causes, I ween,
   Than mumble matins and hald your clayis clean!
   Ye say to the Apostles that ye succeed,
   But ye shaw nocht that into word nor deed!   2030

2031-4   M.

2033-6   *King David . . . King James the First.* The gift of Crown lands
by the saintly David I for the founding of bishoprics and no
less than fifteen abbeys had been noticed by John Bellenden,
in his translation (1531) of Boece's Latin history of Scotland,
as one reason for the perennial difficulties of the royal ex-
chequer: 'Thairfor the wise prince, King James the first . .
said, He was a sair Sanct for the Crown'. Lindsay's comments
on traffic in benefices and taking money out of the country
are from the same passage in Bellenden (Scottish Text
Society, vol. 2, p. 185).

2050   *tholit*, endured; *passioun*, suffering.

2061   *Sanctam Ecclesiam*, Holy Church.
2063-5   M.

POOR MAN: Sir, God nor I be stickit with a knife,
  If ever our Parson preacht in all his life!
JOHN: What if King David were livand in thir days
  The whilk did found sa mony gay abbeys!
  King James the First, Roy of this regioun,
  Said David was a sair sant to the croun.
  I hear men say that he was something blind,
  That gave away mair nor he left behind.
ABBOT: My lord Bishop, I mervel how that ye
  Suffer this carl for to speak heresy!   2040
  For by my faith, my lord, will ye tak tent,
  He serves for to be brunt incontinent!
  Ye cannot say but it is heresy,
  To speak against our law and liberty!
  There is a great commotion. The SPIRITUAL ESTATE *cry, 'Burn*
  him!' CORRECTION *intervenes and addresses* JOHN.
CORRECTION: Shaw furth your faith and feignye nocht!
  JOHN *pauses before saying his creed.*
JOHN: I believe in God that all has wrocht,
  And create every thing of nocht;
  And in his Son, our Lord Jesu,
  Incarnate of the Virgin true;
  Wha under Pilate tholit passioun,   2050
  And deit for our salvatioun;
  And on the thrid day rais again,
  As Haily Scripture shawis plain.
  And als, my Lord, it is weill kend,
  How he did to the heaven ascend,
  And set him down at the richt hand
  Of God the Father, I understand,
  And sall come judge on Doomesday . . .
  What will ye mair, sir, that I say?
CORRECTION: Shaw furth the rest – this is na game!   2060
JOHN: I trow Sanctam Ecclesiam . . .
  But nocht in thir Bishops nor thir Freirs!
LORD: My lords, let be your disputatioun.

F   145

2065   *fra-thine*, henceforth; *disponet*, dealt with.

2070   *gormand*, greedy.

2073–4   M.

2077   *plack*, farthing.
2077   M. SCRIBE does not appear in Kemp's version. Compare other comic complaints in this play about unpaid work.

2080   *pelour*, thief.
2081   *senye*, diocesan court.
2081   M.
2082   *meir*, mare.
2083   *quarrel*, quarry.
2084   M.
2085   *meinye*, company.
2086–96   POOR MAN recites the first words of various legal styles, in parody of the law's formalities and delays: *citandum*, to be summoned; *libellandum*, the pursuer's first plea; *ad opponendum*, the defender's reply; *interloquendum*, decree before decision is given; *ad replicandum*, the pursuer's reply; *concludendum*, conclusion; *pronunciandum*, the sentence.

2092–3   M.

Conclude with firm deliberatioun
How Prelats fra-thine sall be disponet.
MERCHANT (*to* CORRECTION): I think, for me, even as ye first
    proponet,
That the King's grace sall give na benefice
But to a preacher that can use that office.
The silly saulis that been Christis sheep
Sould nocht be given to gormand wolves to keep!   2070
What been the cause of all the heresies
But the abusion of the prelacies?
They will correct and will nocht be correckit,
Thinkand to na prince they will be subjeckit.
LORD: We think your counsel is very good,
As ye have said we all conclude!
SCRIBE: I write all day but gets never a plack!
POOR MAN: Och, my lords, for the Haily Trinity,
Remember to reform the consistory!
PARSON: What cause has thou, false pelour, for to plainye?   2080
Where was ye ever summont to their senye?
POOR MAN: Marry! I lent my gossip my meir to fetch hame coals
And he her drount into the quarrel holes!
And I ran to the Consistory for to plainye,
And there I happent amang a greedy meinye.
They gave me first a thing they call *citandum*,
Within aucht days I gat but *libellandum*,
Within a month I gat *ad opponendum*,
In half a year I gat *interloquendum*,
And then I gat – how call ye it? – *ad replicandum:*   2090
But I could never a word yet understand him!
And then they gart me cast out mony placks,
And gart me pay for four and twenty Acts,
But or they came half gait to *concludendum*
The fiend a plack was left for to defend him.
Of *pronunciandum* they made me wonder fain,
But I gat never my good grey meir again!
LORD: My lords, we mon reform thir consistory laws,

2104–5   M.

2115   *ludging*, lodging.

2119   *the noble nuns*. Hamer reads 'innis', but 'nuns' is clearly meant.
          The heads of convents were often of noble family and affected
          a luxury much satirized.
2121   *dortour*, dormitory; *dourly*, harshly; *dang*, thrust.
2122–2170 M.

2126   *digne*, worthy.

2133   *feill*, information.

Whase great defame above the heavens blaws,
Sa that the Kingis honour we may avance.   2100
We will conclude, as they have done in France –
Let Spritual matters pass to Sprituality,
And Temporal matters to Temporality!

BISHOP: We will not want our profit, by Sant Geil!

LORD: Your profit is against the Common Weil!

VERITY *and* CHASTITY *now press their complaint.*

VERITY: My sovereign, I beseek your excellence,
Use justice on Sprituality,
The whilk to us has done great violence.
Because we did rehearse the verity
They put us close into captivity;   2110
And sa remaint into subjectioun,
Into great languor and calamnity,
Till we were freed by King Correctioun.

CHASTITY: My lord, I have great cause for to complain,
I could get na ludging into this land,
The Spiritual State had me sa at disdain.
With Dame Sensual they have made sic a band,
Amang them all na freindship, sirs, I fand:
And when I cam the noble nuns amang,
My lusty Lady Prioress fra-hand,   2120
Out of her dortour dourly she me dang!

VERITY: With the advice, Sir, of the Parliament,
Heartly we mak you supplicatioun,
Cause King Correctioun tak incontinent
Of all this sort examinatioun,
If they be digne of deprivatioun.
My prudent Lords, I say that poor craftsmen
Above some Prelats are mair for to commend.

CORRECTION (*to* BISHOP): Ye are a Prince of Sprituality;
How have ye uset your office now let see.   2130

BISHOP: My Lords, when was there ony Prelats wont
Of their office till ony King mak count?
But of my office if ye wald have the feill,

149

2135   *For I tak in my count*, For I take in [collect] my rental.

2136   *ane*, one, a single; *beir*, barley.

2138   *my buttock-mail, my cotes*, my ecclesiastical fines for fornication, and my portion of the goods of the deceased to be paid for confirmation of his testament.

2143–4   *I let . . . mule*, Don't think I am a fool in respect of worldly wisdom and success just because I ride on a bishop's mule.

2148   *herriet*, pillaged (see note to 415).

2153   *Carail*, Crail, a port of east Fife.

2164   *the catch*, hand-tennis.

I let you wit I have it usit weill.
For I tak in my count twice in the year,
Wanting nocht of my teind ane boll of beir!
I gat good payment of my Temporal lands,
My buttock-mail, my cotes and my offrands.
Howbeit I dare nocht plainly spouse a wife
Yet Concubenes I have had four or five,   2140
And to my sons I have given rich rewairds,
And all my dochters marriet upon lairds.
I let you wit, my Lord, I am na fool
Forwhy I ride upon an ambland mule.
CORRECTION: I weend your office had been for to preach,
And God's law to the people teach!
Wherefore wear ye that mitre, ye me tell!
BISHOP: I wot nocht, man, by Him that herriet hell!
CORRECTION: Sir Scribe, ye sall, at Chastity's request,
Pass and exame yon three in goodly haist.   2150
SCRIBE: Father Abbot, this Council bids me speir;
How ye have uset your abbey they wald hear.
ABBOT: There is na monks fra Carrick to Carail
That fares better and drinks mair halesome ale.
My Prior is a man of great devotioun,
Therefore daily he gets a double portioun.
My paramours is baith as fat and fair
As ony wench into the toun of Ayr.
I send my sons to Paris to the schools,
I traist in God that they sall be na fools!   2160
And all my dochters I have weill providit.
Now judge ye if my office be weill guidit!
SCRIBE: Maister Parson shaw us if ye can preach.
PARSON: Thocht I preach not I can play at the catch.

2165–70   Lindsay clearly enjoys his sporting parson. After the exam-
           ination of the Prioress a learned Doctor preaches a model
           sermon – too long for inclusion here – on Christian love and
           its duties, and enumerates the Seven Deadly Sins. The Bishop,
           Abbot and Parson, refuse to be edified, and the incredulous
           and indignant Parson exclaims:

> Came doun dastart and gang sell draiff!
> I understand nocht what thou said.
> Thy words were neither corn nor caiff.
> I wald thy tongue again were laid!
> Where thou says Pride is deidly sin,
> I say Pride is but honesty,
> And Covetice of warldly win
> Is but wisdom, I say for me.
> Ire Hardiness, and Gluttony
> Is nathing else but lifeis food.
> The natural sin of Lechery
> Is but true love. All thir are good! ...
> But were they sin, I understand
> We men of Kirk wald never use them!

2166   *ferily*, vigorously.
2167   *tables*, backgammon.
2169   *four-nookit*, four-cornered.
2171–4   Spoken by Correction in Kemp's version.
2172   *guess*, give an account.
2176   *fra-hand*, forthwith.
2179–84   M.
2185   *fleyt*, frightened.

2190   *wame*, belly.

2192   *feignyit*, feigning.

I wot there is not ane amang you all
Mair ferily can play at the football.
And for the carts, the tables and the dice,
Above all Parsons I may beir the prise.
Our round bonnets we mak them now four-nookit,
Of richt fine stuff, if ye list come and look it.   2170
SCRIBE: What say ye now, my Lady Prioress?
How have ye uset your office, can ye guess?
What was the cause ye refuset harboury
To this young lusty Lady Chastity?
PRIORESS (*haughtily*): I do my office efter auld use and wount.
To your Parliament I will mak na mair count.
      CORRECTION *now points to* FLATTERY, *still in the stocks and*
      disguised as a friar, and to PRIORESS.
CORRECTION: I counsel you, sir, now fra-hand
Banis yon freir out of this land.
Yon Prioress, withouten fable,
I think she is nocht profitable   2180
      For Christis regioun.
To begin reformatioun
Mak of them deprivatioun.
      This is my opinioun.
FIRST SERGEANT: Come on, sir Freir, and be nocht fleyt.
The King, our maister, mon be obeyt,
      But ye sall have na harm.
      He takes FLATTERY *out of the stocks.*
If ye wald travel fra toun to toun,
I think this hood and heavy goun
      Will hald your wame owr warm.   2190
      He pulls off FLATTERY'S *habit, so that the motley is revealed.*
GOOD COUNSEL: Sir, by the Haily Trinity,
This same is feignyit Flattery.
      I ken him by his face.
Believand for to get promotioun,
He said that his name was Devotioun,
      And sa beguilet your Grace.

2200   *pavane*, stately dance.

2204   *cow-clink*, whore.

2210   *wary*, curse.

2224   *widdiefows*, gallows-birds, here applied to the sergeants.

2229   *graith*, get ready.

The FIRST SERGEANT *now pulls the* PRIORESS *from among the* SPIRITUAL ESTATE.

FIRST SERGEANT: Come on, my Lady Prioress,
    We sall leir you to dance,
  And that within a little space
    A new pavane of France!   2200
The sergeants pulling off her habit show a gay dress underneath.

SECOND SERGEANT: Now, brother, by the Mess,
    By my judgment I think
  This haily Prioress
    Is turnt in a cow-clink!

PRIORESS: I give my freinds my malisoun.
  That me compellt to be a nun,
    And wald nocht let me marry!
  It was my freindis greediness
  That gart me be a Prioress.
    Now heartly I them wary!   2210
  Howbeit that Nuns sings nichts and days
  Their heart wots nocht what their mouth says,
    The sooth I you declare;
  Makand you intimatioun,
  To Christis congregatioun
    Nuns are nocht necessare.
  But I sall do the best I can
  And marry some good honest man,
    And brew good ale and tun.
  Marriage, by my opinioun,   2220
  It is better Religioun
    As to be Freir or Nun!

FLATTERY: My lords, for God's sake, let not hang me,
  Howbeit thir widdiefows wald wrang me!
    I can mak na debate
  To win my meat at pleuch nor harrows,
  But I sall help to hang my marrows,
    Baith Falset and Deceit!

CORRECTION: Than pass thy way and graith the gallows!

2235   *novelles*, news.

2251   *gragit*, excommunicated.
2252–5 M.

Syne help for to hang up thy fallows,   2230
  Thou gets na other grace!
The gallows are brought in.
DECEIT: Now Flattery, my auld companion,
What does yon King Correctioun?
  Knaws thou not his intent?
Declare to us of thy novelles!
FLATTERY: Ye'll all be hangit, I see nocht else,
  And that incontinent!
DECEIT: Now walaway, will ye gar hang us?
The Deil brocht yon curst King amang us,
  For meikle sturt and strife!   2240
FLATTERY: I had been put to deid amang you,
Were nocht I took on hand to hang you,
  And sa I savit my life!
CORRECTION: With the advice of King Humanity,
Here I determine with ripe advisëment,
  That all thir prelates sall deprivit be!
KING: As ye have said, but doubt it sall be done.
The COURTIERS *lay hands on the* PRELATES.
WANTONNESS: My lords, we pray you to be patient,
For we will do the King's commandëment!
BISHOP: I mak a vow to God, and ye us handle   2250
Ye sall be curst and gragit with book and candle!
The SPIRITUAL ESTATE *is despoiled and is seen to wear motley.*
MERCHANT: We mervell of you paintit sepultures,
That was sa bauld for to accept sic cures,
With glorious habit ridand upon your mules.
Now men may see ye are but very fools!
BISHOP: We say the Kings were greater fools than we,
That us promovit to sa great dignity!
ABBOT: There is a thousand in the Kirk, but doubt,
Sic fools as we, if they were weill socht out!
Now brother, sen it may na better be,   2260
Let us ga soup with Sensuality!

2264	*brether*, brothers.
2264–77	M.
2266	*lift*, sky
2270	*wary*, curse.
2273	*tocher-good*, dowry.
2279	*garmoun*, garment, gown.
2280	*owrlookit*, neglected.
2281	*crookit*, lame.
2282	*singular profit*, self-interest; *suppriset*, oppressed.
2283	*nakit*, defenceless; *disguiset*, ill-clothed.
2285	*abilyement*, dress.
2287	*Salve res publica*, Hail to the Commonwealth.

They go to SENSUALITY.

SENSUALITY: Pass fra us, fools, by Him that has us wrocht,
    Ye ludge nocht here, because I knaw you nocht!
BISHOP: I see nocht else, brether, withouten fail,
    But this false warld is turnit top owr tail.
    Sen all is vain that is under the lift,
    To win our meat we mon make other shift.
    With our labour except we mak debate,
    I dreid full sair we want baith drink and meat.
ABBOT: Allace, this reformatioun I may wary,   2270
    For I have yet twa dochters for to marry,
    And they are baith contrackit, by the Rood,
    And wots nocht now to pay their tocher-good!
PARSON: The Deil may care for this unhappy chance,
    For I am young and thinks to pass to France,
    And tak wages amang the men of weir,
    And win my living with my sword and spear.
GOOD COUNSEL (*to* CORRECTION): Or ye depart, Sir, of this
        regioun,
    Give John the Common-Weal a gay garmoun!
    Because the Common-Weal has been owrlookit,   2280
    That is the cause that Common-Weal is crookit.
    With singular profit he has been sa suppriset,
    That he is baith cauld, nakit and disguiset.
CORRECTION: As ye have said, Father, I am content.
    Sergeants, give John a new abilyement
    Of satin, damas, or of the velvet fine,
    And give him place into our Parliament syne!
    Music. They clothe JOHN *gorgeously and receive him into Parliament. The* ESTATES *sing 'Salve, res publica.'*
POOR MAN: I give you my braid benison,
    That has given Common-Weal a goun;
    But I beseek you, for All Hallows,   2290
    Cause hang Deceit and all his fallows,
    And banis Flattery of the toun,
    For there was never sic a loon!

2294	*by the gait*, out of the way.
2294–314	were spoken in the play at Common Theft's first entrance, before the examination of the clergy, in a scene in which Public Oppression, a typical protector of reivers, betrays him, leaving him in the stocks. The scene interrupts the main action but has been omitted chiefly for want of space.
2294–2347	M. Theft does not appear in Kemp's version.
2295	*thrang*, crowd.
2309	*forlorn*, undone.
2311	*craig*, neck.
2316	*sweir*, loath.
2318	*widdy*, gallows rope.
2322	*limmer*, bold rascal.
2324	*tippet*, a cape fastened round the neck. Hamer and Kinsley in their editions simply translate 'hangman's rope'.
2325	*a fellon rippet*, a great ado. It was from Lindsay that Allan Ramsay learned the trick of writing semi-comic 'last dying speeches'.

THEFT *enters running and finds* POOR MAN *in his way.*

THEFT: Ga by the gait man, let me gang!
  How Deil cam I into this thrang?
  With sorrow I may sing my sang
    And I be tane,
  For I have run baith nicht and day.
  Through speed of foot I gat away.
  If I be kend here, wallaway,   2300
    I will be slain!

POOR MAN: What is thy name man, by thy thrift?

THEFT: Hureson, they call me Common Thift,
  Forwhy I had na other shift
    Sen I was born!
  In Ewesdale was my dwelling place.
  Mony a wife gart I cry alace.
  At my hand they gat never grace,
    But ay forlorn.
  Get this curst King me in his grips   2310
  My craig will wit what weighs my hips.
  The Deil I give his tongue and lips
    That of me tells!
  Adieu, I dare na langer tarry.

The FIRST SERGEANT *recognizes and seizes* THEFT.

FIRST SERGEANT: Come here, sir Theif, come here, come here!
  When was ye wont to be sa sweir?
  To hunt cattle ye were ay speedy,
  Therefore ye sall wave in a widdy.

THEFT: Mon I be hangit? Allace, allace!
  Is there nane here may get me grace?   2320
  Yet or I die give me a drink.

FIRST SERGEANT: Thou art a limmer, I stand ford!
  Slip in thy heid into this cord,
  For thou had never a meeter tippet!

THEFT: Allace, this is a fellon rippet!
  Repent your lives ye plain oppressours,
  All ye misdoers and transgressours,

161

2329   *mak you ford*, prepare yourselves.

2334-44 Common Theft lists the main reiving families of the West
         Border.

2343   *slicht*, skilful.

2346   *fangit*, caught.

2351   *mangit*, mad.

2360   *ill-deedy*, evil-doing

Or else gar choose you good confessours,
  And mak you ford.
For if ye tarry in this land   2330
And come under Correctioun's hand,
Your grace sall be, I understand,
  A good sharp cord.
Adieu my brethren common thieves,
That helpit me in my mischieves.
Adieu Grosars, Nicksons and Bells,
Oft have we faren out-through the fells.
Adieu Robsons, Hawes and Pyles,
That in our craft has mony wiles,
Littles, Trumbels and Armistrangs.   2340
Adieu all thieves that me belangs,
Tailors, Irwins and Elwands,
Speedy of foot and slicht of hands,
The Scotts of Ewesdale, and the Graemes —
I have na time to tell your names.
With King Correctioun and ye be fangit,
Beleive richt weill ye will be hangit!

THEFT *is hanged to a roll of drums. Then the* SERGEANTS *take*
DECEIT *and* FALSET *from the stocks and lead them to the gallows,*
where each makes his speech and is hanged with the same ceremony.

FIRST SERGEANT: Come here, Deceit, my companyoun!
  Saw ever man liker a loon
    To hing upon a gallows!   2350
DECEIT: This is eneuch to mak me mangit!
  Dule fell me that I mon be hangit!
    Let me speak with my fallows!
  I trow wan-fortune brocht me here.
  What meikle fiend made me so speedy?
  Sen it was said it is seven year,
  That I sould wave into a widdy.
  I learit my maisters to be greedy.
  Adieu, for I see na remede.
  Look what it is to be ill-deedy!   2360

2363 *ye hurt my craig*, a common hanging jest.

2364 *wed*, wager; *plack*, farthing.

2365 *knag*, knot.

2373 *upalands*, country.

2378 *rounand*, whispering.

2387 *good cheap*, at a bargain price.

2388 *saip*, soap.

2389 *oyldolly*, olive oil.

2390 *ocker*, usury.

2392 *double-mail*, the 'herild horse' or similar rent in kind mentioned earlier by Poor Man, which might be repeated on the death of the deceased man's widow.

2393 *ell-wand*, the rod for measuring the Scots ell, which was approximately 37 inches.

FIRST SERGEANT: Now in this halter slip thy heid!
Stand still! Me think ye draw aback!
DECEIT: Alas, maister, ye hurt my craig!
FIRST SERGEANT: It will hurt better, I wed a plack,
Richt now when ye hing on a knag!
DECEIT: Adieu, my maisters, merchant men,
I have you servit, as ye ken,
Truly, baith air and late!
I say to you, for conclusioun,
I dreid ye gang to confusioun,   2370
Fra time ye want Deceit.
I learit you merchants mony a wile,
The upalands wives for to beguile
Upon a market day;
And mak them trow your stuff was good,
When it was rotten, by the Rood,
And sweir it was not sa!
I was aye rounand in your ear,
And learit you for to ban and sweir
What your gear cost in France,   2380
Howbeit the Deil a word was true!
Your craft if King Correctioun knew,
Wald turn you to mischance!
I learit you wiles monifauld –
To mix the new wine with the auld,
That fashion was na folly!
To sell richt dear and buy good cheap,
And mix rye-meal amang the saip,
And saffron with oyldolly.
Foryet nocht ocker, I counsel you,   2390
Mair than the Vicar does the cow,
Or lords their double-mail.
Howbeit your ell-wand be too scant,
Or your pound-weicht three ounces want,
Think that but little fail!
Ye young merchants may cry alace!

2400	*perqueir*, thoroughly.
2402	*mense*, grace.
2404	*cankert*, depraved.
2410	*cummer*, trouble.
2414	*webster*, weaver.
2415	*walker*, fuller.
2426	*lorimers*, makers of bits, spurs, metal mountings for bridles and saddles.
2427	*cordiners*, cordwainers.

For wanting of your wonted grace,
    Yon curst King ye may ban!
Had I livit but half a year,
I sould have learit you crafts perqueir   2400
    To beguile wife and man!
SECOND SERGEANT: Come here, Falset, and mense the gallows!
Ye mon hing up amang your fallows
    For your cankert conditioun!
Mony a true man have ye wrangit,
Therefore but doubt ye sall be hangit,
    But mercy or remissioun!
FALSET: Alace, mon I be hangit too?
What meikle Deil is this ado?
    How cam I to this cummer?   2410
My good maisters, ye craftismen,
Want ye Falset, full weill I ken
    Ye will all die for hunger.
Find me a Webster that is leal,
Or a Walker that will not steal!
    Their craftiness I ken.
Or a Miller that has na fault,
That will neither steal meal nor malt –
    Hald them for haily men!
At our Fleshers tak ye na grief,   2420
Thocht they blaw lean mutton and beef,
    That they seem fat and fair.
Adieu, my maisters, Wrichts and Masons,
I need not lear you ony lessons,
    Ye knaw my craft perqueir!
Adieu, Blacksmiths and Lorimers,
Adieu, ye crafty Cordiners,
    That sells the shoon owr dear!
Amang craftsmen it is a wonder
To find ten leal amang a hunder,   2430
    The truth I to you tell!
Adieu, I may na longer tarry,

2433   *the King of Fairy*, the Devil.

2435–46 M.

2440   *pin*, peg.

2443   *my father brother*. Deceit was the brother of Satan, the 'father of lies', i.e. of 'Falset'.

2444   *silly*, helpless.

2447   *wend*, gone.

2449   Hamer asks why Flattery is not hanged with the others and suggests that it was because he was a cleric, Lindsay not wishing to incur a charge of heresy or suspicion that he wanted reformation on the drastic English model; but he first enters the play as a Fool or Vice and is later only a pretended Friar. He is needed to end the proper business of the play, which has been an exposure of folly in all three Estates, and to remind the audience that folly is still very much with them. In case the point should be missed, Lindsay's production closes with an 'epilogue – interlude' in which 'Foly' himself reviews farcically all the themes of the play and chooses as his text, 'The number of fools is infinite'. Such a 'sermon joyeux' Hamer notes, 'was characteristic of the French *sottie*' or fool-play. I have omitted this post-script for its length and comparative superfluousness.

2458–67 M. The last lines given to Flattery by Kemp were these:
         Mark weel! my feres the piper pay,
         But Flatterie slips clean away,
           O aa the world I'm free!

2461   *scaplary*, 'scapulary', a monk's garment covering breast and back.

2462   *genners*, engenders.

2463   *black or blue*, whatever the colour or Order.

I mon pass to the King of Fairy,
    Or else straichtway to hell!
Here he looks up at his hanged companions.
Waes me for thee, good Common Thift!
Was never man made mair honest shift
    His living for to win!
There was nocht in all Liddesdale
That kye mair craftily could steal –
    Where thou hings on that pin!   2440
Sathan resave thy saul, Deceit,
Thou was to me a faithful mate,
    And als my father brother!
Dule fell the silly merchant men!
To mak them service, weill I ken
    They'll ne'er get sic another!
Fareweill, for I am to the widdy wend,
For-why Falset made never a better end!
FLATTERY: Have I not chapet the widdy weill?
Yea, that I have, by sweet Sant Geill!   2450
    For I had nocht been wrangit,
Because I servit, by All Hallows,
To have been marshallt with my fallows,
    And heich above them hangit!
I made far mair faults nor my mates,
I beguilet all the Three Estates
    With my hypocrisy.
When I had on my freiris hood
All men believit that I was good.
    Now judge ye if I be.   2460
I knaw that cowl and scaplary
Genners mair heat nor charity,
    Thocht they be black or blue.
What haliness is there within
A wolf cled in a wether's skin?
    Judge ye if this be true.

169

2467 *famous*, worthy.

2477 *brawl*, a lively dance tune.
2478 *hobbles*, capers.

2480 *or ever I stent*, without stopping.

Music.

DILIGENCE: Famous people, heartly I you require
This little sport to tak in patience.
We traist in God, live we another year,
Where we have failit, we sall do diligence,   2470
With mair pleasure to mak you recompense;
Because we have been some part tedious,
With matter rude, denude of eloquence,
Likewise, perchance, to some men odious.
Now let ilk man his way advance!
Let some ga drink, and some ga dance!
Minstrels, blaw up a brawl of France!
   Let see wha hobbles best!
For I will rin incontinent
To the tavern or ever I stent!   2480
I pray to God omnipotent,
To send you all good rest!
Music. A dance, followed by a march, during which EXEUNT
OMNES.

THE END

Luxury Retail
Management

Luxury Retail Management

*How the World's
Top Brands Provide
Quality Product
and Service Support*

Michel Chevalier
Michel Gutsatz

WILEY

John Wiley & Sons Singapore Pte. Ltd.

Published in 2012 by John Wiley & Sons Singapore Pte. Ltd., 1 Fusionopolis Walk, #07-01, Solaris South Tower, Singapore 138628

Other Wiley Editorial Offices

John Wiley & Sons, 111 River Street, Hoboken, NJ 07030, USA

John Wiley & Sons, The Atrium, Southern Gate, Chichester, West Sussex, P019 8SQ, United Kingdom

John Wiley & Sons (Canada) Ltd., 5353 Dundas Street West, Suite 400, Toronto, Ontario, M9B 6HB, Canada

John Wiley & Sons Australia Ltd., 42 McDougall Street, Milton, Queensland 4064, Australia

Wiley-VCH, Boschstrasse 12, D-69469 Weinheim, Germany

Library of Congress Cataloging-in-Publication Data:

ISBN 978-0-470-83026-0 (Hardcover)
ISBN 978-0-470-83028-4 (ePDF)
ISBN 978-0-470-83027-7 (Mobi)
ISBN 978-0-470-83029-1 (ePub)

Typeset in 11.5/14 BemboAR by MPS Limited, a Macmillan Company, Chennai, India
Printed in Singapore by Markono Print Media Pte Ltd

10 9 8 7 6 5 4 3

Contents

Introduction

Luxury retailing adheres to a distinct business model. This book takes us through its major elements.

It starts with a question that all luxury brands have asked themselves: Where should I sell my products and how can I make sure my brand reaches its customers? While each brand may adopt its own distribution strategy, the essentials are common to all retailers. The differentiator is in the way they deal with their customers. What makes luxury brands unique (as we discuss in Chapter 1) is that their longevity and growth is built on the very special relationship they create with their customers. It is fundamentally emotional: bringing together the name of the brand, its heritage, and the design and quality of its products. This relationship, which traditionally had been built in a top-down manner (the brand talks to the customer; the customer accepts the brand as it is), is now changing. Twenty-first century customers are of a different essence than their predecessors.

Twenty-first century customers respect both the luxury brand and the emotional link they have with it, but also ask to be recognized, addressed as important individuals, and given best-in-class service. The new customer wants personalization—both in the product (can I get my initials on this bag?) and in the service (I was greeted by name!). Luxury brands now have new questions on their agenda: How can we give our customers a memorable experience? How do I integrate my distribution channels so that this experience is translated into a memorable experience that is unique to our brand? How can we give our customers a memorable *brand* experience?

The authors' objective is to introduce readers to all the dimensions needed to ensure this memorable brand experience is made possible. This means that we consider that an experience is not just something that happens in the store. Drawing on the wisdom of Sun Zi's *Treaty of War* (written in 1300 B.C.), it is a holistic strategy whose major objective is to ensure that the customer's mind is won over *before* he or she steps into the store. The goal is to ensure that every part of his or her customer journey is memorable and unique.

This book's objective is therefore to provide readers with answers to the five critical questions a luxury brand manager has to address when setting up such a strategy. As we shall see, these five questions are embedded and the answers will structure the specific brand experience one wishes to build.

Question 1: What Distribution Channel Do I Choose?

The choice is quite simple: There are four major channels to be explored. We will take you through the essentials of each (Chapter 3: "The Different Outlets of Luxury Distribution" and Chapter 4: "The Internet as a Channel of Distribution"):

1. The wholesale channel—from department stores to travel retail and specialty stores.
2. The branded store—which can be either owned by the brand, licensed, or franchised.
3. Internet and e-commerce—currently the most dynamic of channels, but the one that requires expertise that luxury brands tend not to have in-house.
4. Direct sales—which can be very exclusive, as in fashion trunk shows.

As this is ultimately a book about retail management, we then shift our focus squarely on the luxury store. This will lead us to the next question.

Question 2: Where Do I Set Up My Store(s)?

We will explore countries and cities, and discuss flagship stores, megastores, secondary stores, and pop-up stores. We will select the streets where luxury stores simply must be. This will lead to trade area analysis and its application to luxury. (See Chapter 5: "Luxury Store Location.")

We will then step inside the store and answer two further critical questions.

Question 3: What Is My Store Concept?

The store, being the place where the brand meets the customer, needs to have a strong and differentiating design, a specific merchandising strategy, and unique windows that will convey the brand vision to its customers. We will look at the role of the artistic director in designing the store concept and how visual merchandisers will help implement it. (See Chapter 6: "Luxury Store Concept and Design.")

Question 4: How Do I Manage the Store?

A luxury brand store—not very different from other stores—is a mix of a product offer (what products in which store?), a pricing strategy (do I sell my products at the same price in all stores worldwide? how do I price them compared to my competitors?), a set of metrics (what critical indicators should I include in my business plan?), and sales staff (who do I hire? what are their critical competencies? which compensation system should be set up?). This will take us into the details of store management, where we will examine both the commonalities that luxury brands share with all other retail brands and their differences. (See Chapter 7: "Luxury Store Economics" and Chapter 8: "Luxury Retail

Pricing.") Since "retail" as a discipline is a completely new competence for luxury brands, we have included a retail toolbox that can be found in the Appendix.

Luxury brands have discovered with time that customers are not necessarily loyal, given the growing competition between brands. The Internet and other major consumer megatrends have empowered customers. Customers now ask the luxury brands to respect them, to engage them in conversation and to reenchant their world. Luxury brands, therefore, are being asked to shift their erstwhile inward focus to their customers instead. This opens new questions for luxury brand managers, one of which is key—the loyalty issue. The luxury store has a major role to play here, because this is a major battleground of the brand experience.

Question 5: How Can I Build Customer Loyalty and Provide a Memorable Brand Experience?

Luxury brands have understood that they should not just wait for customers to enter their stores, but must build a long-lasting relationship with them. They also know that the store—and now the Internet—is where they meet their customers. This gives new importance to what happens on the floor and to how customer journeys are to be designed. This leads brands to design specific customer relationship strategies that encompass both the development of important communication strategies and the excellence in customer experience that their customers are looking for (Chapter 10: "The Importance of Stores in Customer Relationship Building," Chapter 11: "Building Loyalty in Luxury Brands," and Chapter 12: "Advertising and Communication").

The Retail Model

It will come as no surprise to the reader that, given our perspective on the critical role played by retail in the present luxury brand business model, we have put retail management in a central position.

Figure I.1 describes this.

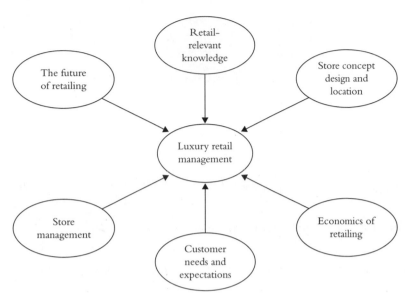

Figure I.1   The Critical Dimensions of Luxury Retail Management

This book's content follows the structure of this illustration: It starts with the relevant knowledge about retail activities, which generally comes from mass-market retailing or specialty store situations but provides valuable insights for luxury brands. We have included customer needs and expectations: What does a consumer expect when he or she enters an exclusive luxury brand store? What does the customer expect, for instance, from the staff, and which retail procedures are acceptable or unacceptable for him or her?

On the right side of the graph are two very important topics that could each justify a complete book: Store concept design and location (as an integral part of the brand identity and positioning) and the economics of retailing; that is, dealing with the basic ratios one must have in mind to effectively run a store.

The left part of the graph is more down to earth: How should one run a store? What are the most important ratios? Which key performance indicators must be gathered and analyzed every day, every week, and every month? It also deals with the future of retailing, which is not just a projection of what might happen in the future, but a description of what must be done right now to respond to the fact

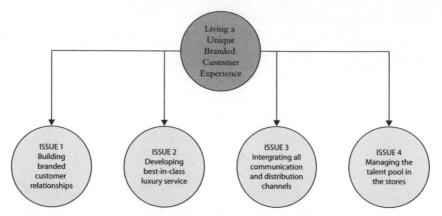

Figure I.2   Living a Unique Branded Customer Experience

that large numbers of customers are more and more regularly buying their products on the Internet.

We have stated a number of basic questions about luxury retail activities. Answering these questions will lead us to identify four critical issues being faced by luxury brands today, which they are only now starting to address:

Issue 1: Building branded customer relationships
Issue 2: Developing best-in-class luxury service
Issue 3: Integrating all communication and distribution channels
Issue 4: Managing the talent pool in the stores

Achieving this may take a few years for most luxury brands, but it can give a strong competitive edge for smaller, more agile brands. These major issues constitute what customers are now looking for the world over as Figure I.2 shows.

We will end our luxury retail journey by suggesting luxury brands should also look into three future issues:

Future Issue 1: Inventing new store formats to develop the emotional bond with the customers.
Future Issue 2: Dealing with the China Retail Footprint, which may be growing too fast.

Future Issue 3: Inventing twenty-first century luxury retail, by making each store visit a new experience for customers (Chapter 13: "The Future of Luxury Retail").

Before setting out on this journey we will review the essentials to understand what makes luxury brands so different and why retail has become a critical element for them. We will therefore undertake to define luxury and its specificities and introduce the reader to brand positioning and brand power (Chapter 1: "Luxury and Brand Power").

Chapter 1

Luxury and Brand Power

Victorious troops will first win and only then go to battle while
defeated troops will first go to battle and then only try winning.

—Sun Zi

In a book on luxury management, one generally expects to find a
chapter on retailing or retail management in which the subject is
discussed and key issues are explored. However, retail management
includes many issues—too many (and complex ones at that) to be dealt
with in a single chapter. Concepts such as visual merchandising, store
design, and store economics, to name just a few, all merit detailed analysis on their own. Developing luxury retail store activities, or staffing or
managing individual stores, are not small tasks. Each deserves a
comprehensive review.

Who is likely to be interested in such a thorough investigation of "luxury retailing"? The obvious answer is every manager in the luxury field who is responsible for developing the worldwide presence of a given brand. But let's not forget all the people who work the floor of a retail store and want to develop a career in this field and hone their instincts and skills. And we speak of retail stores in general and not just luxury stores. That's because many of the concepts applicable to luxury retail are very welcome in the specialty retail field as well.

In writing this book we have endeavored to offer the broadest possible overview of the sector while providing a compendium of the tools required to improve daily performance and forward planning.

A Definition of Luxury

It is impossible to speak of luxury without providing a definition for this concept. Many experts discuss the meaning of this word and cannot agree on a final definition accepted by everybody.

The first distinction to make is between luxury and fashion. For some people, a brand in the field of textiles or accessories simply starts out as a "fashion" brand and is only considered as a "luxury" brand when it has achieved stability and the quality of being timeless. According to that theory, a fashion brand has to be creative and come up with new ideas, new concepts, and new products every season in order to attract the interest of the consumer. As it develops classical models that sell year-round, which become permanent best sellers with a signature style, its status moves from fashion to luxury. While this distinction between a fashion brand and a luxury brand is a valid one, it is misleading because even a fashion brand that has achieved luxury status, such as Chanel or Dior, must come up with new designs each season, and present them in new ways in order to retain consumer interest.

In the following sections we start looking at the difficulty of providing a definition of luxury, then look at several approaches to distinguishing different types of luxury.

Why Is It Difficult to Come Up with a Definition?

The concept of luxury has fluctuated over time. In the Middle Ages, people thought of luxury objects as unnecessary and superfluous. A luxury object would be much more sophisticated than the standard product used to satisfy the same need. At that time, luxury objects were only targeted at "the happy few" and would give them a way to differentiate themselves from the crowd.

Today the word *luxury* carries a much less negative connotation. It is not considered superfluous or targeted to a very small group of individuals. A new concept has emerged—the concept of branding, so that a luxury object is one that carries a brand that is well known, credible, and respected. As the brand signature comes into the picture, the concept of exclusion (that it's not for everybody) disappears and the focus is much more on the quality of the product offering.

Another element that may have contributed to this more positive perception of the luxury concept could be the rise of an intermediary luxury, which in fact is targeted to almost everybody. So what remains in the mind of the consumer is that luxury products are sophisticated, expensive, have a reasonably high quality, and bear a very strong and attractive brand name.

The Different Approaches to Luxury Another way to differentiate between the definitions of luxury is by looking at the criteria that different individuals use to distinguish one luxury product from another.

- In terms of *perception*, the consumer decides what is and what is not a luxury object. Today, they would not speak of "conspicuous waste" as Thorstein Veblen did, but would speak of quality of service in a sophisticated environment.
- In terms of *production*, the manufacturers themselves decide whether they want their products to be part of the luxury world. Accordingly, they make sure a luxury product is the work of a careful craftsman, sold in a very sophisticated environment, and promoted in an exclusive way, with major emphasis on the description of the brand and its core values. However, at a different level, Hugo Boss is perceived by the general management of the brand as a very sophisticated way

of manufacturing and selling slightly upscale fashion products. And in another way, Zara, with emphasis on their very selective retail network, based in the very best locations in every city and on the flow of new designs being delivered every other week in all these stores in the world, can still be considered, from the point of view of Zara management, as a luxury activity.

- In terms of *social and individual behavior*, a luxury product would be described by sociologists as an item that makes its user stand out from the crowd. Individuals would probably speak in hedonistic terms and describe how the ownership of a specific luxury item gives them individual satisfaction and genuine pleasure, possibly reflecting the sophistication of the objects they have acquired or plan to purchase.

Behind all these different definitions is an underlying element: the brand itself and its specific values. A product has its own technical and aesthetic characteristics—but it also carries a brand. This brand identity must be coherent and consistent with what the product represents and should bring an additional value without betraying it.

A Set of Luxury Values Another approach to the definition of luxury is to list the different components that a luxury object should include.

- Underlying the concept of luxury, there is the notion of *exclusivity*. A luxury product should be rare and slightly difficult to acquire. It should of course be available, but give the feeling that the purchaser is "in the know," can identify what makes it so different from other products or other brands, and can demonstrate that he or she has better taste and is more sophisticated than the standard customer.
- An obvious characteristic of a luxury object is its *quality*. It should be better looking. Its warranty should be clear and generous. The packaging should be sophisticated and the object should be priced relatively high, or at least clearly above the price level of a similar mass-market product.
- An additional facet should be a form of *hedonism*: It should be pleasant to own and use, providing a very personal sense of satisfaction.
- *The brand image* is the last component. It should be renowned, but it should also be unique, different, and strongly positioned.

But ultimately luxury is always about status. A luxury professional should never forget the business she or he is really in: providing customers and clients with status, directly or indirectly, in whatever form or shape.

Ultimately, customers will pay the high prices of luxury because, through all these different characteristics, a luxury object fulfills all the emotional, symbolic, and experiential needs of the customer. This is what exclusivity, quality, hedonism, and brand image are about.

The Different Types of Luxury Rather than embark on a lengthy discussion of one single luxury concept, it may be more efficient to list different types of luxury.

- *Authentic luxury* refers to objects that are clearly different from mass-market products because they were created by means of craftsmanship: They may have an added durability, they may be easier to use, and they also have a rewarding brand identity. A true luxury product will be somewhat timeless and will be pleasant for the owner to handle or use, thanks to an infinite number of sophisticated details and craftsmanship values. Its price would certainly not be cheap and its identity would provide much more than the economic value it represents: It is not so much an economic proposition as it is an object with aesthetic components that bring additional emotional value to its owner.
- *Intermediary luxury* (one of the authors coined the phrase "Luxe Populi" in an unpublished book[1]) products refer to products that are imbued with traditional luxury status in terms of creativity, communication, and coherence in the management of the brand identity, but are in fact upgraded traditional middle-of-the-road consumer goods. These are not the result of individual craftsmanship. They are positioned in the upper middle range of the price scale and produced in relatively large quantities by automated factory processes, yet their brand identity is carefully developed and controlled over time.
- *Eccentric luxury* refers to products that are practically individual creations and are truly distinct from the standard. Ferrari is a good

[1]Michel Gutsatz, *Luxe Populi/Developing Luxury Brands*, July 2002.

example: Although a Porsche would be an authentic luxury product, a Ferrari provides an added dimension of eccentricity. It is manufactured in very small quantities and the Ferrari Corporation seems to claim the right to its own freedom and creativity. They do not manufacture standard automobiles but individual collector's items, some of which never to be seen on a normal country road.

As Jean Louis Dumas, the late chairman of Hermès, said one day, "A luxury brand must respect three conditions: It should stamp beautiful objects; it should select its customers and promote them as individual promotion agents; it should be able to decide freely and without any constraints what it wants to do." There is perhaps no better definition of eccentric luxury.

- *Sensible luxury* is almost not a luxury at all or a special case of intermediate luxury at best. Zara represents this segment: creative products changing very rapidly in an efficient way, with customers finding psychological satisfaction in buying and using these quick-moving products. The price is very reasonable and the brand identity is carefully managed and promoted, with a clear long-term view.

As we will see, the Zara business model is very effective. But if, from the point of view of the manufacturer, many luxury status tools are being used, we are in fact in a category that should be included in intermediary luxury—and may not even be part of this intermediary luxury, but simply sophisticated and effective mass-market brands.

Zara is probably a bad example because most readers might say that this brand has nothing to do with the luxury field. We accept this point of view, but with the concept of "trading up," many luxury tools can be useful for mass-market brands. We are also in a continuum, and Zara is at the end of this continuum and Gucci or Chanel at the other end.

Brand Positioning and Retail Efficiency

To explain main changes in the retail field, the concept of the "wheel of retailing" has been used for several decades. It was described for the first time by Jerome McCarty in 1960. According to this concept, newcomers generally use price to enter a new retail market by starting as the cheapest store in the area. Then, as they become successful, they upgrade their services, and they improve their store presentation, which, one way or another, they then have to charge to the consumer by increasing their retail prices. They can thereby run their business profitably, but in so doing, they leave the door open to the next round of newcomers who arrive on the scene with lower prices to give the wheel of retailing another spin.

This concept explains how the landscape of mass market retail has moved over time from local stores to supermarkets and then to discount stores. In such cases a long-term retail position is never obtained and retail brand preferences have little value. Their positioning differs over time as brands are moved by the wheel of retailing, with their relative prices changing to absorb efforts to improve services while reflecting the price aggressiveness of newcomers.

Luxury is probably the only field in which the wheel of retailing does not seem to work. In luxury, the consumer preference results from the strength and the attractiveness of the brand: The stronger the brand, the greater the price premium for the retailer. In fact, the brand's strength can provide either a volume advantage at price parity or a price premium.

This was described for the first time by Andrew Willeman and Michael Jary in their book *Retail Power Plays*.[2] As illustrated in Figure 1.1, they put the concepts of relative price and relative volume on a graph. A given brand will generally be represented by a straight line with the volume decreasing regularly as the relative price increases—thereby providing an opportunity to measure the strength of a given brand. The stronger it is, the more to the right would its relative volume/relative price line appear. The advantage of such a location on the right of the graph is that it can command a higher price, a higher volume at a given price, or a bit of both, as indicated in Figure 1.1.

How can we explain this phenomenon? A luxury purchase is an inspirational act with many criteria unrelated to the single price variable.

---

[2]Andrew Willeman and Michael Jary, *Retail Power Plays* (New York: New York University Press, 1997).

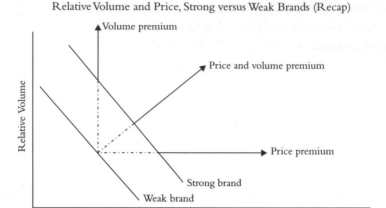

Relative Volume and Price, Strong versus Weak Brands (Recap)

Figure 1.1   Brand Power versus the Wheel of Retailing
SOURCE: Andrew Willeman and Michael Jary, *Retail Power Plays* (New York: New York University Press, 1997).

By purchasing a luxury product, a consumer wants to enhance his or her self-image and self-esteem as well as reinforce a sense of peer group membership (either actual or desired).

From the point of view of a given luxury firm, the strength and the attractiveness of a given brand is good news, providing ample opportunities for tremendous profit, either as a result of a higher volume of sales (higher market share) or from a higher price and margin than its competitors. But part of such additional profits must necessarily be reinvested in advertising or public relations to reinforce the brand identity and keep this consumer preference alive and meaningful.

As we look at the graph, we notice that over time there should be a balance between increased market share and increased price premium. The temptation is quite strong, of course, to cash in on the advantage and raise prices—but in the long run, this could jeopardize customer loyalty and regular repeat purchases. In that respect, the volume premium variable must not be forgotten.

The situation is easier for stores like department stores or luxury multi-brand specialty stores (for example, Colette in Paris). They must use the brands' recommended prices and can only cash in on the strength of their own retail brand to look for additional volume.

This brand power, as it applies to luxury retail activities, reduces sales volatility and therefore provides greater sustainability of profits. Obviously, the stronger the brand power, the higher the sales per square foot in a given location and the lower the rent as a percentage of forecast sales. For a strong brand, almost every retail location opportunity can become profitable, and the stronger the brand the stronger the maneuverability of its retail strategy.

In fact, as we integrate the concept of brand power, the retailing field can be divided in two subcategories:

1. A category in which the retail brand plays a secondary role and the wheel of retailing explains the major shifts in market shares and in consumer preferences.
2. A category in which the wheel of retailing plays almost no role and the brand power is a critical variable. This includes the largest part of luxury retail brands and some specialty retail brands as well—those that have been able to create a strong *brand preference* (the interest of consumers for a given brand—awareness, knowledge, and favorable attitude for the brand in such a way that the consumer is almost ready to intend to purchase).

This book deals with issues related to brands that are able to or seek to create a strong brand preference.

Retail as a Source of Prosperity

There is something very particular in retailing. If it is possible to operate a store in a given city, for example New York or Paris, without major advertising budgets, and do it with a very satisfactory profit level, then this performance can be duplicated in London or in Milan, again and again.

In the first step, when a store is doing well somewhere, it is very important to constantly improve performance, fine-tune the product offering, check price levels, and organize the customer relationship management. It then becomes possible to open a new store elsewhere: The business plan would be done on the basis of the pilot store results. If it is clearly profitable and has a positive cash flow, it is possible to find a bank that will provide part of the money necessary to rent an adequate store in an effective location and finance its setup and decor. If the second store works just as well as the first one, then a third store can be opened, then a fourth, and so on.

It is not surprising that in many countries like Sweden, Spain, or France, the wealthiest people (or those among the wealthiest) come from the mass-market retail field. Think of the Fournier and Defforey families in France, the inventors of the hypermarket concept and the creators of Carrefour, or Ingvar Kamprad in Sweden, the founder of IKEA, or Amancio Ortega, the founder of Zara in Spain. They all started with one store, then another, to eventually create large world-wide retail groups. They constantly thought about how they could improve their retail operations and generate new ideas or new practices across the globe.

Do these mass-market examples also apply to luxury? The answer is yes, the same process applies: When one has a brand and store concept that is very profitable, nothing can stop the growth and the opening of additional stores. Two observations follow:

1. If a large Ralph Lauren store is very profitable in New York and if its sales per square foot are very high, the same can probably happen in London, and then in Paris. And in Paris, if the large Ralph Lauren store on the Right Bank is profitable, then there is an opportunity to open another large store on the Left Bank, which is exactly what was done in 2011. Effective and profitable stores are just another form of money machine. So, when Hermès had only one very profitable store on the Right Bank of Paris, it made sense to also open a store on the Left Bank, which they did at the end of 2010.

2. If a store has existed for a long time in a city and no replicas are planned, this probably indicates that the first store is not as profitable as it could be. How profitable is, for example, the very large flagship store of Sonia Rykiel in Paris? Not that much! How profitable is the Balenciaga store on Avenue George V in Paris? Probably not that much either. In such cases, the priority is to work on the existing brand concept and, above all, the merchandising of these stores.

Sometimes luxury brand executives forget that the name of the game is to come up with products that customers like and purchase within an effective store concept. It is useful to remind ourselves of this at this early point in this book.

Retailing: For Which Type of Products and with What Logistic System?

When one speaks about luxury retailing, one may think about a jewelry store located in New York on Fifth Avenue or a fashion store located on Via Monte Napoleone in Milan.

But retailing concepts can apply to a much larger category of products or trade situations. There is in fact a continuum between stores selling material products (the customer comes out with a shopping bag and some products), sites selling products that are partly material and partly immaterial (a restaurant, for example, provides its customers with food and services and the customer in turn comes out of the place with a specific experience), and entities selling products that are completely immaterial (for example, a private bank or an insurance company). At first sight, these situations seem very different, but they share some of the same characteristics for the client, who takes in:

- The atmosphere of the place and its specific environment.
- The quality of the service, the warmth of the interaction with the staff, and the way he or she was treated—as a standard or as an exceptional customer.
- How the product or service was offered, was presented, and was made available.

Whether we are talking about a bank, a restaurant, or a fashion store, location, as well as store concept and staff interaction, are all very important to the overall service expected and obtained. The same criteria for excellence apply and the way customers evaluate the quality of services is almost identical.

Luxury hotels work this way, too. They need to be located in a very special place, be decorated in a special way, develop a specific atmosphere, and provide sophisticated service, every single day of the year.

But can an individual bank outlet be considered a luxury retail location? Probably not, but a private bank with one single outlet in

Geneva can certainly be considered as such, and will define its own concept, its own atmosphere, and its quality of service accordingly.

So, what is the difference? The same process applies to stores that provide material services (a perfume, a dress, or a watch), for stores that provide a service slightly material and slightly immaterial (a luxury restaurant and a five-star hotel), or stores that provide exclusively immaterial services (an investment bank specializing in high-net-worth individuals). In this book, we provide effective tools for the development and management of the different types of retail structures.

Retailing is not only a pure marketing activity. It must deal with logistics and precise organization management. Any effective retail organization requires a 100 percent foolproof system. This exclusive brand power is only available to those who have organized *a logistics system* that works in any possible situation.

One of the authors worked in a company where the initial logistic diagnostic, as seen by the retail store operators, was as follows:

- U.S. retail stores unpack every incoming product box due to:
  - Incomplete or incorrect shipping information (for 30 percent of the volume) and advanced shipping note missing.
  - Products coming from one of the factories (20 percent of incoming volume) not labeled at all, which forced the retail organization to invest in a labeling hardware system.
  - Ten percent of incoming merchandise not matching the order.
- Tokyo and Hong Kong retail operators unpack every box due to:
  - A need for a special quality check on every item (products that had been approved by European quality control teams but that were considered unfit for Japanese and Chinese luxury consumers).
  - A need to relabel every product to fit high Asian standards.

Most people, reading this after the fact, would probably think that it could not have been that bad, but this was the actual situation. It happened because:

- European factory people had never thought about the specific needs of Japanese or American retail operators and final clients.

- Logistics systems had never been clearly and completely applied to systematic procedures.
- The very high number of process steps had never been clearly identified and carefully organized.
- Different factories were using different identification coding systems and that the consolidation of logistics was not foolproof.

The system was not transparent enough, not robust enough, and not really predictable. It had too many opportunities to fail. It was unacceptable at the receiving end, which is to say, at the shop level.

A committee was created with IT specialists, logistic experts, product development managers, factory and quality control staff, and retailers from different parts of the world. It came up with a list of recommendations and a request for a set of completely new procedures. A very precise timetable was set; procedures were set forth in detail; new manufacturing and quality control processes were created; investments in new IT, labeling, and logistic systems were decided; and over a period of two years, a new foolproof plan would be implemented.

As this company went into the analysis of the supply chain processes, it described the level of control that different competitors had, according to them, in the system. This is presented in Table 1.1.

We felt that we could publish their evaluation sheet because the situation and therefore the comments are completely outdated. But the point is that a smooth and effective retail operation is only possible if:

- All stakeholders from suppliers to subcontractors and internal factories are completely coordinated, work with the same set of objectives, and use the same procedures.
- The system is user-friendly and has been developed with full understanding of retail operators' requirements and full approval of back office staff.
- The procedures are smooth, foolproof, and have been tested and retested over time.

Table 1.1   Different Business Logistic Models

	Raw Material Sourcing	Production	Distribution	Comments
Bally	medium control	low control	full control	improvement needed?
Ferragamo	medium/ high control	low control	full control	too much leverage on suppliers?
Gucci	medium control	medium control	medium control	open but effective system
Prada	medium control	full control	full control	strong control of suppliers
Sergio Rossi	medium control	medium control	medium control	improvement on the way
Valentino	medium control	very low control	full control	priority to growth

SOURCE: 2003 confidential document. Probably most findings are outdated today, as most companies have put major emphasis in improving their logistic systems to be in line with retail excellence objectives.

- Investments on systems and on factory equipment have been made to provide enough flexibility and assure long-term usage, whatever the expected growth in sales volume or number of stores.

Only then can we speak of an organization that can take full advantage of its brand power and concentrate on its major task: to give the customer a memorable experience.

Chapter 2

The Distribution
Models of Luxury

If you control your distribution, you control your image.
—Bernard Arnault, President, LVMH

P utting a chapter about distribution models this early on in a
book about luxury retail might seem a little out of place. Most
readers are likely to have expected a lengthy examination of
brand development through store concepts or visual merchandising
before launching into this arguably dry subject. But in reality, brand
development boils down to defining the best system to present branded
products to the end customers, convincing them that they should buy,
by acting in a way that is so pleasing and rewarding that they will come
back for a new experience and buy again at a later date. This means that

we have to first understand why, when, and how luxury brands—which traditionally were production companies operating only a few stores—decided to move into retail and how their decisions about distribution channels are made.

Starting by looking at luxury retail from a historical perspective, we will see how brands, in order to develop a worldwide presence, have understood the importance of having their own stores. This leads us to describe the specific challenges of retailing for the luxury firm.

We then outline the major choices open to luxury brands when they make decisions about their distribution strategy. You will understand that the brand's life cycle and its different categories are the two most critical dimensions to be taken into consideration, given that the unique objective of a luxury brand is to control its image. This has been the driving force behind the development of retail in luxury. It has led most brands to control their distribution and it has further led them to understand that it is also a way to control margins. Cutting down intermediaries leads, of course, to capital expenditure (setting up a store is expensive) but it also leads to increased profitability if correctly deployed.

Retail: A New Business Model for Luxury

Retailing: A Historical Perspective

Retailing is probably one of the oldest professions in the world. Once people realized that they could not personally furnish themselves with all the items needed for their own survival, they located other individuals who could gather a selection of sought-after products that they, in turn, could sell at a profit. This process of sourcing and selecting different items to present a wide range of products, and then facilitating their acquisition by others, seems to be as old as the world. Later, in the Middle Ages, as commerce developed, retailers from the same trade would often gather in the same street. They felt they were better off next to their main competitors, believing that customers would visit them as part of a destination shopping trip, where all the stores located in the same street stood a similar chance of being visited. They reasoned that those who had set up shop elsewhere, on their own, would simply not be visited during a shopping trip and would miss out on potential sales. Being located away from other retailers but perhaps close to where people lived was mainly an advantage for those serving people's daily needs such as food products—in other words, "convenience shopping."

This difference between convenience shopping and destination shopping has always existed and explains different strategies in terms of location. The fact that similar traders wanted to be close to each other and concentrate their individual pulling power is not very different from what happens today with the concentration of luxury stores in the same areas of major cities.

The original event that deserves mention here is the creation, in 1851, of the first department store in the world, Au Bon Marché, in Paris. The idea was that for the first time a single store would sell both ladies' and men's ready-to-wear, as well as shoes and kitchen wares, all at the same time. As usual, when an idea is good, it is rapidly copied, and in 1856 the first department store was created in New York: Macy's.

Over time, the look and the system of department store merchandising was very much affected by technical innovation. In 1869, the first elevator was installed in Paris in a department store, making it easier for customers to move from one floor to the next, while making it possible to present merchandise in four or five different departments.

Another innovation, dating from 1892, shaped the look of all department store buildings in the world—the escalator. The escalator enabled customers to move from one floor to another at their own pace, without the wait that using an elevator involves. Escalators created the look of most department stores today: a central well with a large and impressive hall, sometimes crowned with a cupola, and escalators reaching up and down in the middle, enabling customers to move from floor to floor as they pleased. In 1895 the first escalators were installed in Harrod's in London.

In 1915, the first Japanese department store was created in Tokyo: Mitsukoshi Nihonbashi.

Another very important date is 1919. The first air-conditioning system was installed in Abraham & Strauss in New York. From that point on, department stores no longer needed windows. Air-conditioning made it unnecessary to have windows for air circulation or doors that opened onto the street, therefore enabling stores to be part of a shopping gallery or shopping center. Individual stores no longer required windows either, except as a stage for product presentation. Since then, the appearance of department store buildings as we know them has pretty much stabilized.

In 1922, the first shopping mall, the Country Club Plaza, was created in Kansas City, and the look of the present store system has remained relatively unchanged for almost 90 years with very few innovations, with the exception of the first duty-free shop, which opened in Shannon Airport in Ireland in 1957.

On the other hand, we must note the introduction of the first electronic cash register in 1970 and the first optical scanner in 1975. Prior to that time, it was difficult to predict that every product, sold somewhere in the world, would have its own code that could be read easily by a machine.

Today's department stores, shopping malls, individual shopping galleries, or duty-free galleries are in fact the result of 150 years of retail innovation and development.

The Challenge for Luxury Brands: Distributing Their Products

As they develop internationally, luxury brands will use different systems. They will have one or several retail stores in their own countries but they may start wholesale activities abroad. They may also shop-in-shop develop their own departments in department stores. If and when the brand develops strongly abroad, it may then be time to conduct a larger part of their activities in directly operated stores.

At a given time, most brands use a mix of retail systems: They will have some wholly owned stores as well as franchised or joint venture stores (all considered directly operated stores), then shop-in-shops and corners in department stores.

For perfume and cosmetic brands, most sales are done at the wholesale level, as well as through department store counters (or assimilated corners). They sometimes use freestanding stores in very special locations: This is true for Dior and Estée Lauder in Moscow and Dior in Hong Kong. Conversely, some brands, like Mac, Shu Uemura, Joe Malone, and By Terry have developed a large part of business in directly operated stores.

Watches are also slightly different in their distribution mix. Fifteen years ago, Ebel developed a large number of retail stores, but it did not work out and they had to close them and get back to a wholesale model. Yet today Rolex and Bréguet are concentrating a large part of their activities on their own retail stores. Bréguet has directly operated freestanding stores in major cities around the world, using them as showrooms and flagship stores that complement the work done on the brand by a select number of independent retailers. Rolex seems to concentrate their own flagship stores in a select number of countries, like, for example, China.

The point here is that there is no such thing as a unique business model. Watches, perfumes, and cosmetics generally use wholesale models. Very upscale ladies' ready-to-wear and accessory lines generally work with directly operated stores and department stores, but they also develop wholesale activities. Even in a book discussing luxury retail management, it is important to mention the relative importance of different distribution systems, according to the products and the priorities of different brands. We examine all these issues in the next chapter and in Chapter 7.

Five Major Trends in Luxury Retailing

At this early stage, a list of the major changes occurring today in luxury retail is in order.

1. Contrary to what one might think, the different retail systems are becoming less standardized: Some brands specialize in directly operated stores, others use a fully wholesale strategy. Even the types of stores can vary from one brand to another. The retail strategy for each retail brand requires creativity and independence. Doing exactly what the major brands are doing does not necessarily make sense for smaller brands.
2. The communication between the store and the consumer has become individualized. We discuss this in detail in Chapter 10.
3. Innovation has become key. Different types of stores or retail strategies may be more effective in Korea or in China. Other systems may be better adapted to the United States. There is obviously a need for a clear retailing platform for a given brand, but each country should have the opportunity to slightly depart from the rule.

4. The paradox of luxury is that the market is worldwide, but each brand must also be developed locally. The strength of Tiffany in the United States is a challenge for Cartier. Probably, for Cartier, American development may require retail strategies that are not necessary in Europe, or even could be viewed as counterproductive in Europe.

5. Brand communication must be organized at different levels: There is a worldwide brand identity strategy, but in each country, a compatible retail sales communication must be developed. This way, the consumer will receive different bits of information from different sources, all being coherent, but building a complex set of values, potential, and brand characteristics.

In a way, brand development happens at two complementary levels: at the worldwide level, but also at the level of each retail outlet.

Retail: A New Business Model for Luxury

Retail activities are not necessarily the major thrust of luxury brands. Perfumes and cosmetics brands mainly use the wholesale model. That is to say, their products end up in perfume shops and in department stores and they will be presented as one alternative choice, compared to many others present on the shelf.

Wholesale and retail models require very different marketing strategies, as described in Table 2.1.

Table 2.1 Differences between Wholesale and Retail Models

	Wholesale Distribution	Retail Stores
Product line	narrow	large
Product objective	blockbuster	part of a whole
Advertising and promotion	pull	push
Price elasticity	strong	limited
Customer link	reduced	strong (CRM)
Logistics requirements	limited	key

- For wholesale, the point is not to sell a wide product line, but rather an individual product that will have enough strength to stand on its own. On the contrary, when a brand has its own stores, it should provide a large offering so that any customer entering the store can find a product that he or she likes.
- The name of the game, in a multi-brand perfume shop, is for a given brand to present a blockbuster that customers easily identify as an attractive product. On the contrary, in a mono-brand retail shop, a blockbuster does not provide a balanced contribution to the merchandise selection: It overshadows the individual products that must be individually geared to a specific market segment.
- Retail and wholesale models require different advertising and promotional thrusts. In a wholesale model, media advertising is a priority to convince the consumer, confronted with a large selection of products in a given store, that brand X is more desirable, more modern, more prestigious, or simply more adequate. In a retail model, media advertising is necessary to bring consumers into the store, where the "push" is up to the shop assistants who use their convincing power, and their individual sales arguments to make the difference.
- In the wholesale model, the consumer, confronted with many brand offerings, uses price as a selection criterion. In the retail model, although the consumer will not buy if the product he or she wants is overpriced, he or she will not use price as a selection criterion between different items within reasonable limits.
- In a retail model, a strong individual link between the consumer and the brand will be created over time through customer relationship management (CRM): The customers will be identified, their names and addresses registered, and their preferences and their shopping patterns noted. It is then possible to develop a strong relationship and organize specific promotional programs just for them. In a wholesale model, most customers remain unknown and unidentified, therefore making customer links difficult to create for any single brand that is only part of a larger merchandising offer.
- Logistics requirements are quite different between the two systems. In a wholesale model, part of the logistics tasks, like warehousing and delivery to each individual outlet, is done by the retail operator. In a retail model the tasks are the exclusive responsibility of the brand owner.

In this section, the retail model may seem to be presented as a new model. It has, in fact, always existed; however, some of the strongest shifts in the luxury industry have been the increasing shift of brands from a wholesale to a retail model.

Gucci is certainly a case in point. In 1993, with sales around 200 million euros, it was selling through its own stores in Europe, but in the United States and Japan it was in fact a wholesale brand. In the United States, aside from a flagship store in New York, it was selling through 500 "doors" in department stores. The product assortment was limited, focused mainly on shoes (in particular the Gucci loafer) and some ties and scarves. Products were presented at department store counters or in corners that were more or less identified. In Japan, 250 department stores carried the brand. It was then decided to pull out of most of these stores and to stay only in the most upscale and large volume ones, exclusively in the form of clearly identified "shop-in-shops": This would allow the merchandising mix to be enlarged, particularly with ladies' products and ladies' ready-to-wear, and in such stores, the volume could be increased more than 10 times. In 2010, with sales above 2 billion euros, Gucci had 49 doors in the United States and 44 doors in Japan: The brand model has changed completely, to the advantage of a retail one.

Because of the impressive increase in sales and profitability, some experts have been fast to jump to the short-sighted conclusion that this example, and a few others, was a clear indication of the superiority of the retail model versus the wholesale one. We, frankly, don't reach the same conclusion; to us the facts suggest that different brands require different strategies, which means that any coherent system can make sense.

A case in point is Ralph Lauren, which is also a very strong success story, but with a different model. They speak of a "flexible integrated model" that encompasses retail, wholesale, and licensing, with total annual sales in the vicinity of 3.5 billion euros and a net income of 280 million euros. It is therefore more profitable than Hermès, which is not a bad performance for a first-generation brand, still chaired by its founder. They use an integrated approach to advertising and marketing, but in each zone they have a mix of directly operated stores, and franchised stores, either managed directly or with the help of local exclusive distributors. Sales are divided as 55 percent at wholesale, 40 percent at retail, and 5 percent from licensing royalties, with only 23 percent of operating income coming from directly operated retail stores.

Compared to the 49 Gucci stores in the United States, Ralph Lauren claims 8,611 doors in its wholesale segment in the United States and Canada. It has, nevertheless, only 120 doors in Japan, where its policy is not so different from that of Gucci. In fact, for Ralph Lauren, the stated wholesale segment corresponds to 11,000 doors. In the retail division, Ralph Lauren operates 153 full retail stores (134 in North America and 19 in Europe) and 158 factory stores.

Ralph Lauren uses licensing for fragrances (L'Oréal), eyewear (Luxottica), and watches (Richemont) as well as for men's tailoring clothing (Dealers), men's underwear and sleepwear (Hanes brands), and men's Chaps sportswear (the Warnaco Group).

They also use exclusive distributors to develop their wholesale activities in many countries including Japan, Korea, Hong Kong, China, and Singapore, as well as Columbia, Ecuador, Peru, Bolivia and various other countries in Central America and the Caribbean.

The Ralph Lauren system is a diversified approach to luxury. Of course, all products will end up in stores, but not necessarily in directly operated ones: They use wholesale, local distributorship contracts, and licensing to continuously improve the quality of their product presentation and the economic soundness of their corporate growth model.

Writing a book on retail, our tendency would be to strongly recommend a retail model. But things are never that simple. In the development of a luxury brand, several phases make sense at different times. Even in the case of Gucci, the existence of 500 "doors" in the United States before 1993 generated very strong brand awareness in the country and, with a limited investment cost, a strong presence and preference among American customers. With that level of preference, the opening of freestanding stores and large shop-in-shops was no longer a costly and risky venture. Thanks to a strong customer base, those stores could open with confidence and were rapidly above break-even. The opening of freestanding stores from scratch would have been a much more uncertain and costly venture. In principle, Ralph Lauren could one day move to a full retail store operation: They now have the credibility and the business volume to do it.

In the luxury world, opening stores is the costliest and the riskiest way to get started. To be in a key location in every major city of the world requires very expensive key money outlays, plus a lot of direct staff on the payroll, without mentioning the financing of large inventories. Is it effective? Of course it can be, as it has been for Gucci. But for many brands, using department stores, exclusive distributors in given countries, and licensing operations may be just as effective — or even more effective — and certainly cheaper.

The Development of Retail Activities in Luxury

How important are retail activities for major luxury brands? In the last 10 years, luxury companies have clearly developed their retail activities. Between 2000 and 2009/2010, many major groups have doubled their number of directly operated stores: Some, like Bulgari, have more than doubled, going from 126 in 2000 to 276 in 2009. Many brands have also increased the size of their average store.

In Table 2.2, we discuss Bulgari, Gucci, Louis Vuitton, and Tiffany. For Cartier, specific figures on sales are unavailable, so we have used the consolidation of Cartier and Van Cleef & Arpels, knowing that most of the sales (probably in the vicinity of 2.4 billion euros) come from Cartier.

The table clearly illustrates the following points:

- Retailing and retail stores have been a major activity and a major strategic concern for luxury goods.
- In this sample of six brands, the total number of stores has gone from 922 to 1560: Managing, staffing, and controlling those stores has therefore become a major aspect of managing a luxury brand.
- Business has not been simplified, now that luxury brands rely very heavily on their own retail structure. It is clear, for example, that during the same period from 2000 to 2010, the average sales per store slightly decreased, while running them did not become any easier.

Table 2.2   Example of the Extension of New Stores for Major Brands (Estimates of Sales and Number of Stores)

	2000	2003	2007	2009/2010
Bulgari				
Sales in million €	376	759	1,091	926
Number of stores	126	182	207	273
Cartier and **Van Cleef**				
Sales in million €	1,500 (E)	1,994	2,435	2,688
Number of stores	250	250	301	364
Gucci				
Sales in million €	1,200	1,800	2,300	2,266
Number of stores	143	174	233	283
Louis Vuitton				
Sales in million €	1,500 (E)	2,200 (E)	3,700 (E)	5,000 (E)
Number of stores	284	317	390	440
Tiffany				
Sales in million €	1,334	1,600	2,342	2,167
Number of stores	119	141	184	220

(E) Indicates estimates by the authors.
SOURCE: Annual reports and official documents.

Choosing a Distribution Model

Many outsiders believe the only way to develop retail activities for a brand is to own 100 percent of the stores and to sell no product outside of this system. There is in fact only one brand doing that, Louis Vuitton, but due to the brand's incredible success, people think this is the only viable retail model.

While Louis Vuitton is undeniably successful, its model is not necessarily right for everybody. As they want their products to be sold only in their own stores, Louis Vuitton has made the decision not to offer perfumes and cosmetics that require substantial visibility to be sold wholesale to department stores and select perfume shops. They sell sunglasses in their own stores but cannot sell optical frames, as this would require them to have in-house opticians or to sell to a large selection of independent optical stores. (Chanel, for example, through a license contract with Luxottica, sells optical frames in many optical stores.)

Also, the policy of selling products exclusively in a company's own stores precludes a brand's presence in independent duty-free outlets. Louis Vuitton does make an exception to this rule that allows their products to be found in DFS stores (duty-free shops) at airports and in their downtown Galleria complexes, but, that being said, DFS happens to belong to the LVMH group. As a singular exception, Louis Vuitton products can also be found in independent downtown and airport duty-free shops in South Korea.

This system of selling exclusively in one's own retail stores is therefore quite limited. It requires a very attractive brand that can stand on its own almost everywhere on the world. Probably only 8 to 10 brands in the world are strong enough to use that strategy. For less powerful brands, the only solution is to have a mix of distribution systems.

The advantage of working only with directly operated stores is that supply chain and distribution systems can be centralized. In that case, deliveries can be almost automatic, based on a strong centralized information system that monitors sales and inventory online and provides frequent systematic deliveries. With this system, stores are generally divided into several categories (A, B, or C) according to their size and their volume and with adjusted merchandising collections. The bigger stores will feature a very large range; whereas smaller ones will sometimes have a limited ready-to-wear collection or an even more limited number of product categories.

For other brands, the solution relies on a mix of their own retail stores, department stores, and wholesale activities, so that the merchandise can be visible and easily available.

Cartier is a good example of this mixed distribution system. They have their own stores, presenting a very large collection of products. They also have shop-in-shops and corners in department stores. Yet a large percentage of their watches are sold wholesale to independent jewelers. A limited collection of their basic jewelry products can also be found in a small number of independent jewelry stores. Their own stores give them the image of a strong brand, but they use independent retailers to give them additional volume and a strong presence in places where watches are also sold. They also have their own separate sales forces for perfumes and for optical frames that end up in independent outlets. Their challenge is to make sure that consumers find their product in varying locations which all promote the same overall image of quality and scarcity everywhere.

For a company that wants to distribute branded products to the end consumer, three broad possibilities exist:

1. Create a brand retail store that will sell such products to the end consumer.
2. Sell those products at wholesale to dealers and retailers including department stores that will in turn offer them to the end consumers in their own ways and in accordance with their own conditions.
3. Reach an agreement with department stores or potential franchisees so that products will be presented in their outlets in a way that is either in accordance with the brands' standard merchandising procedures or in a way that is similar to what happens in a full-fledged, directly owned brand retail store.

What is the best system? It all depends. If a firm is selling ladies' leather belts, it would not make sense to have their own mono-product stores. Their belts are much better off in a department store, presented in the ladies' ready-to-wear section or at a multi-brand counter with many different products from different competitors. But what about gloves? Like belts, gloves could be sold in a multi-brand environment—but in Italy, in every major tourist city, one can find stores that exclusively sell a large variety of gloves that attract consumers by the sheer diversity of their products and extensive variety of colors. However, brands like Chanel or Gucci, with very large product assortments, seem to be better merchandised in mono-brand stores, even though in many cases their products are also sold in department store shop-in-shops.

What is the best economic system? There is no single answer to this question. It all depends on the type of products, the attractiveness of a given brand, and its expected volume in a given trade area. When operating a retail store, one works with fixed costs, independent of the level of sales, for example, yearly rental costs, sales staff salaries, and other miscellaneous fixed costs like a telephone line or electric power. On the contrary, if one is selling the same products at wholesale to retailers and to department stores, one would incur no fixed costs at all, but obviously the retailers would request a retailers' margin: The brand would make a relatively smaller percentage of gross margin on a product sold through a retailer rather than in its own store. The choice is therefore between a relatively lower margin and no fixed costs or a higher margin but straight fixed costs.

One may say that for low volume brands, the wholesale system is more profitable and that for high volume brands the full retail system seems to make more economic sense. But other considerations must also be taken into account: the importance and the visibility of a given trade area, the level of priority of a given city for a given brand, and, of course, the availability of cash to start the heavy up-front investment needed for a new retail store.

To reach a better understanding of the issues brands face when choosing their distribution channels, one should consider two major questions:

1. How much control do I have over my distributors/distribution? And as a consequence, what part of the margin do I want to control?
2. What distribution channel must I use for my different categories?

The Control Issue

How can you control your distribution? How can you make sure your products are displayed in the right environment? How can you be sure that they are in good locations, next to the right brands? That they are being sold by salespeople who respect the product and are knowledgeable about the brand and its history? How can you make sure that customer information is fed back into your business? And that deliveries are received on time, so that the new collection is displayed appropriately, worldwide?

It very much depends on how many intermediaries there are between the brand and the final customer. The more intermediaries there are, the less you control your distribution.

There are four main ways to sell your products:

1. Sell them in your own company-owned stores (COS): the zero-intermediary solution.
2. Sell them through a franchisee, a duty-free operator, or a department store: the one-intermediary solution.
3. Sell them through a licensee: the one-plus intermediary solution (the licensee may work with another company that specializes in retail).
4. Sell them through a wholesaler: the two-intermediary solution.

Once again, the choices that a luxury brand makes are very much dependent on the brand life cycle:

- At the outset, the brand usually starts with one company-owned store and will distribute its products through selected retailers, mostly multi-brand stores. When entering a new market, this will be done through local agents or a distribution agreement: Bluebell and Dickson Poon are distribution companies used by European brands wanting to enter the Asian markets.
- When the brand grows, they will develop their company-owned stores and simultaneously move from the distribution agreement to a franchise or a joint venture. In new, developing markets like Russia, franchisees will be the solution: In December 2000, Hermès opened a 2,430-square-foot store in Moscow with the help of a franchisee, JamilCo.[1] The Russian company took on the entire investment outlay for the project, including construction costs, while Hermès managed the interior design. The two Moscow Gucci stores are managed by a franchisee, Mercury Distribution. Another fascinating case is that of Singaporean

---

[1]Since the beginning of 2011, several brands have announced that they would change their business model, choosing to develop in Russia by themselves. In January, Prada announced the termination of its cooperation with Mercury in anticipation of opening its own stores in Moscow. In May, the exclusive distribution contract between Hermès and JamilCo was terminated. Luxury brands that operate directly in Russia are Christian Dior, Louis Vuitton, Chanel, Swatch Group, and Hugo Boss (among others).

Club 21,[2] the distributor of Armani in the United Kingdom, the United States, and Asia (Singapore, Malaysia, Thailand, Taiwan, Hong Kong, and Australia) under franchising agreements.

- Ultimately, once the brand considers itself to be strong and the market as ripe, it will buy back the franchisee or the joint venture and set up a 100 percent subsidiary: This has been the major trend over the past 10 years for global brands like Gucci, Louis Vuitton, and Armani.[3]

Ultimately, control of distribution will rest on five major distribution channels (see Figure 2.1):

1. Company-owned stores in major markets (through subsidiaries).
2. Franchisees in developing countries (that are more controllable than licensees or simple distributors).
3. Shop-in-shops in department stores, so as to totally control the visual merchandising, sales, and customer relationship. Only very strong brands can manage to do this, such as Polo, Ralph Lauren,

---

[2]"Christina Ong, the wife of the Singaporean oil tycoon Ong Beng Seng, can take much of the credit for giving London its gloss as a fashion capital in the 1990s. Club 21, her retail empire, has an annual turnover in excess of £50 million through franchises with some of fashion's most covetable designer names— Giorgio Armani, Emporio Armani, Prada, Donna Karan, DKNY, Guess, and the jeweler Bulgari. As well as owning considerable chunks of London's most desirable retail real estate, Ong has cleverly captured today's money-spending, culture-hungry visitor to London in other ways. She owns two of the city's most stylish hotels—the Halkin, opened in Belgravia in 1991, with staff dressed by Giorgio Armani, and the new, hip Metropolitan Hotel, which opened . . . on Old Park Lane, where the staff uniform in The Met Bar is navy DKNY." (*International Herald Tribune*, March 15, 1997.)

[3]Gucci has had an extensive such program:

July 2001: Buys the remaining 35 percent of the Australian joint venture with FJ Benjamin Holdings Ltd.

February 2001: Buys back the Spanish operations (three stores) from its franchisee.

May 1998: Buys back the Korean franchisee Sung Joo International Limited (nine stores and nine duty-free stores).

April 1998: Buys 51 percent of the stock of Shiatos Taiwan Co. Limited, their Taiwan franchisee (nine stores and one duty-free store).

and Louis Vuitton—others tend to manage corners which will be very much under the influence of the department store itself.

4. Duty-free stores, because even though the costs are high, sales here are significant. But quality and image control may deteriorate over time in this environment unless the brand keeps strict control of these operations. For these reasons, Gucci set up its first non-Italian duty-free store in Heathrow in January 1999—900 square feet were added to its Rome and Milan duty-free stores; Chanel opened its first duty-free stores in 1999 in Heathrow terminals at 1,100 square feet each, but Prada is no longer present.

5. In watches, jewelry, perfume and cosmetics, and eyewear: Brands progressively select the best multi-brand stores, those that are in line with their brand image.

Distribution Channels and the Margin Issue

Image control is not the only issue when distribution is concerned.

Figure 2.2 shows that the final average retail price of luxury goods is five to six times the cost to the brand. Splitting it between wholesaler and retailer minimizes profit for each intermediary. The tendency is therefore to only have one intermediary (when necessary), be it the department store, the franchisee, or the duty-free operator. In that

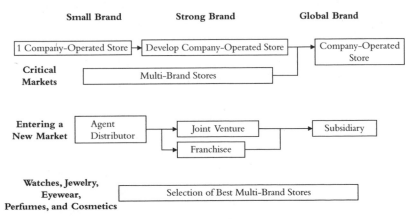

Figure 2.1 Distribution Control and the Business Life Cycle

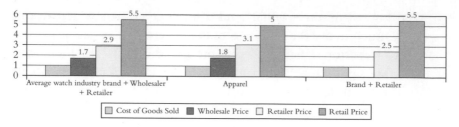

Figure 2.2   Average Margins in the Luxury Industry

case the margin will be split between the brand and the retailer, mostly on a basis that leaves a 2.2 multiplier to the retailer. The brand itself will then have a multiplier of 2.5 instead of 1.7.

Of course, the optimal solution for the brand is to get rid of the retailer altogether, in order to capture the whole margin. But there is a cost to this: the cost of managing the retail operations—a lease and personnel costs.

Choosing Distribution Channels Depends on the Core Business of the Brand

In all product categories multi-brand retailers exist that once were the natural outlet for luxury brands. At their beginnings, these mostly had a handful of flagship stores in major cities and relied on two channels to distribute their products: independent retailers and department stores. This is the wholesale trade that is critical for brand development. Two cases are instructive: Gucci and Bulgari. The differences seen between them depend mostly on the different core businesses of these brands. There are numerous luxury watch retailers—one of Bulgari's core businesses—that the company can tap to distribute their products. No equivalent distribution exists in other product lines, save eyewear and fragrances.

- Bulgari's initial strategy was primarily to grow its wholesale business, which represented 45 percent of its sales in 1997 and 51 percent in 2000. This corresponds to the strong focus the brand put on its watch and perfume businesses. The number of watch retailers was increased tenfold between 1993 and 2000, whereas the company-operated stores were only multiplied by four.[4] Interestingly, the sales per square foot of Bulgari-company-operated stores decreased over the same period: They went down from $3,900 per square foot in 1993 to $2,700 per square foot in 2000. Opening stores will naturally drive your sales but there is a limit to store growth: store profitability.

A change in strategy became evident in the early 2000s with the opening of numerous mono-brand stores to develop the jewelry and accessories business, which is the core business of the brand. The number of company-operated stores (COS) by Bulgari went from 72 in 2000 to 166 in 2009, while non-COS (franchisees/wholesale/travel retail) went from 54 to 107.

- Gucci's strategy was different: they had a very sound base of 64 stores in 1990—what was then considered *the historical distribution network*—to which the department stores, duty-free locations, and franchisees had to be added. It was only in 1997 and 1998 that the network of company-operated stores was grown significantly to 83 and then 126 stores, both by buying back franchisees and by opening new stores.[5] Since then openings and buying back franchisees has brought the number of company-operated Gucci stores to 317 in 2010 and franchisee stores to 43 in 2001 (down from 77 in 1997—figures after 2004 are no longer available). This led Gucci's directly operated stores to represent 73 percent of its sales in 2004.

This strategy requires significant investment, which necessitates high store profitability. Return on invested capital (ROIC) is a good measure of this. It decreased steadily for Gucci during that period: 34.6 percent in 1997; 28.9 percent in 1998; 28.3 percent in 1999, and 25.5 percent in 2002.

Achieving visibility requires that the brand be distributed through many channels, the choice of which being largely dependent on the

---

[4]Between 1993 and 2009 Bulgari stores grew from 33 to 166 and wholesalers' stores (excluding watch resellers and perfume doors) from 57 to 107. Watch and jewelry third-party retailers represented 800 doors and there were more than 17,000 perfume doors and 12,000 eyewear doors in 2008.

[5]Gucci figures on sales by distribution channel group franchisees with wholesale, contrary to Bulgari figures.

product lines. Only company-operated stores, franchisee stores, and shop-in-shops (company operated) guarantee that all product lines are displayed. All other channels (top end multi-brand stores, independent retailers, department stores, or travel retail) will carry only a limited number of lines, supporting brand awareness but not displaying its complete image. Figure 2.3 synthesizes this.

Armani is a brand that has developed very specific retailing strategies for different product lines. Their products are divided into seven categories:

1. Giorgio Armani
2. Armani Collezioni
3. Emporio Armani
4. Armani Jeans
5. Armani Exchange
6. Armani Junior
7. EA7

The first two lines, Giorgio Armani and Armani Collezioni, can be found almost exclusively in directly operated stores or department store shop-in-shops. Armani Jeans and EA7 (a sports line) are basically whole-sale lines. Emporio Armani has some directly operated stores but can be found in many shop-in-shops and department store corners. Armani Exchange is a retail brand in the United States but a wholesale line in Europe and in Asia. So the system is based on a balanced product selection, adapted to different retail channels, that changes over time.

Leather Goods	Shoes	RTW	Tablewear	Writing Instruments	Fragrances	Watches	Jewelry	Eyewear
Company-Operated Stores Franchisees Shop-in-Shops								
Top End Multi-Brand Stores			Independent Retailers	Independent Retailers	Independent Retailers	Independent Retailers	Independent Retailers	Independent Retailers
Department Stores Corners	Department Stores Corners	Department Stores Corners	Department Stores Corners	Department Stores Corners	Department Stores Corners	Department Stores Corners	Department Stores Corners	Department Stores Corners

Figure 2.3   Distribution Channels per Category

What about smaller luxury ready-to-wear or accessories brands? They generally have a large flagship store in their home city, and 10 to 20 company-operated stores in the world's major cities, but in most places they rely on department store shop-in-shops and corners to build as strong an international presence as possible. For their corners, they sell their merchandise at wholesale and their direct contacts with major department store purchasing or merchandising managers are essential to achieve their yearly sales budget. They also sell their products to individual multi-brand stores, but department stores remain a vital part of their retail strategy.

The balance in distribution channels is therefore a balance between different pros and cons, each of which will be favored in a different period of the brand's life cycle (see Table 2.3).

Table 2.3 Pros and Cons of Different Distribution Channels

	Pros	Cons
Company-operated stores	Brand image building Full product range displayed	Capital employed Store profitability in flagship stores
Franchisees	Brand awareness building Full product range displayed	Loss of control of image
Shop-in-shops	Brand image building Brand awareness building Full product range displayed	
Top end multi-brand stores	Brand image building	Limited range display No image control
Independent retailers	Brand awareness display Turnover growth	Category display Loss of control of image unless strict selection
Department store corners	Brand awareness building Turnover growth	Category display No image control in certain department stores
Travel retail	Strong flow of customers Turnover growth New customer base	Image control in multi-brand stores and in airport shopping malls

Chapter 3

The Different Outlets of Luxury Distribution

Distribution can be viewed as an exchange system between many independent organizations, each with its own objectives.
—*Hans Mülhbacher*

When we think about luxury goods, we immediately think of large and impressive stores in the center of Paris or Milan. Unfortunately, such stores very often lose money, and brands have difficulty paying the rent. It is therefore important to realize that most luxury goods products, if we include perfumes and cosmetics, watches, and wines and spirits, are actually sold at wholesale to independent retailers or department stores. Even for ready-to-wear and accessories, department stores play a key role in the development of many brands and are a major source of profitability for them.

We begin this chapter by describing all the different retail situations as they exist. We then compare the full retail system to a mix of retail and wholesale, and finally we go into more detail to describe department stores, factory outlets, travel retail, and other distribution vehicles.

Definition of the Different Systems

Let us begin by providing definitions of the different types of retail stores or the varying setups that a brand can own or negotiate with different types of retailers or store operators:

- A **freestanding store** is an outlet standing on its own with direct access to the street as well as street-facing display windows. The store owner negotiates the rent independently and does whatever he wants in his own location.
- A **shopping center retail store** is an independent retail outlet located in a shopping center. Here, the brand owners pay a rent, generally fixed, but in some cases with a small percentage of sales to pay for common promotional activities or help in the financing of the center. Such retail stores can also be subdivided into two categories: The first is *outlets in shopping centers*, where customers walk from one store to another, with customer flow being very dependent on the variety of stores in the center and the general appeal of the different brands offered in the center. The second is *outlets in retail parks,* where individual outlets are located in the same commercial location, but with their own entrances and parking, so that each brand must attract its own customers. Customers will largely be pulled by the diversity and the attractiveness of the brands available in the entire retail park, so each brand will need to ensure that their own clients consider their brand attractive enough to park in their lot. This second model requires the brand to be more of a "destination" brand to justify the extra effort customers will make to drive specifically to their lot.
- A **shop-in-shop in a department store** is a retail outlet located in a department store, but presented almost as a freestanding store, with

walls on at least three sides of the store and an open door with direct access to and from another part of the department store.

In a shop-in-shop, the brand generally owns its own merchandise and pays its own sales staff directly. It does not pay a fixed rent but works on the basis of the department store's margin. Generally, with a shop-in-shop setup, the brand does not have its own cash register. After a customer has made a purchase, he or she must go to the central cash register with a sales slip to pay, then come back to the shop-in-shop to pick up the purchase. Sometimes, shop-in-shops have their own cash registers, but they are always linked to the department store cash system, which takes in the retail margin and gives the brand the retail amount minus this retail margin.

In a shop-in-shop system, the advantage for the brand is that they have an economic system based solely on variable costs: They do not have to pay a fixed rent and the only fixed cost they incur is the sales staff salaries. Another advantage is that they do not have to attract their own customers but can benefit from those customers who have already been drawn by the department store's own pulling power and promotional program.

Shop-in-shops in department stores are generally limited in size, but sometimes they can be huge, as is the case of Louis Vuitton in the Matsuya department store in Tokyo or Chanel in Daimaru Osaka. In both situations, the shop-in-shops have two floors and the Chanel in Daimaru even has its own elevator to go from the first to the second floor.

- A **counter in a department store** is a location given to a brand in a department store that is not clearly identified and where the department store owns the products and pays for the staff. In this case, the department store operators can decide on how they want to price the products, what the merchandise assortment should be, how much space it will occupy, and which activities they want to employ in order to generate sales.

- A **corner in a department store** is a system that is halfway between a counter and a shop-in-shop. In a corner, the location is slightly identified as belonging to a given brand, but even if it is separated by two or even sometimes three walls, it will open to the department store open floor. In a corner, sales staff is generally paid by the brand but the merchandise belongs to the department store. A corner is, in fact, a location where the brand is given a limited identity but remains part of the department store's visual merchandising. For example, branded men's suits are often presented in corners so that the variety of brands appears as part of the complete department store offering.

Special cases of corners are, for example, stands for perfumes and cosmetics in the ground floor of department stores. Usually, each brand has its own stand setup, clearly identified as part of the brand but in an open-space environment. Watches are also often presented in department stores with a system of corners where each brand has its own well-identified counter with its own staff presenting the brand in a relatively open space.

- **Factory outlets** are described further on in the book but broadly speaking, they are a special type of shop-in-shop, not within a department store, but within a special structure of operators organizing a space dedicated to discount sales of different brands.

What is the most effective system? Here again, it all depends on the strength of a given brand and on its own priorities. What can be said is that every brand uses a mix of systems, from straight department store counters to freestanding stores. For each brand the mix of retail outlets will result from the different economic systems and will correspond to a balance of fixed costs and variable costs.

Another system is the **franchised store**. In this case the brand, by contract, gives the right for an outside individual to build and operate a store in a given location in a given city. For example, a fashion brand may be contacted by a wealthy individual who wants to open a mono-brand store in the city of Kiev, Ukraine. In the franchising contract, he will have an exclusivity for the city of Kiev (or for all of Ukraine) and will commit himself to buy a minimum amount of products for each season and to have no other products in the store that sells that brand's products. The brand may not have listed Kiev as a priority location but may be very happy to let a local investor go ahead with it instead. The brand would get money from the products sold each season and would also ask for a royalty on retail sales (generally 3 to 5 percent of net sales). The brand would also make sure that the retail store environment is approved by headquarters and that the store design is identical to a Paris or a Milan store. For the consumer, there would be no difference between that store and a fully owned one—they would find the same products, with the same large selection, the same store design, the same show windows and the same shopping bags as in a fully owned store.

This system has a very big advantage for the brand as it enables the development of retail operations without any investment costs. Of course, such local investors generally look for strong brands that they believe can sell very well in their territory, but they would also be ready to buy the merchandise and follow instructions. And given the (understandable) reluctance of outsiders to invest in a store in Ukraine, Kazakhstan, or Malaysia, this makes perfect sense. The franchisee can develop the business, provide volume and visibility to the brand, and satisfy the need of being present everywhere in the world.

Are there possible drawbacks for a brand to develop by franchising? Not many, provided that franchise store locations are carefully planned and the franchising contract gives the brand enough control on local operations, and that brand representatives visit those stores regularly to make sure instructions are complied with. (The worst-case scenario would be if a franchisee was having difficulties selling the brand in his store and then brought in other unbranded products, or worse, other brands, to meet his expected trading volume. However, this would only happen if the franchisee feels he or she is never visited and not controlled by headquarters.)

Therefore, the franchising system, if well controlled, is relatively effective and productive. But if there is a major change in the brand strategy, the franchising system creates constraints that are difficult to overcome. A case in point is Benetton, as can be seen in Table 3.1.

In 1998, Benetton was a very strong brand with sales of 1 million euros at wholesale and with their own retail stores. They had developed mainly through franchising and they were very happy to claim the opening of more than one store every day. Most stores were small (800 to 1,000 square feet) and were generally franchised stores. In a given city like New York, several franchisees had been given, as

Table 3.1 Sales Performances of Different Upscale Mass Fashion Retailers (in billion euros)

	1998	2010	Average Annual Growth
Benetton	1.0	2.1	8%
Gap	1.7	10.5	16%
H&M	3.3	14.2	13%
Zara	1.6	12.5	19%

SOURCE: Annual reports.

exclusive territory, a small part of Manhattan. Then newcomers like H&M or Gap came in with much larger stores, with sizes between 5,000 and 10,000 square feet, and locations geared to a very large population base. Benetton could not react: They could not convince some of their franchisees to open larger stores since their exclusive territories were too small to justify them. They would have had to negotiate with four or five different franchisees to close their stores in order to enlarge the exclusive territory of one franchisee, who could then open a new, larger store. To further complicate matters, the different franchising contracts had different durations and different timing clauses. As a result, from 1998 to 2010, Benetton continued with much smaller stores than those new competitors and lost an opportunity. If they had been the owners of all their retail outlets, the change in store size would have still been difficult, but at least possible.

Another retail system is to have a local partner run a retail store with a franchise contract, but to do it though a joint venture where the luxury brand has the majority of the capital (at least 51 percent) and the local partner no more than 49 percent. In this case, the brand has much stronger control of the operations and can make major strategic shifts if necessary. Of course, in this scenario, the luxury brand must finance 51 percent of the start-up investment and absorb part of the losses during the first years of operation, if there are any.

Last but not least, as we have seen in many annual reports, luxury brands often mention the number of their company-operated stores (COS). At first sight, one may think this means fully owned stores. In fact, it is not always the case. By company-operated stores, people sometimes include all department store shop-in-shops that they manage directly, all joint venture franchised stores where they have a majority, and sometimes they also add independent franchised stores for which they believe they have full control.

Department Stores

In countries like Japan or the United States, department stores are the primary retail channel to sell luxury goods. In these two countries, more than 75 percent of all luxury perfumes and cosmetics are sold in department stores. This is also the channel through which many luxury fashion brands, with few freestanding stores, also sell a majority of their products.

For perfumes and cosmetics in some countries like France, Italy, and Germany, most sales are done through small perfume shops, but in Japan, the United States, Canada, Australia, or the United Kingdom, department stores are the major, if not almost unique, sales outlets. Therefore, perfume and cosmetics marketing plans are always divided in two very separate programs: one for perfume store countries and another for department store countries.

For fashion, even in countries where department stores may not be the only major sales outlets, department stores remain important because they tend to be opinion leaders and actively look for innovative new brands to promote and develop. The store's brand merchandising managers regularly visit the likes of Paris and Milan to look for new ideas or scout new brands. When they find a new brand they like, they may end up distributing it before the brand's management has ever even visited their country. Department stores can therefore provide convenient and easy access to a given country by becoming the first export outlets for new brands.

Department stores can be defined as retail establishments that specialize in satisfying a wide range of the consumer's personal and residential durable product needs while at the same time offering the consumer a choice of multiple merchandise lines at variable price points in all product categories. Department stores usually sell products including apparel, perfumes, furniture, home appliances, or electronics in a sales area of at least 25,000 square feet. In a department store, no single product category accounts for over half of the total sales area.

Over the past 10 years, department stores have generally not performed outstandingly, having been adversely affected by the development of luxury goods freestanding stores on one hand, and the growth of new mass market "selective" brands like Gap, H&M, Zara, or Uniqlo on the other. Nevertheless, they remain a very important partner for luxury brands.

Let's now take a look at the department store situations in four countries—the United States, Japan, the United Kingdom, and Canada—plus some additional countries.

Department Stores in the United States

Although department stores were first created in Europe (Au Bon Marché in Paris and Harrod's in London), they have developed considerably in the United States. In 2009, the top 10 U.S. department store chains managed 6,810 outlets in the country. That year, U.S. department stores generated sales of $124 billion—but with almost no growth compared to 2004. In fact, their global sales decreased by 6 percent from 2008 to 2009, as they were significantly impacted by the September 2008 crisis, even more so than U.S. retailing as a whole, which still managed to grow 1 percent in 2009.

Table 3.2 provides statistics for major U.S. department store groups.

One can see a clear concentration of operators as these top 11 groups represent 90 percent of the total market. While chains like JC Penney, which is positioned at mid-range, or TJX Cos or Bon-Ton, which are positioned in the lower end of the market, are important for not too selective perfume brands, they are not essential for luxury ready-to-wear and accessories. We therefore concentrate our discussion on Macy's, Neiman Marcus, Nordstrom, Saks Fifth Avenue, and two specialty stores: Bergdorf Goodman and Barney's.

Macy's Macy's was the first department store created in the United States and today it exists as a conglomerate of different department stores. In 2006, it merged with the May Department Stores company, changing its legal name from Federated Department Stores to Macy's, Inc., which includes two major department store brands: Bloomingdale's and Macy's.

Table 3.2   Top American Department Stores (2009)

	Number of Stores	Total Sales ($ billions)	Sales per Outlet ($ millions)	U.S. Share (percent)
Macy's	852	22.2	26.1	18.9
Kohl's	1,059	16.5	15.5	14.0
JC Penney	1,103	15.1	13.7	12.8
Sears Holdings	842	13.7	16.3	11.7
TJX Cos	1,803	13.5	7.5	11.5
Nordstrom	176	6.9	39.3	5.9
Dillard's	312	6.0	19.1	5.1
Belk	310	3.3	10.6	2.8
Neiman Marcus	71	3.1	43.2	2.6
Bon-Ton Stores	282	2.9	10.3	2.5
Saks Fifth Avenue	108	2.6	24.0	2.3

SOURCE: Annual reports.

Macy's manages the New York store at Herald Square, which is the biggest in the world. They position themselves as "the American department store" and try to attract consumers from the mid-range to the top end.

Bloomingdale's, purchased in 2006, is a very upscale department store with only 38 stores in the United States and a strong concentration on the East Coast. It is very strong in European fashion.

Nordstrom Nordstrom is the largest independent store in America. It was created by John Nordstrom, who opened it as a shoe store in Seattle in 1901.

Today, their 176 stores are heavily located on the West Coast. The emphasis is on upscale fashion and a strong commitment to customer service. They have a strong customer loyalty program with four different levels. Level 2 is for customers spending $2,000 a year, who are invited to private shopping events. Level 3 is for customers spending $10,000 a year, who get a personal concierge (who will assist with ticket reservations or party planning, for example) and free alterations.

Level 4 is for customers spending $20,000 a year, who are given tickets to fashion shows and can host a private party in the store for their personal friends.

Neiman Marcus Created in Dallas in 1907, Neiman Marcus is the upscale department store of the Southeast. Alongside Saks Fifth Avenue, it holds the position of one of the top luxury department stores in the United States. It was a family business for many years, but today belongs to the private equity firm Texas Pacific Group.

The group is divided into several divisions: a speciality retail division, which includes the 40 Neiman Marcus stores plus Bergdorf Goodman (later discussed in our section on specialty stores) and a chain of contemporary boutiques called CUSP. They have recently developed 26 *Last Call* clearance stores that are developing rapidly. These 26 stores vary in size from 20,000 to 42,000 square feet, and Neiman Marcus cardholders receive a 5 percent discount on products already priced for clearance sales. Neiman Marcus department stores publish lavish catalogs (in those catalogs, it is often possible to buy special limited series of luxury cars like the Maserati Quattroporte or a BMW 700 with the Neiman Marcus logo) and organize fashion shows. This gave them the opportunity to launch Neiman Marcus direct, a strong mail-order and Internet service.

Saks Fifth Avenue Rooted in New York on Fifth Avenue, the group has grown to 52 locations across the country, strongly concentrated on the East Coast. Luxury goods are its strength, with an emphasis on service: All products can be returned within a period of three months without any questions, and sales staff are not allowed, at the end of the day, to indicate to consumers that the store is closing; they have to attend to them as long as needed.

Saks developed a new concept of lower-end *Off 5th* stores, where they sell excess Saks inventory as well as Saks' own brand products that are produced specifically for these outlets. They have been so successful that they now have 55 of them, where they try to sell "luxury in a loft environment."

The Specialty Stores Specialty stores are much smaller than department stores and present a more limited selection of products. They generally specialize in fashion and accessories and have a very upscale positioning. For a fashion brand, they are particularly interesting as they provide a top image entry into the United States and can accept a lower level of sales per square foot when the luxury and creative statement of the products bring something special to the store. In that respect, we should mention Bergdorf Goodman and Barneys.

- *Bergdorf Goodman:* Started as a tailoring shop, the store was opened at the present location of Fifth Avenue and 58th Street in Manhattan in 1928, in the former mansion of Cornelius Vanderbilt. Today, it is renowned as a specialty fashion store. It contains major shop-in-shop boutiques for Chanel, Armani, Gucci, and Yves Saint Laurent. In 1990, Bergdorf Goodman launched a men's store across the street from the women's fashion emporium.
- *Barneys* started in New York in 1923. It now has 13 brick-and-mortar stores in major U.S. cities. The New York store is located on Madison Avenue at 59th Street, a very popular area for tourists, and is close to the very top luxury brand stores like Calvin Klein, Tods, and Hermès. It could be considered as a full-line department store for fashion with a basement specializing in perfumes and cosmetics.

  Barneys is well known for its very strong creative spirit and its sometimes outrageous store windows. It is also constantly searching for and discovering new design talents. Barneys' fashion director has been called one of "the most influential people in fashion" by *New York* magazine. She was the first to bring to the United States Alber Elbaz, Proenza Schouler, Olivier Theyskens, and Goyard, among many others. It is undoubtedly a store that everybody in the fashion world should know and respect.

Department Stores in Japan

In the past 10 years the 279 major Japanese department stores have witnessed a very long period without growth. This is the result of not only the global retail environment, but also of the stagnation, if not of the Japanese economy, then of Japanese consumption in general. During the past 10 years, when visiting Japan one was told, "department stores have now been without growth for 47 consecutive months," then 53,

and so on. As a result, many groups have found themselves in difficult financial situations and have merged—causing the names of major
department stores to have changed regularly. Table 3.3 provides a list of
the major Japanese department store groups.

Japanese department stores play a very important part in the development of luxury goods in Japan. For reasons that are explained later,
it is very costly to start freestanding retail stores in the country, which
is why most brands, including Louis Vuitton, Chanel, and Gucci, rely
heavily on department store shop-in-shops for their presence and their
sales performances. It could be said that for almost every top European
brand, the majority of sales are generated through department stores.
The following are the most important groups.

Mitsukoshi–Isetan–Marui This group was formed by the 2008 merger
of two major chains, Mitsukoshi and Isetan, which then merged with
Marui-Imai in 2009. Mitsukoshi was a very traditional trading company
created in 1673. Its Mitsukoshi Nihonbashi store in Tokyo dates back to
1904 and is one of the largest stores in the world, with sales of 253 billion yen. The chain has six major stores (Tokyo Nihonbashi, Nagoya,
Tokyo Ginza, Sapporo, Sendai, and Fukuoka) out of a total of 16, and
foreign stores in China (Shanghai and Hong Kong) and Taiwan.

Isetan, with a corporate slogan "Isetan gives new meaning to fashion,"
is an extremely fashion-focused chain, with 58 percent of total sales coming from apparel and accessories. It has 10 stores in Japan including the

Table 3.3 Major Japanese Department Store Groups (2009) (in billion yen)

	Sales	Net Income
Mitsukoshi–Isetan–Marui	1,427	4.7
J. Front retailing (Daimaru-Matsuzakaya)	1,097	7.2
Takashimaya	926	11.7
Seven and 11 Holding (Sogo, Seibu)	922	14.2 (operating income)
Hankyu	N/A	N/A
Tokyu department stores	556	3.9 (operating income)
Kintetsu	N/A	N/A

SOURCE: From Jean Barthélemy: "Challenges and Opportunities of European Retailers in Japan 2007,"
Working Paper; and Nikkei, 2010.

Tokyo Shinjuku main store, with sales of 246 billion yen (representing more than half of the group sales) and other stores in Tokyo, Chiba, Niigata, and Kanagawa, among others. It also has stores in Bangkok, Kuala Lumpur, and Singapore.

The merger of 2008 is probably the result of financial difficulties in the two chains and in Isetan in particular. It is sure that it will add efficiencies in terms of infrastructure and management resources. But the main assets of the group are the two very strong brands of Mitsukoshi and Isetan, the first one corresponding to a very upscale positioning and the other one to a strong fashion image. It would be difficult to merge the brands, except outside of Japan, so the profit improvement program should rely on general sales increase. Mitsukoshi can probably develop its apparel and fashion sales. Isetan tries to attract younger customers with the opening, in Shinjuku, of an "Isetan girl" new space. Marui Imai can probably be better integrated.

Daimaru and Matsuzakaya Daimaru, based in Osaka, and Matsuzakaya, based in Nagoya, merged in 2007 with a new head office located in Tokyo. Daimaru was founded in 1920 and has seven main stores including two in Osaka, one in Kyoto, and one in Kobe. Total sales were 470 billion yen in 2007 with the three major stores representing 58 percent of the total (Kobe 22 percent, Osaka Shinsaibashi 18 percent, and Kyoto 18 percent), with the four other stores representing the remaining 42 percent. It is a strong

Table 3.4   Mix of Sales for Mitsukoshi and Isetan (2009) (in billion yen)

	Mitsukoshi	Isetan
Apparel	33.4%	47.3%
Accessories	13.1%	11.3%
Household	15.8%	13.9%
Sundry goods	5.2%	3.9%
Foods	28.2%	19.4%
Others	4.0%	5.2%
Total	657 BY	132 BY

SOURCE: Annual report, 2009.

fashion group with 45 percent of total sales coming exclusively from this type of merchandise. Matsuzakaya has a very large store in Nagoya but also a well located one in Tokyo. The merger company, J. Front retailing, could develop into a very strong operator.

Takashimaya Takashimya was considered with Mitsukoshi to be of the most exclusive and upscale department stores in Japan. It is the only major chain that did not merge in the past 10 years. The group was created in 1829 in Kyoto as a retailer of apparel and cotton cloth. It manages 18 stores in Japan, but also has outlets in New York, Paris, Taipei, and Singapore.

Sogo and Seibu Sogo and Seibu merged in 2000 as the result of the financial difficulties of Sogo, which had developed extremely rapidly between 1985 and 1995. Seibu, another strong group, began as a private railways operator and started in the 1920s to build department stores close to its own projected railway stations. It had to sell its activities on December 2005 to the diversified retail group of Seven & 11 Holdings (which had changed its name from Ito-Yokado) to become the fifth-largest retail group in the world. Its main activities are in small convenience food stores (7-Eleven and Ito-Yokado) as well as an internal bank (Seven bank). The total group had an operating income of 227 billion yen in 2010. It could certainly finance the growth of the two brands, Sogo and Seibu.

Seibu has a more luxurious image than Sogo, but Sogo, in its aggressive growth program, developed major retail operations in China (Beijing and Hong Kong), Taiwan, Indonesia, Malaysia, and Singapore.

Despite these mega-mergers, the economic situation of these Japanese department stores has not yet stabilized. Luxury brand operators must hope they can develop and find new growth patterns in the future. After several years of stagnation, if not decline, luxury sales in Japan will develop again only if consumers start visiting those department stores more frequently, since they generate most of the luxury sales in Japan.

Department Stores in the United Kingdom

Like the United States and Japan, department stores in United Kingdom are a major channel of luxury products in the country.

Harrods Harrods deserves to be mentioned first, since with 90,000 square meters, it one of the largest department stores in the world. Although its motto is "All Things for All People, Everywhere" it is clearly an upscale store, organized across 330 different departments. It was owned by the very famous Mohamed al Fayed before he sold it to Qatar Holdings.

Selfridges Selfridges, the second-largest department store in London, with 50,000 square meters, first opened in 1909. It recently opened 3 new locations; Manchester Trafford Centre, Manchester Exchange Square, and Birmingham, and can therefore consider itself a British department store chain.

John Lewis Partnership Originally a London draper's founded in 1864, John Lewis is a profit-sharing partnership, which means that all employees are stake-holding partners in the company, providing a unique incentive to deliver good customer service. Although it has wide appeal (having been elected Britain's favorite department store in 2007), it is definitely favored by old money, traditional clientele. Its major outlet in London is the Oxford Street branch. Peter Jones is a slightly more unique proposition, being located in Sloane Square, at the heart of one of the most affluent neighborhoods in London. The product and brand range there is therefore perceived to be higher-end.

House of Fraser House of Fraser has 62 stores across the country and Ireland. The flagship store, House of Fraser, is located in Oxford Street in London. Over the years, House of Fraser has purchased a number of famous regional stores such as Jenners of Edinburg, Howells of Cardiff, David Evans of Swansea, Rackshams of Birmingham, and is rebranding its stores under the House of Fraser name. Dickins & Jones (Regent Street, London), D.H. Evans (Oxford Street, London), Army & Navy (Victoria, London) and Kendal's in Manchester have all disappeared or been rebranded. House of Fraser is trying to reposition itself at the top end of department store retail, with a strong focus on designer brands. Harrods, although privately owned by Qatar Holdings, purchases its merchandise through the House of Fraser purchasing center.

Debenhams Debenhams has 157 stores in the United Kingdom and Ireland. It manages approximately 1 million square meters. They have a strong presence in women's wear, menswear, children's wear, and health and beauty. They have their own brands as well as those of third parties. They are broadly mid-market, presenting design and quality at affordable prices. They are perceived to be very middle class, but the "designers at Debenhams" campaign (which predated the "Karl @ H&M" promotion by almost a decade) created a more fashion-forward image. They had sales of 1.6 billion euros in 2009 with a net profit of 85 million euros. The company is public and is listed on the London stock exchange.

They have developed outside of the United Kingdom and Ireland through strong franchises and are present in Romania, the Czech Republic, Cyprus, Bahrain, the United Arabic Emirates, Kuwait, South Arabia, Qatar, Iran, India, Singapore, the Philippines, and others.

Department Stores in Canada

Canada is a strong department store country. Major chains are present at a national level. These stores are, 90 percent of the time, located in shopping centers. In a standard shopping center, the two largest competitors, the Bay and Sears, will generally be found at opposing ends of the center.

The Bay The Bay operates 92 department stores across the country. The oldest commercial corporation in the world, incorporated by English royal charter in 1670, it was originally set up as trading posts in the far reaches of northern Canada and opened its first department store in 1881 as The Hudson Bay Company. The price points tend to be middle to upper market with certain stores carrying higher-end assortments. It could be compared to Macy's in the United States.

Freestanding flagship stores exist in major cities like Toronto, Montreal, Vancouver, Calgary, Ottawa, and Winnipeg. Stores have a large selection of products and often feature special designer lines. Such flagship stores have a very upscale environment. They are well known for their emphasis on service. They often feature a restaurant, hair salons, and optical stores within the store.

Sears Sears operates a network of 196 stores, 195 dealer's stores, 38 home improvement stores and 108 Sears travel offices. Compared to its operations in the United States, Sears is much more upscale in Canada, resulting from its purchase of Eaton's, a chain of department stores which were a social institution in Canada. Eaton's filed for bankruptcy in 1999 and was converted into Sears in 2002.

Sears stores attract both their traditional blue-collar customers (especially in their home improvement stores) and more upscale customers in Canada. Their shopping mall stores are similar to The Bay in terms of product offering, selling apparel, perfumes, beauty products, and home products. Their consumer base is nevertheless slightly more masculine than that of The Bay.

Holt Renfrew With only 10 stores located in Toronto, Ottawa, Montreal, Calgary, Vancouver, and Edmonton, Holt Renfrew is a very upscale chain of department stores and would be positioned a bit between Saks Fifth Avenue and Barney's if they were in the United States. They generally feature shop-in-shops of brands like Louis Vuitton, Gucci, and Tiffany. Services at the larger locations include valet parking, a concierge, a personal shopper, made-to-measure items and a gourmet restaurant.

For a perfume or a watch brand distribution channel, the focus should probably be between The Bay and Sears. For more upscale products, Holt Renfrew, with its five or six small city center stores would certainly be an attractive alternative.

Other Particular Countries

In this subsection, we quickly describe three countries where department stores may not be the major channel for the sale of luxury goods.

France Two major chains (excluding Bon Marché) operate in France: Galeries Lafayette and Printemps.

Au Printemps was created in 1865 and currently has 23 department stores with total sales above 1 billion euros in 2009. It was part of the luxury and distribution group PPR, but in 2006 it was sold to the family group of Maurizio Borletti (who used to own the Italian department stores La Rinascente) and the Deutsche Bank capital investment group.

Since that purchase, the main store on boulevard Haussmann was completely renovated. In the building dedicated to fashion, a vast atrium was built at the center to give the store more elegance and light. The Haussmann store has 435,000 square feet of selling space and welcomes from 40,000 to 100,000 visitors a day. It is estimated that 25 percent of customers in the Haussmann store are foreign tourists.

The motto of the Printemps stores, "Modernity and Tradition," is not particularly informative, but the gist of it is to be extremely creative and come up with new ideas and new products all the time.

Galeries Lafayette, created in 1891 at the corner of rue Lafayette (which explains its name), belongs to a family group. The group, which includes another department store, BHV, plus 50 percent of the retail chain Monoprix, had total sales of 5.1 billion euros in 2009.

Galeries Lafayette encompasses 60 stores and had sales of 2.5 billion euros in 2009. The flagship store, Galeries Lafayette on boulevard Haussmann in Paris, generates sales above 1 billion euros with a floor space of 700,000 square feet. It can handle more than 100,000 visitors a day.

Both chains of department stores are very creative and focus heavily on fashion. They carry most of the top brands, either in open corners, counters, or in shop-in-shops. But if they represent an important part of fashion sales, they sell less than 10 percent of all perfumes and cosmetics purchased in France.

Russia The TSUM in Moscow, owned now by Mercury Distribution, a major luxury brand distributor in Russia (see Chapter 2), was erected in 1908. It was nationalized in 1920 and was named Mostorg, then TSUM (central department store). In 1995 the store was restructured and in 2007 a new building extension was finished, providing a total space of 600,000 square feet.

It is the largest store in Eastern Europe and certainly the most fashionable. It carries more than 1,000 brands including Gucci, Prada, Dolce & Gabbana, Bottega Veneta, Yves Saint Laurent, and Alexander McQueen.

Seasonal collection appearances are supported by strong advertising campaigns with world famous stars like Mila Jovovich, Naomi Campbell, and Mathias Lauridsen. Celebrities like Caroline Herrera and Victoria Beckham participate in TSUM to introduce their newest collections to guests and clients.

The store hosts an ice vodka bar, a Moet & Chandon champagne bar, a Hennessey cognac bar, a cigar room, and a gourmet restaurant.

Spain The case of Corte Ingles is definitely worth mentioning. It is the only department store group in the country and represents more than 50 percent of all Spanish sales of some luxury brands.

Privately owned, this group, created at the end of World War II, generated sales reaching above 17 billion euros in 2009. The department stores are only a part of the total, as the group also manages supermarkets (Supercor and Hipercor) as well as a travel agency and retail stores specializing in do-it-yourself home improvements, optical frames, and telephones and computers.

The department store activities alone represent more than 9 billion euros in sales, with 140 different stores in Spain and 5 in Portugal. It is present throughout Spain and has a strong position in Portugal as well.

The stores at the centers of major cities are very upscale, with very strong perfume and cosmetics activities (for some brands, more than 50 percent of their Spanish perfume volumes), and a strong presence in fashion and jewelry. It is impossible to be in Spain without having a strong position in Corte Ingles.

■ ■ ■

The 26 department store chains just described are the world's foremost customers of fashion and perfume brands. They all feature shop-in-shops and corners of major luxury brands and many luxury groups' employees end up as sales staff in those department stores.

Strangely enough, with the notable exception of Debenhams and Sogo, department stores are almost always concentrated in one or two countries. This seems to represent the public's strong affinity with such "national heroes" as Mitsukoshi, Neiman Marcus, or Galeries Lafayette. To be successful abroad, department stores are better off if they can take advantage of a strong presence of residents from their own countries (which is the case of Japanese in Asia), a specific set of national lines that they can promote in their new country, and a specific national atmosphere where they can communicate to the local customers. It is also worth noting that department stores will have developed in different cities of the same country for almost 150 years. During that time, they have created strong recognition among residents and a strong brand preference.

Their value as a local partner of worldwide luxury brands is undeniable.

Factory Outlets

In the past, factories would have a small store on the premises where they could sell overstocks or items rejected by their quality control. These factory outlets sold products at very low prices. Most products would be purchased for cash with a no return, no exchange policy. The factory outlet was a small location taken from the factory floor, with no effort made to make it fancy or different.

Around the late 1960s and early 1970s, the concept of providing a new type of factory outlet "shopping center" was developed. The location would be outside of any city, in an open field were real estate costs would be minimal. Over time the outlet centers were able to bring in top brands and form something that looked like a standard shopping center, further away from any urban center, but still quite welcoming. Then bus shuttles were organized to take people, including tourists, from the center of major cities and bring them to the outlets free of charge, on a ride that could take 45 minutes to one hour.

Factory outlets were started in the United States in 1969. Two VF Outlets started in Reading, Pennsylvania, and North Dartmouth, Massachusetts. Today we can count 216 American factory outlets, operated by such major players as, for example, the Chelsea Property Group, which owns and manages 50 centers. The second most significant operator, Tanger Outlets, created by Stanley K. Tanger in 1981, now operates 33 centers, representing 2,200 individual brand stores and 10 million square feet of commercial space (see Table 3.5).

The largest centers, for example, Woodbury Common Premium Outlets in the state of New York or Orlando Premium Outlets in Florida, have 850,000 square feet and 770,000 square feet of gross leasable space: They are as big as the biggest department stores.

Table 3.5 Largest Factory Outlet Groups in the United States

	Number of Centers	Gross Leasable Space (in square feet)
Chelsea Property Group	50	18,000,000
Tanger Outlets	35	10,000,000
Prime Retail Outlets	22	8,000,000
Craig Realty Group	10	2,750,000
Horizon Group Properties	5	1,150,000
Ariel Preferred Retail Group	6	1,300,000
AWE Talisman companies	3	1,000,000
	131	42,550,000

SOURCE: *Value Retail News*, November 2009.

In Europe, as can be seen in Table 3.6, the picture is also very impressive. In Europe today there are 190 outlets, with major group McArthur Glen stating that its sales are above 2 billion euros.

Consumers in those centers are either quite young (50 percent are between 20 and 39 years old) or retired. Tourists are also a very interesting target, as their average purchases are two to two and half times higher than those of domestic customers.

Over time, the merchandise presented in such factory outlets has changed.

On top of overstocks or out-of-season items, some stores are now manufacturing special products exclusively for this channel at very interesting prices. Factory outlets are also used by some brands to test new accessories, new models, or new colors at low risk. If successful, they would then be introduced to the main exclusive retail stores.

Almost every brand except the very upscale ones uses factory outlets to unload some of its overstock. Brands like Coach, Ralph Lauren, and Burberry are strong users of the system, which can also be utilized as a way to attract a younger consumer to a brand.

Over the years, factory outlets have become a unique distribution channel that can be effectively employed to promote a brand to this very specific population target.

Table 3.6   Largest Factory Outlet Groups in Europe (2008)

Leasing Companies	Nationality	Number of Centers	Gross Leasable Space (in square feet)
McArthur Glen Europe	British	18	3,050,000
Value Retail	British	9	1,960,000
Neinver	Spanish	11	1,730,000
Concepts and Distribution	French	9	1,240,000
Fashion District Group	Italian	3	1,230,000
Realm Limited	British	12	1,140,000
Freepart	British	3	1,120,000

SOURCE: *Global Outlet Project Directory*, 2008.

Travel Retail

A large percentage of luxury goods are purchased by people traveling. For perfumes, for example, it is estimated that more than 20 percent of worldwide volume is purchased in duty-free outlets. For cognac and ties, too, duty-free purchases account for up to 15 percent of worldwide sales.

An estimate by the specialist research firm Generation puts the total duty-free market in 2008 at 30 billion euros (41 percent from Europe, 27 percent from Asia, and 24 percent from the Americas). Of this total, wines and spirits account for 5 billion euros, fashion luxury goods and accessories, 10 billion euros, and perfume and cosmetics, 9 billion euros.

Most duty-free stores are located in airports, where people generally have time on their hands and cash in their pockets. These stores represent a good opportunity to provide discount prices and real customer savings in a sophisticated environment. In the days when travel itself was less common, this was a discount market reserved for the privileged few. Even now that everybody travels, it has retained some of its luxury characteristics because traveling by plane or on cruise ships remains a relatively upscale activity.

The Travel Retail System

Travel retail operators work on two basic conditions. As the products they sell have not really entered the country, they are not liable for import duties. As they are not sold "within the country," they are not subject to a local distributor's margin. But while local duty-free operators do not pay import duties or local taxes, they do pay airport commissions, which can be two to three times higher. Table 3.7 illustrates the workings of the duty-free system.

As Table 3.7 shows, if, for example, a perfume company sells its product in a store in Germany at a retail price of €105, its export price may actually be €26.20, as indicated in the last column, the difference being accounted for by a large distributor's margin and an advertising and promotional budget. When the product is sold directly to the duty-free operator at, say, Frankfurt airport, the perfume company can invoice it at a price of €32; that is, at almost double the price it would sell for if it has to go through the German distributor's cost structure. Thus, everybody is gaining; the customer gets a better deal, and the manufacturer sells at a higher export price, even if there is no advertising budget built into the structure.

Table 3.8 explains how the system works from the duty-free operator's perspective.

When the duty-free operator purchases at 32, it receives only a 20 percent margin; most of the difference between the export price and the duty-free retail price goes on commission paid to the airport operators. In fact, airports have two major sources of income: landing and parking costs for planes, and duty-free commissions; in many cases the latter provide more than half of the total airport revenues.

Table 3.7 Duty-Free Pricing System

	French Retail Domestic (€)	European Duty-Free Retail (€)	German Retail Price through a Local Distributor (€)
Full retail price	100		105
Retail without value-added tax (19.6%)	83.61		
Duty-free retail price		80	
Wholesale price	50		52.5
Export price		32	16.2

Table 3.8   Price Structure for the Duty-Free Operator

	Total Amount	Percentages
Airport retail	80	100
Airport commission	32	40
Operator's margin	16	20
Export price	32	40

Duty-free operators work with an airport concession generally awarded to the highest bidder. Such concessions can last from three to seven years, but the majority are for seven. In preparing their bid, the major operators study their forecast volume of business based on the number of planes, the destinations and the nationalities, and the types of travelers (tourists versus business travelers, for example), and commit themselves to give a commission (which can range from 35 percent to 55 percent of their sales) and sometimes also a flat minimum for each year of the concession.

In general, for a large-volume airport this bidding process is very competitive, with most of the worldwide operators participating.

Operators factor into their bids considerations such as new slots that may be given for new destinations or new airlines, and they use their own estimates of nationality and travel type mix for each of the luxury product categories: Japanese customers smoke more than American customers, but they smoke mainly Mild Seven, the highest-selling cigarette brand in Japan. Americans buy whiskey and cognac and, for cognac, their preferred brands are Hennessy and then Remy Martin; and so on. Operators can then prepare a business plan with their best estimates of sales and the maximum concession fee they can offer the airport authorities.

Given the very high airport commissions (which can be more than half of the duty-free retail price) it can make more sense to build downtown galleries in countries like Hong Kong, Guam, Singapore, and Panama, where there are no import duties and the business model will work without the payment of large airport concession fees.

But in this case, duty-free operators are back to square one: They are in the official territory of the domestic distributors, unless they can put pressure on their brands and find middle ground. Of course, even these downtown stores are the result of the specific duty-free system that pertains in each country.

For fashion and accessories the brands are found in retail shop-in-shops in major airports (like when Harrods' merchandise is sold at Heathrow Terminal 1). Does it give them a good image? Not necessarily a top one, but if they are not there and most of their competitors are strongly there, they just look bad.

Chapter 4

The Internet as a Channel of Distribution

The founding principle of NET-A-PORTER.COM was and is to create the balance between content and commerce.
—*Natalie Massenet*

T he Internet is now a major communication and/or distribution channel that luxury brands have been investing in—but their attitude toward the Web is somewhat complex. This chapter takes us through the intricacies of the love/hate relationship luxury brands have with modern communications. Our starting point is a turning point: How did yoox.com and its business model change luxury brands' perspective on e-commerce?

If we wish to understand the cultural differences that exist between luxury and the Internet we should start by going back a few years to track the evolution of this love/hate relationship. We will then examine the present state of things in the industry, which mixes the use of the Internet as a communication device with some e-commerce facilities, and will undoubtedly change in the coming years. Finally, we will explain the intricacies of digital marketing and give seven rules of Internet and social media that all brands should obey to develop their business using the Web.

An analysis of the current Internet strategies leads us to two major conclusions:

1. Luxury brands should integrate their communication and distribution channels.
2. The Internet and social media are nothing but a tool at the service of a customer relationship strategy.

Introduction: The Yoox.com Issue

During the 2009 Milan Fashion Week, a man caused a sensation. Federico Marchetti, CEO of Yoox, was installed in the first row of the fashion shows.

Why this honor?

Because Federico Marchetti has made Yoox a key player in the luxury sector, with a total revenue of $214 million in 2010. A review of the story of Yoox will allow us to understand the innovative business model that was formed.

Yoox started in 2000, creating one of the first Web discount outlets, offering Italian luxury and fashion brands a means for disposing of unsold stock of previous seasons through an elegant Web portal. The logistics are designed to provide customers with a service that equals the expectations of the brands themselves. In this first phase, Yoox positioned itself as a reference in e-discount, the key element of its business model being the fact that *Yoox pays its suppliers only after the sale is made*— and therefore does not have to bear the costs of maintaining stock.

In a second phase, Yoox set up *a strategy of differentiation*: It offered creations from new designers as well as designer objects, and books.

Two important features characterize this new offer: The merchandise is sold at full price (no discounts) and capitalizes heavily on the "Made in Italy" image. "Our soul is Italian," says Federico Marchetti. In this second phase, *Yoox positioned itself as a key player in the fashion sector*—and left behind its discount-only image.

After acquiring know-how in matters of e-commerce, Yoox *outsourced two important functions*: Selection and packaging of goods was entrusted to Norbert Dentressangle, and delivery to UPS.

Yoox found it possessed valuable savoir-faire when luxury brands (finally) started studying the question of Internet sales. To do this they had to find a professional operator, which was Yoox Services, a subsidiary of Yoox. In 2006, the e-commerce website, Marni, was launched followed by others "Powered by YOOX": Emporio Armani, Diesel, Dolce & Gabbana, Jil Sander, Valentino, Bally, Dsquared, Miss Sixty, Costume National, Emilio Pucci, Stone Island, and CP.

Yoox has also recently developed—using its privileged relationships with brands as a real strategy for training in the field of brand management and e-commerce—the creation of a Masters course in e-fashion at MIP, the Politecnico di Milano business school, with scholarships offered by Armani.

The yoox.com website is an excellent example of modern e-commerce sites, featuring information, videos of runway shows, and exclusives. There is a dedicated eco design space, Yooxygen, too. It lacks only the "Community" dimension to be complete.

This business model is successful because it is built around four strategic advantages:

1. *A full-fledged, integrated e-commerce offer*: This is a real (new) know-how that luxury brands would not know how to deploy and needs specially trained employees.
2. *The trust built around a customer-supplier relationship*—and a keen knowledge of the sales of each brand.
3. *The use of technology that is fully controlled in-house*: RFID chips for referencing products, proprietary e-business tools, design studio, and so on.
4. *An image projecting expertise in fashion, and discounts*: Everyone therefore finds what they are looking for—well-known brands at discount prices, niche brands, exclusive products, vintage, and so on.

A Short Review of the Love/Hate Relationship That Luxury Brands Have with the Internet

In the luxury industry, the Yoox.com example has been a trigger. Luxury groups have been giving ample thought to their Internet strategy, with a common concern: Why, when for the past 20 years their strategy has been structured around a business model of distribution control, would they abandon a very promising distribution channel into the hands of external operators? Why should they not also control e-commerce margins to keep their profitability at its current very high levels (see Chapter 7)? With CAPEX costs growing with the necessary opening of exciting new stores in ever more expensive locations, why forgo the possibility of bringing in cash through a distribution channel whose costs are so low compared to a store?

But this is only possible if the luxury brand acquires this new know-how—that of e-business—just as it has, over the years, acquired retail know-how. This explains why luxury groups have opened the hunt for e-business expertise, in very different manners:

- The Richemont Group acquired www.net-a-porter.com, considered to be one of the most successful e-business fashion companies, in 2009.
- LVMH has nurtured one of the best e-commerce websites in its brand portfolio—sephora.com—and has been the owner from 2000 to 2009 of e-luxury.com, the very first multiluxury brand e-commerce site. This has given them great insight into the Internet and e-commerce.

This brings us a long way from the year 2000. Ten years ago, in the early years of the century, luxury brands considered the Internet as an alien—because they had believed that luxury and the Internet had two very different cultural backgrounds (see Figure 4.1).

At least two characteristics—the virtual issue and the control issue—have been instrumental in the love/hate relationship luxury brands have with the Web and they are essential to understanding the four major phases this relationship has gone through.

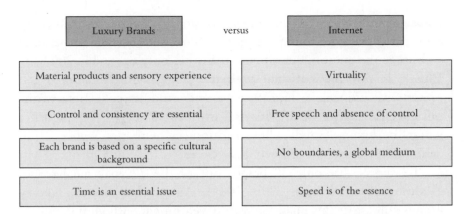

Figure 4.1   Cultural Background of Luxury Brands and the Internet

Let us quickly deal with the virtual issue: If the essence of a luxury product is "feel" and "sense," luxury marketers and sales-persons thought luxury could only be bought in a store; that a customer had to touch and feel the product and that the presence of a sales assistant was essential. This is, of course, important but not essential: Consumer studies (more on that later) have proven that luxury consumers are quite eclectic and will buy any luxury product on the Web if the website is sufficiently attractive and functional.[1] This argument was for years a decoy—the real concern was elsewhere: *Luxury brand marketers and executives alike feared (and still fear) that a strong uncontrolled Web presence would endanger their brand equity—because they would lose control of the brand into the hands of netizens.* Which is true. Because of this fear, we have witnessed four phases—which we will illustrate using interesting studies realized by L2, an Internet think tank devoted to tracking, analyzing, and measuring luxury's relationship with the Web (72 were analyzed in their 2010 report).

---

[1]This has been addressed by luxury sites with extraordinary photo quality, 360° pictures, and virtual mannequins, and so forth, transforming the Web experience into something unique that sometimes is not available in the stores.

Phase 1: No website. The Prada website was famous for consisting only of "Opening Soon" for many years—it only opened a perfume website at the end of 2005 and the main site only opened in 2007.

Phase 2: An institutional website. This is where a brand can present its essence, its history, its events, and its collections without ever getting in touch with its customers. They are kept at arm's length by luxury brands whose relationship with the Web is of an aristocratic nature—top down. Just revere.

L2 shows that only 39 brands out of the 72 analyzed have an e-commerce site (versus 32 in 2009): Almost half the top luxury brands still are at this phase of Web development, although they may have developed a social media presence.

Phase 3: An e-commerce site. Once the Internet has been recognized as a distribution channel in its own right, brands have embedded e-commerce sites into their institutional websites (this is where the yoox.coms of this world come into the picture). More than half the luxury brands today are at this stage of their Internet development (see the Hermès website case study).

Having reached Phase 3 leads brands directly to Phase 4: "Those that sell are more likely to be present on multiple platforms, boast larger communities, and interact more frequently with fans and followers. E-commerce-enabled brands are also more adept digital marketers and more likely to use email and paid search to drive traffic to sites and stores."[2]

Phase 4: A top-down social media presence. All those Internet-savvy luxury brands have jumped on the social media bandwagon. They all have Facebook pages, they Tweet, they have iPhone and now iPad apps: 90 percent of the brands analyzed by L2 were on Facebook in 2010 (versus 79 percent in 2009), 48 percent were on Twitter, 55 percent were on YouTube, and 39 percent had developed smartphone apps.

They multiply the touch points. *But they do not engage with their customers; they do not have conversations with them.* They still control the message and the relationship—and quite often their social media presence leaves something to be desired, as we will see later.

---

[2]Luxury Digital IQ Report, L2, 2010.

Building a Website Consistent with the Brand Image: The Hermès Case

Luxury brands have a major issue when reaching the e-commerce phase: building a website that is completely consistent with the brand values and the brand image. The "best-in-class" example is undoubtedly Hermès.

Hermès is a brand that knows how to take its time—its e-commerce website didn't open until in 2008. This site is a marvelous reflection of the intelligence of the brand. From the outset, the home page establishes the basic elements of the aesthetics of the brand, which are each references to the "global vision" (or ethics) of the brand:

- An off-center logo, slightly tilted. Where so many brands display them head-on, forcefully, Hermès does not need to proclaim its presence.
- The use of drawing and writing: Hermès is a brand that attaches importance to hand made, to the gesture—that of the craftsman as well as the designer.
- A mood that is both romantic and unconventional: Hermès arouses the imagination of its customers.
- The use of the color orange and the orange box, emblematic of the brand.
- The faint dashed strokes that one sees on all pages—a saddle stitch—symbolizing its trade.

The next Web page shows the coachman, who has alighted from his coach. He has come to deliver our purchases and he leads us toward the world of Hermès. You will discover the meaning of the word *sabrer* ("strike/cut with a sword"), and the work of the *sabreuse*, the symphony of tools; you are invited to emotionally vibrate to the Hermès diaries of the Baroness Nica de Koenigswarter, discover the horse-tricycle of Napoleon III from the Emile Hermès collection, and much, much more. . . . The website conjures a poignant and

(continued)

exceptional stroll through the world of craftsmen, materials, and anecdotes of the mark.

When advancing toward the boutique, escorted by a forest of ties that unfold in step with the mouse, we find drawings, inscriptions, and the products laid out in staggered array.

This site is a feast for the senses. The eye as well as the ear is captured by it continuously: The brand expresses its world vision, its ethics as well as its aesthetics. Its products are well displayed; a purchase is the direct consequence of the emotion felt while one travels through it—even though the products sold online are very (one might say frustratingly) limited.

Digital Marketing: A Framework

Although most brands—faced with the complete novelty of the Internet medium—have built their online presence by adding new layer upon new layer, the time has come for luxury brands to completely reconsider their Web business model.

Over the past 10 years, luxury brands have developed a Web presence much in line with their standard organization and traditional business model, with the addition of two independent or near-independent layers:

1. A sales layer, including: stores + department store shop-in-shops + duty-free stores + e-commerce website + wholesale.
2. A communication layer, itself made of: corporate brand communication + customer relationship management (CRM) + social media presence + mobile presence. These are just tools that should be at the service of a global customer relationship strategy.

The standard organizational chart of a luxury brand separates sales from marketing and sometimes even from communication, which reports to the creative director. Unfortunately, this leads to difficulties in integrating a customer relationship strategy across departments—which leaves it as the sum of communication strategy + CRM strategy + Internet strategy + sales strategy.

Contrary to its traditional cultural background, which starts from the brand and its equity, we suggest a complete reversal. We believe that in order to face the demands of their Internet-savvy customers, luxury brands will need to refocus and rebuild their Web business model starting from the most critical actor of the twenty-first century: the customer. This means that the entire value chain has to be rethought.

The traditional value chain (see Figure 4.2) is an inside-out one: The brand identifies the core competencies from which it derives its business model, then identifies its offer, chooses its distribution channels, and finally reaches out to its customers.

The new value chain (see Figure 4.3) is an outside-in one: The brand starts by identifying and segmenting its core customers and their needs, defining the brand experience(s) it wants to share with them, and only then building its offer and the business model.

This means that building a specific and identifiable customer relationship becomes a critical issue for each brand. Let us see how this can be done.

There are five critical phases in building a relationship between a brand and its customers:

1. Attracting
2. Engaging
3. Retaining
4. Learning
5. Relating

Each of these phases needs specific levers that will help build and maintain the relationship. Figure 4.4 shows but a few of these levers,

Figure 4.2   Traditional Inside-Out Value Chain

Figure 4.3   The New Outside-In Value Chain

ATTRACTING This is the primary role of the brand—its history, its stories, its images, and products	**ENGAGING** *On the Web*: Intuitive interface and navigation Interactive content User-generated content *In the stores*: Relating to the Sales Assistant
RETAINING *On the Web*: Transaction capability Efficient circulation Digital communities Novelties *In the stores*: Clienteling New product	**LEARNING** *On the Web*: Information capture Continuous preference updates *In the stores*: Sales assistant listening capacities and feedback
RELATING *On the Web*: Personalized and customized communications Digital communities Real-time interactions *In the stores*: Clienteling Personalized products	

Figure 4.4   Critical Phases in Building a Relationship and Their Levers

which all tell the same story: Stores and the Internet should be considered simultaneously because they are complementary.

Start with the Customers: Why Are They Online and How Do They Use the Internet?

All recent studies of the patterns followed by Web surfers show that they:

- Enter the Net looking for information.
- Then move to forums, focusing on their topics of interest.

- End up engaging with people with whom they share interests and passions.

Conclusion: People have passions they want to pursue on the Net and they end up sharing them with others—*The web is a world of communities*.

The involvement of a member of a community will depend on two factors:

1. The relationship the person has with the core online activity of the community: The more central the activity is to the person's self-concept, the more likely the person is to pursue and value membership in the community.
2. The intensity of the social relationships the person possesses with the other members of the community.

Four types of community members can therefore be defined[3] as evident from Figure 4.5.

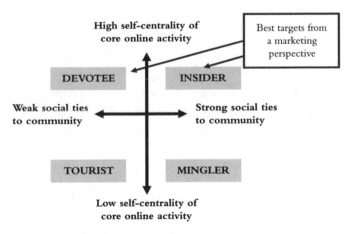

Figure 4.5 Four Internet Communities

---

[3]R. Kozinets, "E-Tribalized Marketing? The Strategic Implications of Virtual Communities of Consumption," *European Management Journal*, June 1999. This pioneering article on online communities is still a major reference in consumer habits studies.

Case Studies

These stories are old, given Internet-time and even brand-time. But they are still extraordinarily topical: Each luxury brand should ponder them so as to understand the potential the Web represents in customer relationship building.

Meet the Krugistes

Late in 1998 Remy Krug, CEO of Krug Champagne, was invited to a cyber champagne tasting by *Wine Spectator*. As he told one of the authors: "It was suggested to me by my daughter. But I really did not find the idea attractive. Champagne has to be shared!"

To his surprise hundreds of Krug lovers were connected— with a Krug bottle alongside, sometimes alone, sometimes as a group—ready to welcome him. They were ready to share with him their knowledge and passion for the brand and the products. "It was a unique experience," he said.

The Web is full of emotion.

Meet the Sephoracoholics

Sephora opened its first U.S. boutique in Soho in July 1998.

In December 1998 on Alt fashion's website people were raving: "When is Sephora coming to Minneapolis? I am Sephoracoholic!"

Words are created to name something of importance: Having coined a word shows how people relate to a brand or a retailer.

The Web is full of emotions.

The Internet: Some Facts and Figures

Let us look at a few facts from various sources that clearly demonstrate the importance of the Web for consumers:

- A report from the Center for Culinary Development tells us that Generation Y (the 75 million Americans between 13 and 28, called "Millennials" by some) is radically changing American eating habits. This is the wired generation that uses the mobile phone to download recipes, share brands and good deals, and create a real online food subculture.

- A Cap Gemini study[4] shows that consumers, thanks to the Internet, enter a car showroom "with a level of knowledge that provides a position of power that can be on par, or even exceed, that of the salesperson." They know about all the models displayed, their advantages and shortcomings; they know the current prices and the margin of negotiation possible.[5]
- Recent Edelman studies[6] on Trust show that "Conversations with your friends and peers" are both used *and* credible as a source of information—much more than "company web sites," "communications issued by companies," and "corporate/product advertising" (the least credible).
- Wave 3 by Universal McCann (2008) gives us some further insights:
  - 57 percent of active Internet users in the world are part of a social network.
  - 73 percent read various blogs.
  - There were about 184 million bloggers in the world in 2008.
  - 26.6 percent of Internet users read blogs that express their opinions on brands.
  - 36 percent of Internet users have a more positive opinion of brands that have a blog.

This shows that *the Internet transforms customers into experts who will trust their peers more than traditional sources of authority, such as advertising or the brands themselves*. It also shows that *bloggers have a real impact on brands and their reputation*.

---

[4]"Am I Being Taken? Inside the Dealership: The Impact of Consumer Negotiation Preferences and Strategy," CAPGEMINI, 2008.

[5]This study also shows that the salesperson's style will ultimately affect the sales experience and its final result. Based on academic studies, it identifies two major styles:
1. Customer-oriented style: putting the welfare of the customer first, with the objective of increasing long-term customer satisfaction.
2. Sales-oriented style: putting the close of the deal first—which may lead to sacrificing the long-term customer satisfaction to the probability of making an immediate sale.

[6]Edelman Trust Barometer, Europe, 2010.

The Seven Rules of Internet and Social Media

Luxury brands wishing to exploit Internet and social media to their potential should implement seven fundamental rules.

Rule 1: Internet and Social Media Are a Dialogue—a Conversation between a Brand and Its Customers

It takes two to conduct a conversation. The Web should be used to create a noncommercial dialogue with customers on subjects like practical advice through forums and online services. This is one of the best ways to develop a sense of belonging.

Example: The Huggies Forum does not sell diapers. It gives free advice, has a virtual baby room creator, shows how to time contractions and how to massage a baby, and helps with the selling of used baby products.

Rule 2: Accept Loss of Control

Social media is predicated on two-sided involvement. This must lead brands to accept reciprocity of information, share content with their customers, and accept criticism. While building the relationship with customers, brands should use case studies saying: "This is what happened.". . . "This is how we did it, or solved the problem." This helps build credibility.

Example: When trying to rebuild their Web image, the Davos World Economic Forum posted pictures and videos from their huge content base on Flickr and YouTube. Immediately, some of them were copied and transformed—especially by political opponents of some leaders depicted there. But this helped build the credibility of the WEF.

Rule 3: Know Your Customers

This is critical: Most brands have developed customer segmentations, more often than not based on demographics or sales. Best practices suggest that these segmentations should be sophisticated and include levels of engagement or involvement with the brand.

Example: Lego's customer segmentation consists of five segments:

1. **The Covered Households**—all those who are susceptible to the purchase of a Lego product.
2. **The Active Households**—those who bought in the past 12 months.
3. **The Connected Community**—those who actively connect with the brand by visiting the website or a store (approximately half of the active households). When an active household connects to the brand, the average spend almost triples!
4. **The 1:1 Community**—members of the Lego Club, registered adult fans, or catalog online database members (approximately half of the connected community share their personal data). When an active household becomes 1:1, average spend increases five times.
5. **The Lead Users**—the Lego Universe Partners, the fan community that engages in co-building new products, for instance.

This shows that spending increases as consumers move up the pyramid—and that the brand engages differently with each segment.

Rule 4: Measure, Measure, Measure

Pure players from the Internet have developed this rule, which is surprisingly new for the industry: Always measure the results of any action.

Most brands which are active online use Net Promoter Scores (NPS) that help in measuring promoters (brand advocates, for instance) versus detractors (those who complain about the brand). This is quite important: Most brands only measure overall satisfaction and satisfy themselves with 95+ rates. All recent studies show that a good metric must measure both brand approval *and* brand disapproval. This has led to the adoption of both loyalty metrics and referral economics: How loyal is the customer to the brand *and* does he or she refer (or detract) customers to the brand?

Example: Lego uses Net Promoter Scores to measure the capacity of the brand to promote different referral rates. Four dimensions are measured: product experience (immediate post purchase), online experience, store experience, and customer service experience.

Rule 5: Have a Dedicated Internal Team—Including a Community Manager

Method: The brand should build a strong internal team to build internal capacity, bridging internal departments and organizational silos. When it comes to everything that concerns the Web, a few basic rules should be observed:

- Act fast.
- Join the conversation.
- Keep the channels alive and interesting.
- Grow your digital footprint.
- Establish channels before the crisis (it *will* come).

This needs real internal involvement: Social media need employees to be involved and a professional community manager hired. He or she is a brand ambassador and is clearly responsible for the brand image—especially in a crisis period.

Example: On Kenneth Cole's Twitter feed, a tweet, signed by the creator himself (or, at least, "an authorized person"), read on February 3, 2011: "Millions are in uproar in #Cairo. Rumor is they heard our new spring collection is now available online at http://bit.ly/KCairo-KC."

This was in the midst of the Egyptian revolution. Tens of thousands of protesters gathered daily in Tahrir Square demanding true democracy—and in the thick of it, the American fashion brand latched on to this movement for its own marketing. This tweet traveled around the Internet, prompting both outraged comments and messages of approval. Suddenly the virtual world was split: On one side were those who said the tweet was in the worst possible taste, criticizing the irresponsible brand; on the other were fans (mostly American), who found the message amusing and reaffirmed their commitment to the brand.

Kenneth Cole, after admitting (half-heartedly) that he did not wish to offend the Egyptians, finally posted an apology (just as discreetly) on Facebook.

Rule 6: Social Media by Itself Doesn't Sell

May 2009: A report by Knowledge Networks gives advertisers, marketers, and researchers a clearer picture of the motivations and attitudes of social media (excluding blogs) users in the United States:

- 83 percent of the Internet population (ages 13 to 54) participates in social media—47 percent on a weekly basis.
- Less than 5 percent of social media users regularly turn to these sites for guidance on purchase decisions.
- Only 16 percent of social media users say they are more likely to buy from companies that advertise on social sites.

Rule 7: Social Media Is about an Integrated Strategy That Develops Brand Awareness/Brand Image/Customer Relationship—and Eventually Sells

The Internet is not about having a corporate website, an e-commerce site, using a blog, having a Twitter account, a Facebook page, a YouTube account, using e-mail or texting: It's *about using* all *of them in an integrated manner*. All brand initiatives must be integrated, branded, and consistent.

These 7 rules lead us to a first major conclusion: The idea of *integrating the different channels of distribution* for a brand is critical today.

A recent McKinsey study, "The Promise of Multi-Channel Retailing," reinforces this idea by recalling some essential facts and offers some ideas:

- *Fact*: In the United States only 25 percent of drugstores, 40 percent of distributors, and 60 percent of dealers specializing in fashion regained their pre-crisis growth rates in the five years after the recession of 2001. No brand can now afford to wait that long.
- *Information that is too often neglected:* Consumers who buy and use multiple distribution channels spend much more than those who are satisfied with a single channel. The example of fashion is instructive: The ratios range from 1 to over 5!
- *Why do so many brands not make the grade?* Because they believe that integrating distribution channels means a replication of the "boutique/magazine" on the Internet, or the creation of a sales representative who only reproduces what can be found in the store, hoping that by multiplying the availability of products the customer will buy more. This is a big error: *Each channel is unique! It must correspond*

to a specific offer and complement the other channels, through services offered, information available, and a knowledge of consumer expectations.

- *Example: JCPenney.* "JCPenney has leveraged its legacy as a successful catalog merchant into a tightly integrated cross-channel commerce offering. Stores are outfitted with Web kiosks, and all point-of-sale terminals have Web access so customers can easily purchase product categories, styles, and sizes not available in stores. JCPenney is even testing a system that allows customers to scan coupons in the store that have been sent directly to their mobile telephones. What's important is that each of these channels builds upon JCPenney's overall 'fashion at a value' brand equity by highlighting exclusive brands and deep promotional pricing."[7]

The future lies in a strategy driven by the CEO (the question of the accountability for such a strategy is clearly posed), a reasoning where distribution and communications are closely interlinked, and multiple channels including the mobile phone.

Case Study: When Will Brands Grasp the "Social" in Social Media?[8]

In a recent A.T. Kearney study of Interbrand's Top 50 Global Brands, they analyzed 1,115 posts on Facebook that had 60,570 replies across the top 45 brands, which boasted an aggregate total of 70,016,541 fans. The results are fascinating:

- Five of these brands have no presence on Facebook.
- Seven—including Gucci and Louis Vuitton—allow only company-initiated conversation.
- Only *one* routes fans to an unfiltered Facebook wall—the 45 others initially choose to restrict consumers and fans to a filtered selection of company posts only!

(continued)

---

[7] "The Promise of Multi-Channel Retailing," *McKinsey Quarterly*, October 2009.
[8] Adapted from "Socially Awkward Media," A.T. Kearney, Executive Agenda, 2010.

This means that these brands (among which are luxury brands) use social media as a variant of traditional marketing: a one-way communication channel—which is digitally irrelevant.

But there is more.

Eighty-nine percent of consumer replies on Facebook go unanswered—"*Gucci, for example, did not respond to a single consumer reply within the past three months*"—and only 11 brands responded to more than one customer!

When brands respond, only 15 percent of these answers invite further conversation. This translates as "we acknowledge you, but please do not bother us!" which is definitely *not* a conversation and has nothing to do with learning. *This means that most brands do not really want to relate to or learn from their customers*. We are a far cry from the five phases described earlier and there is ample room for improvement.

Once again we are faced not only with a fear of loss of control, but with what can be labeled "marketing laziness": 71 percent of company posts were promotional—offering discount coupons, free prizes, and other amenities.

On the other hand, the 5 percent of company-to-consumer posts that engaged in discussions are really insightful. They show that there are three major techniques—all involving emotional connections—that work:

1. Invoking nostalgia—like discontinued products and history of the brand.
2. Engaging in product discussions and soliciting evaluations or even new colors, flavors, and products.
3. Rallying around common causes.

Revisiting the Brand Internet Strategies

Earlier in this chapter we showed the four phases luxury brands have gone through in the development of their Internet strategies. A recent study[9] suggests identifying four distinct strategies, depending on the customer relationship (top down versus a conversation) and on the brand's channel strategy (mono-channel or multi-channel), as shown in Figure 4.6. Two axes structure these strategies: the sort of customer relationship the company wishes to build (is it top down? is it a conversation?) and the channel strategy adopted (is it mono-channel? is it multi-channel?).

Most luxury brands today are still implementing multi-channel and top-down strategies. What the study shows is that Strategy 4 (multi-channel plus conversation), which is a high-engagement profile strategy, generates higher revenue growth (plus 18 percent versus less than 10 percent for the others), higher gross margins (plus 15 percent versus less than 3 percent), and higher net margins (plus 4 percent versus negative net margins) than all the other strategies. The conclusion we reach is that, even if this strategy is difficult to implement—because it leads the brand to reinvent itself in its organization—it is the most rewarding for business.

This leads us to our second major conclusion: Luxury brands need to first define and structure their customer relationship strategy: This is the cornerstone of all Internet strategies.

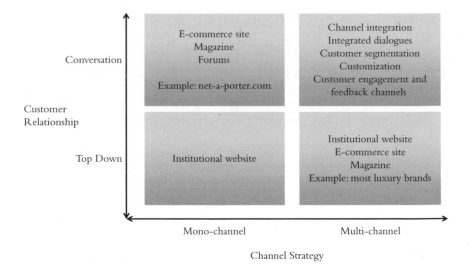

Figure 4.6   The Four Brand Internet Strategies

---

[9]"The World's Most Valuable Brands: Who's Most Engaged?" Wetpaint & Altimeter, July 2009.

Chapter 5

Luxury Store Location

In a real estate context where every square meter counts, the ultimate luxury is *wasted* space. Space that is not "productive"—not shopping—affords contemplation, privacy, mobility, and luxury.
—*Rem Koolhaas*

A t first glance, the problem of store location for luxury outlets is very simple. One should be next to where the major brands of the industry are already located. Luxury retail seems to have taken the old system of the Middle Ages, when it was deemed better to be next to the competitors.

But with which type of store? A store of what size? And to do what? Also, trade area analysis, although more useful for specialty store chains or mass-market operators, is still not useless in this environment. Last but by no means least, the cost of renting a store in different countries must also be assessed and analyzed.

What Kind of Store?

We will start by looking at the different types of stores in general, then focus specifically on luxury, and discuss what the ideal number of stores in a given city is. We will complete this section by looking at stores as cultural institutions, doing much more than just selling products.

The Mass-Market Model

For mass-market retail, we distinguish three types of retail stores: those selling products corresponding to destination shopping, those selling products corresponding to convenience shopping, and those dealing with intercept products.

1. *Destination shopping products* are those that consumers purchase according to a complex planning process and for which they are ready to go out of their way to buy. An automobile would be the perfect example of a destination purchase. The same is true for a baby's crib, for which parents-to-be are ready to travel a few miles in order to purchase it before their baby is born.

2. *Convenience shopping products* are those that you may need at the last minute and that you want to find in a place that is as close as possible to your home, or on your way from your office to your home. The "just ran out of" butter or salt are typical convenience shopping products.

   Convenience shoppers are price inelastic. They do not look at the price and want to spend as little time as possible buying. On the other hand, for destination shopping, customers are very price conscious: They plan their shopping trip in advance and would drive 5 to 10 miles more if they were sure to find the same product, in a similar product environment, at a significantly lower price.

3. *Intercept shopping products* are those products than you don't need urgently and for which you would not be ready to drive 10 miles to find. This can be the case, for example, of a duplicate of your apartment key, new soles on your best shoes, or a box of cigars. You need them, but you don't need them immediately and you would not go out in the middle of the night to find them. In your mind, you

know that the next time you go to such-and-such a place, you will encounter a cobbler or a cigar store and that is when you will get new soles for your shoes or the cigars missing in your humidor. Those stores are not destination places, but they must be on the way to or within a major shopping center, or close to a public transport station and similar locations.

In fact, these three product types end up being part of two different shopping situations:

1. *Shopping that is part of regular routine* is a special case of destination shopping in which customers are organized in such a way that they concentrate, for example, once a week on their grocery food purchases or once a month on their bulk food purchases. These are special cases of destination shopping, and when the consumer has selected a given shopping trip procedure, he or she is no longer extremely price sensitive, at least in the short run. For these routine weekly errands, people are ready to drive up to 30 miles to get the products they need. In special shopping situations like the back-to-school purchase of books, pens, and seasonal dresses, they are ready to drive up to 100 miles.

2. *Convenience as part of a destination shopping trip* is also a retail situation. To make a duplicate of their own apartment keys, people can generally wait until the next weekly trip to the supermarket or the shopping mall. Stores that make duplicate keys and shoe repair stores are basically convenience stores, but if they can be found as part of a destination shopping ritual, and are visible and have easy access, they can be integrated into the process of weekly destination shopping.

In the United States, this is the reason major shopping centers try to have department stores as *anchors*: Their purpose is simply to bring customers into the shopping mall. Once they are finished with their destination shopping, consumers can go around and visit other stores. They will probably end up buying things they did not plan to buy and will also take the opportunity for some intercept shopping.

For luxury brands, the same concepts apply, but as a function of the attractiveness of any given brand. The stronger it is, the more the shopping situation becomes a destination procedure. If the brand is relatively weak, it should plan to provide convenience as part of a destination shopping trip for another brand.

In China, for example, real estate developers coming up with new luxury shopping complexes have a tendency to first visit the management teams of very strong brands and offer them a store at a very low, nominal rent. They know that if they can attract three or four major brands with very high consumer pulling power, they will then have no difficulty renting space to other brands, knowing that customers would flock to such shopping centers. The system makes a lot of economic sense, but it is nevertheless unfair since the weak ultimately pay the rent for the very strong brand operators.

The Case of Luxury: Different Types of Stores

As indicated previously, the main criterion for luxury goods is the pulling power that each brand can obtain. But different types of retail outlets may correspond to different marketing objectives.

Flagship Stores They have a name, which is self-explanatory. These stores are not just there to make money, but to present the brand in all its facets and promote it. As well as being stores that sell products, they are showrooms where journalists, licensees, or foreign distributors can see the full brand collection and get an idea of how it should be presented and promoted.

Flagship stores would have first been created in the home city of that brand. The large Hermès store on rue du Faubourg Saint Honoré in Paris is a good example of this. Flagship stores in Paris are traditionally the very old retail stores, if not the original outlets, and they provide a complete product assortment for the brand. They are not only high volume retail stores, but institutions in themselves. Chanel on rue Cambon in Paris is also a flagship store; it is actually the original store (extended over time, of course) and presents the full Chanel merchandising concept. Dior on avenue Montaigne in Paris is also a large flagship outlet in the original location.

But in the past 10 years, as brands became global, managers extended the concept of flagship stores further. The very top brands decided to have flagship stores not only in their hometowns, but also in major cities where the business was considered a priority: Tokyo, Hong Kong, New York, and Shanghai, for example. For each geographical zone, this extension of the flagship concept anticipates that the opening of a major store would be a "diamond in the crown" that serves as a brand statement for the region, a merchandising example for everybody, and a public relations showcase.

A final point on this subject: A real flagship store should not only be a public relations exercise; it should be packed with people, it should sell products, and it should be profitable.

Megastores This is another concept developed around 1995 in the luxury sector. Megastores are huge stores of at least 8,000 square feet.

The definition of megastores overlaps with that of flagship stores: Many flagship stores are megastores, but some are not, and megastores are sometimes created with a different objective than flagship stores.

Creating a megastore has nothing to do with the origin of the brand or the idea of creating an institution. It is a show of force: Brand X wants to show everybody, including competitors, journalists, as well as clients, that it is able to create a huge store in a given city and make money. It is a demonstration of strength and ambition. The idea is not so much to have a big store, but to have a store that is bigger than anybody else's.

Of the 15 stores listed in Table 5.1, eight are located in Asia, where showing strength is part of the game. Only Armani in Milan and Louis Vuitton in Paris could be considered as worldwide flagship stores. But many others act as regional flagship outlets trying to personify the priority of a given territory.

What is clear is that the development of megastores looks a bit like a battle of giants in which only the very big ones can compete and make money. The small brands, and even the medium brands, cannot join the game—they have to remain on the sidelines.

Another consequence of this battle of giants: There is a strong incentive to develop products in every product category. Selling nothing but handbags in a 20,000-square-foot store would be boring if not ridiculous. To remain in the megastore game, it is necessary to present a full collection of products, including ready-to-wear. Megastores are a strong incentive for big brands to have a full merchandising assortment.

One could argue that, as they develop these huge stores, brands seems to be looking at themselves the same way as the early department stores did back in the 1880s, or more precisely, the specialty stores that were defining their business, but with all products of the same brand. Will megastores continue to develop? Probably, as long as

Table 5.1   Examples of Megastores (and selling space in square feet)

Spazio Armani	Milan	65,000
Chanel	Ginza building, Tokyo	61,000
Louis Vuitton	Champs Elysées, Paris	36,000
Louis Vuitton	Omotesando, Tokyo	31,000
Prada	Aoyama, Tokyo	28,000
Tod's	Omotesando, Tokyo	25,500
Prada	New York	23,000
Louis Vuitton	1 East 57, New York	19,000
Christian Dior	Omotesando, Tokyo	15,500
Hugo Boss	Champs Elysées, Paris	13,500
Hermès	Ginza, Tokyo	13,000
Chanel	57th Street, New York	9,500
Louis Vuitton	Plaza 66, Shanghai	9,500
Prada	Hong Kong	9,000
Cartier	Champs Elysées, Paris	8,000

SOURCE: Specific press articles.

they can be profitable and brands want to show their strength in their priority markets. We should also remember that they are much more than stores, as they tend to become real institutions in the cities where they are located.

Institutional Complements

In a way, these are the opposite of megastores. When brands accomplish a large part of their sales at wholesale, they need to reinforce their images with small stores that make a statement, showing the consumers that the brand is much more than a plain wholesale operator, but also a real institution like the big guys. These institutional complements do not need to be huge: They can be 600 to 1,200 square feet, but they must be developed in top locations.

Many watch manufacturers have such institutional complements. They present the full brand environment, as opposed to independent jewelers who can only show part of the global image since they have to deal with many products from many different sources. Having a prestigious address in a given city reinforces the strength of the brand and provides a guarantee that the after-sales services can be of top quality.

But such stores will only benefit from the best locations. When major watch manufacturers open institutional complement stores in Shanghai but on the wrong side of Huai Hai Zhong lu, or in the basement of Plaza 66, they're missing the point.

Temporary (Pop-Up) Stores

These are a recent development, an invention often attributed to Comme des Garçons, that has been copied by many others. The idea was to rent a large retail space, slightly out of the way (a destination place) so that the rent is low and the risk limited, and sell products in a warehouse environment while hosting complimentary events, perhaps including the presentation of vintage items, to make the customer visit a very worthwhile and entertaining one.

Such a temporary store should be able to make money, particularly if the rent is very low and if the museum pieces and the special themes are strong enough to attract the customers. Moreover, it can also be a very effective public relations tool. In a similar vein, during the busy Christmas season, a store may develop a very nice theme that journalists can write about in their magazines or their newspapers.

It was in February 2004 that Comme des Garçons opened the first pop-up in Berlin, called a "guerrilla store" or "propaganda store." This was followed by many others in Barcelona, Helsinki, Singapore, Stockholm, Ljubljana, and Warsaw. These were temporary boutiques where products are displayed on stands or low tables without sophisticated fixtures, often located in noncommercial areas, in reaction against the hypercommercial growth of city centers: "The location will be chosen according to its atmosphere, historical connection, geographical situation away from established commercial areas or some other interesting feature," stated the manifesto of the brand.

The shop in Berlin had all the features of a discount store. The concept has clearly evolved into a true concept store with its merchandising codes and its "architecture." It has retained only the ephemeral temporary quality of the first guerrilla store and choice of location.

Many other brands (Evian, Wrangler, Gap, Nokia, Levi's, Louis Vuitton, and Target, to name a few) have since adopted the idea of pop-up stores, often without due consideration, preferring to create an event rather than a means to strengthen the value of the brand.

We can suggest a typology of pop-up stores, showing how a brand can use pop-up stores as a powerful means of development.

- A method to strengthen rarity: This is the privileged option of luxury brands. For 10 years they have been losing their luster by multiplying boutiques and expanding their customer base. They have lost the sense of rarity—which is one of the fundamentals of luxury—believing that pricing and enhancements to their images are enough to justify their luxury positioning. The pop-up stores are a way of recreating rarity: a temporary shop offering an ephemeral and exclusive collection. Louis Vuitton is the brand that has best understood this aspect: The Japanese pop-up store with Comme des Garçons (that's right) is a perfect example of this strategy—open in Tokyo from September 4, 2008 to mid-December, it showcased a series of six limited-edition bags.

- A means for the brand to make itself desired in a place where it was hitherto absent: This was the case with the Comme des Garçons guerrilla stores and is now the case with Target's pop-ups, called Bullseye Bazaar. The retailer is absent from a number of large cities like New York and Chicago. Based on its "chic & cheap" concept, it borrows the idea of rarity from the luxury market: designer products created by famous designers at discount prices, available in limited series.

- A way to test a new retailing concept: This is what Procter & Gamble is trying to do with the Look Fab Studio, an itinerant pop-up store in Canada. All the Procter & Gamble beauty products are grouped together (Pantene, Cover Girl, Olay, Nice'n Easy, Crest, Venus) in a spot where professional stylists provide advice about skin care and colors, and offer mini makeovers. All services are free and there are no products on sale. For the first time, a global P&G Beauty offer can be found under one roof—a precursor of future shops, perhaps?

- A means to launch a new product: This is the most common case, and we think the most uninteresting. A brand organizes an event, and instead of proposing a press conference or a "people" event, sets up a temporary store where consumers can discover the new range. That is what Gap did in San Francisco in April 2009 to launch its 1969 Premium Denim Jeans range—a pop-up store open for five months. Glaceau did the same for 10 days in New York to launch VitaminWater10.

Table 5.2 indicates, in the case of China, that an important driver for people entering a store is to have fun. Store visits are probably considered as a part of entertainment. It can be seen in this table that an average Chinese women spends 9.3 hours a week visiting stores.

It is common in China for two friends to call each other and say, "Let's go and visit fashion stores." To a lesser extent, this entertainment side of retail exists in other countries as well. In that respect, the pop-up store seems to be a very good idea.

Also worthy of mention is Hermès, which opened a temporary store in Paris, from May to December 2010, with a leather specialist working on leather pieces in the store's show window.

If they can provide good entertainment, a strong public relations story, and a good level of sales, pop-up stores seem to be an interesting innovation.

Volume Stores As we move in this subsection from one store to another, one should not forget that the objective of a luxury retail store is to make money. Management should carefully design the ideal store with a reasonable size and with most of the merchandising variables carefully tested: Should accessories be separate or should they be

Table 5.2 Shopping and Entertainment

	Hours per Week Spent Shopping	Number of Stores Visited per Week
China	9.3	4.6
United States	3.6	3.1
France	3.0	2.5

SOURCE: *Shanghai Daily*, cited in Michel Chevalier and Pierre Lu, *Luxury China: Market Opportunities and Potential* (Hoboken, NJ: John Wiley & Sons, 2009).

included with ready-to-wear? Are they selling more next to men's suits or next to shirts? Should shoes be sold in a specific place?

As one store in another given city may look different from the flagship store in Paris or in Milan, people tend to forget that each brand has its best selling practices that they must use everywhere.

Coach, for example, uses factory outlets to measure at the outset how new models in different shapes and colors perform, before they decide to sell a finalized item in their genuine stores. The idea of using test stores to measure the impact of different merchandising tools and to define the ideal store presentation to improve volume and consumer satisfaction makes a lot of sense.

How Many Stores in a Given City?

According to the balance of destination and convenience shopping for any brand, there should be an ideal number of stores in a given city. We spoke earlier of Benetton, which was stuck in 1995 with too many small stores in many cities. What would have been for them the ideal number of outlets?

As outsiders, we tend to see that when a brand has a major flagship or megastore in a given city, it seems very reluctant to open another one: Probably management wants to make sure that the flagship store does well and is reluctant to take the risk of a second opening for many years. Hermès had only one store in Paris—their flagship store—and a very small corner in the Hilton hotel on the Left Bank (and half a store on avenue Georges V, which they shared with the Motsch hat brand), whereas Salvatore Ferragamo had more than 10 stores in the same city. They probably lost some business opportunities. At long last, Hermès now has a second store on rue de Sèvres. For many years Louis Vuitton had only one megastore in Shanghai, and three stores in Beijing, until they opened two additional stores in Shanghai, one in April 2010 and the other in 2011. Maybe a flagship store, with its very large pulling power, reduces the need for a second (convenience, volume) outlet. But most major cities have different shopping magnets and luxury shopping areas.

As we move from one single store (located in the very best location or in an outstanding place) to several, then the need for a more systematic analysis of trade areas becomes key.

"A Store Should Be a Place of Worship" or an "Institution"

The words of Donna Karan tell the whole story. She speaks of "modernity," "sensuality," and "drama." It is true that a luxury store should be much more than a straight place to present products and sell them.

In fact, a well-managed luxury outlet organizes presentations and special events. On the walls, it presents iconography in the form of advertisements or snapshots of celebrities endorsing the products. The music used in the store should convey the story of the origin of the brand. There is sometimes a special scent coming from the leather of the products and the brand presents a sort of "sainthood" in the way it promotes the image of the designer or the star, or both, who created the brand.

To conclude this section on stores in a way that can be applied to both institutions and a volume provider, let us take the example of the Sephora store in Champs Elysées in Paris. It is a huge store with sales in 2010 in the vicinity of 100 million euros. But it is much more than a store: It is also a meeting place. On an average Saturday, 17,000 people enter the store, compared to 6,000 on a Monday: When the young generation decide to go to a movie in a nearby theater, they arrange to meet in Sephora. The store has a very high average ticket: 90 euros. As it is such a meeting place on Saturdays and Sundays, the percentage of people leaving with a purchase is quite low (conversion rate of 23 percent, or around 4,000 tickets), whereas on Monday it is much higher: Around 33 percent of visitors purchase, or around 2,000 people. Running such a store is not only about selling products and running the cash register; it is about making sure it remains an institution and stays the best meeting place in the avenue. To do this it is necessary to organize special events that single out the store as something very special for the customer.

In Which Cities in the World
Do You Place Your Stores?

What is specific to luxury is that consumers buy in their home country, but also abroad. A Japanese customer may buy a Hermès tie in New York, a French citizen may buy an Italian perfume in Germany, or a Swede may buy a French perfume while on vacation in the Canary Islands, a territory of Spain. The net result of such individual behaviors is that for a luxury brand to exist and be credible, it must be available in almost every country of the world.

When a luxury brand is not available in the United States, in Japan, or in France, it looses part of its strength and its attractiveness. Spaniards would rather buy a Cartier or a Bulgari piece of jewelry than a Suarez one, because they know that although Suarez has a very strong signature in Spain, it is unknown in New York or in Germany and will not impress their foreign friends. So, in a way, no major luxury brand can remain local: It must perform on a worldwide stage. Brands that are starting out can be local at first, but only provided they give indications that they plan to develop outside of their own country.

Where are brands located in the world? In a study by CBRE, Richard Ellis has looked at the answer. They have studied the location of 280 global retailers (mass and luxury) and come up with Table 5.3.

Table 5.3   Location of 280 Global Retailers

1	United Kingdom	58%
2	Spain	48%
3	France	46%
4	United Arab Emirates	45%
5	Germany	45%
6	China	42%
7	Russia	41%
8	Italy	41%
9	Switzerland	40%
10	United States	39%
11	Belgium	38%
12	Austria	38%
13	Canada	37%
14	Japan	37%
15	Saudi Arabia	37%

Source: CBRE, Richard Ellis, Global Retailing 2009.

This table yields several surprises: First is the fact that the United States is not at the very top of the list, and comes after the United Arab Emirates, for which Dubai has become a key location. Second is that Spain comes up almost at the very top of the list, and before Germany and Italy. This can be explained by the fact that in Spain, rents are very reasonable (as we will see later) and also by the fact that Spain has two cities that are on everybody's hit list: Madrid and Barcelona. Also, the fact that China and Russia seem to be better destinations for global retailers than the United States is quite unexpected.

In this sample, retailers were from the clothing, footwear, and the luxury retail sector. On average, the luxury retailers were present in 27 countries (compared with an average of 14 for the other sectors of the sample).

In the total sample, 40 percent of store openings were realized outside of the home market and this figure was probably much higher for luxury brands.

The study also analyzed how brand managers integrate new developing markets and decide to build stores in a new country. Different brands frequently converge at the same time to a given location: The reason for this may be the opening of a new luxury shopping center. People sometimes wait until they have a strong opportunity in Buenos Aires or in Vietnam, for example, and will all open their first store in those countries at the same time and in the same location with the consolation that if it goes sour, they would not be the only ones to have made the mistake. As a result, country developments tend to happen in waves.

Table 5.4 gives the same results by major cities. In the total by cities, things are more logical, with towns appearing in the ranking as a function of their attractiveness, as well as their rental cost.

But how do retailers decide to go into one city rather than another and what criteria do they use? Jones Lang Lasalle have developed a transparency index to assess the security of different countries where it may be more or less dangerous to invest in a retail store. In that respect, Jones Lang Lasalle tries to define the different levels of risk for occupiers, the security of debt financing, and the stability of property valuations.

Table 5.4 Location of 280 Global Retailers

1	London	59%
2	Paris	50%
3	New York	47%
4	Dubai	46%
5	Madrid	44%
6	Moscow	42%
7	Berlin	40%
8	Munich	40%
9	Barcelona	39%
10	Tokyo	39%
11	Singapore	38%
12	Hamburg	38%
13	Hong Kong	38%
14	Milan	37%
15	Beijing	36%

Source: CBRE, Richard Ellis, Global Retailing 2009.

The transparency index is based on five criteria:

1. The availability of an investment performance index
2. The availability of market fundamentals data
3. The listed vehicle financial disclosure and governance
4. Regulatory and legal factors
5. Professional and ethical standards

The idea is that when global retailers invest in a given retail property abroad, they should be clear about its value, they should be able to sell it later at an acceptable price, they should be able to find stable local debt financing propositions, and they should be sure that the regulatory and legal elements of the deal are clear for everybody and that there would be no unexpected surprises at a later stage.

Table 5.5 lists a selection of countries. One can see the nine countries that correspond to the highest transparency index in the first column. It is interesting to note that countries like Germany, Italy, Switzerland,

Table 5.5   Geographical Situations of Retailing Activities (Transparency Index)

High Transparency	Transparency	Semitransparency	Low or Opaque
1. Canada	10. Ireland	29. Russia tier 1 cities	65. China tier 2 cities
2. Australia	11. Hong Kong	34. Russia tier 2 cities	
3. United States	12. Singapore	44. South Korea	77. Vietnam
4. New Zealand	13. Finland	49. China tier 1 cities	79. Cambodia
5. United Kingdom	14. Germany	50. India tier 1 cities	81. Algeria
	15. Denmark		81. Syria
6. Netherlands	16. Spain		
7. France	17. Austria		
8. Sweden	18. Norway		
9. Belgium	19. Italy		
	20. Switzerland		
	21. South Africa		
	22. Portugal		
	23. Malaysia		
	24. Czech Republic		
	25. Poland		
	26. Japan		

SOURCE: Jones Lang Lasalle, Real Estate Transparency index, 2009.

or Japan only make it to the second column—"transparency"—because their environments for doing retail real estate deals is apparently not always as simple as could have been expected.

In the "low" or "opaque" transparency index one can notice the second tier of Chinese cities as well as Algeria and Syria.

But Jones Lang Lasalle goes one step further. Instead of putting the blame on one country or another, they show that their transparency index correlates strongly with per capita gross domestic product, corruption levels at an estimated point, and to the overall outlook of the business environment. The point here is that as countries develop and improve their political stability and democracy, they become more transparent, making it easier for foreigners to invest securely in local real estate. But the most interesting point demonstrated is how, at comparable levels of economic development and democracy, some countries just happen to be less transparent and less secure than others for foreigners who want to invest in real estate.

So, should luxury retail be worldwide? Without any doubt, yes. But, as in many other subjects, a word of caution seems to be necessary and welcome.

Trade Area Analysis

Let us begin with an economic analysis, then a geographical analysis, and then finish with the possible applications of such tools for luxury goods.

Economic Analysis

Today, before people decide on the location of a supermarket, they carefully look at criteria of purchasing power, trading area adequacy, and trade growth potential. If they have access to a helicopter, they will also look at the flow of automotive traffic, the stops, the bottlenecks, and the exit patterns: The information is that detailed. They then ask special consultants to run economic analyses for them. The data available is so precise today that the general manager of a brand told us that he operates 80 stores in Seoul and the group headquarters based in Europe tells him where the specialized retailing consultants have decided the 81st store should be, without his having ever gone to the city.

The zone purchasing power exists today for almost every housing block in the world:

- Income by block
- Number of private telephones by block
- Number of credit cards and percentage of cards overdue
- Number of burglaries and houses broken into in the block

People can then define a *trading area adequacy* as a function of the buying power index and the retail sales in the area. With this approach, it is possible to define:

- A *net trade adequacy*, taking into account the under-stored areas.
- A *store saturation measure*, using an index of saturation that is the ratio of the number of consumers in the trading area multiplied by the average expenditure in the category and divided by the number of retail square feet: This gives, for each commercial zone worldwide, an estimate of the sales per square foot in the zone.

This will be mitigated by trade growth potential that takes into account the economic trend in the area, income forecasts, and an already established income sensitivity to purchase increases in the category.

Geographical Analysis

Economic data must be balanced by a basic geographical analysis. Each trade area is in a way specific, and its structure could have very different impacts on, for example, a large furniture store, an isolated supermarket, or a large shopping center with an extensive assortment of merchandise.

The Urban Structure

Several theories have been given to explain the way a city develops.[1] One theory speaks of concentric zones, as in Figure 5.1. Zone 1 represents the central business district; zone 2 is a zone of transition; zone 3 is working-class homes; zone 4 is middle-class homes; and zone 5 is commuter's homes. As one can see, this is quite theoretical and applies exclusively to the United States.

A second theory is based on the sector system as indicated in Figure 5.2.

In this system, zone 1 remains the central business district, but zone 2 becomes wholesale and low-class manufacturing and zone 3 is low-class residential, while zone 4 remains middle-class residential, and zone 5 is considered to be upper-class residential.

A third theory is that of a multiple nuclei system as presented in Figure 5.3. In that case, zone 1 is the central business district, zone 2

---

[1]Ronald E. Gist, *Retailing Concept and Decision* (New York: John Wiley & Sons, 1968).

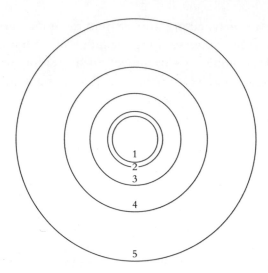

Figure 5.1 Concentric Zones of City Development

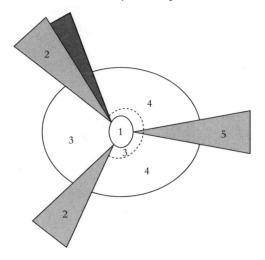

Figure 5.2 The Sector System of City Development
SOURCE: Ronald E. Gist, *Retailing Concept and Decision* (New York: John Wiley & Sons, 1968).

is wholesale manufacturing, zone 3 is low-class residential, zone 4 is middle-class residential, zone 5 is upper-class residential, zone 6 is heavy manufacturing, zone 7 is an outlying business district, and zone 8 is a residential suburb.

What is the best theory? None are, but the three should be used together to explain specific developments in one city or another. By

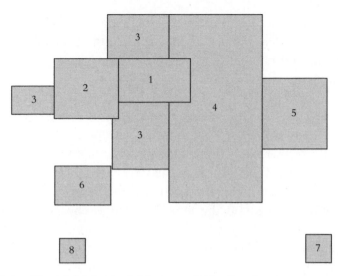

Figure 5.3   The Multiple Nuclei System of City Development
Source: Ronald E. Gist, *Retailing Concept and Decision* (New York: John Wiley & Sons, 1968).

looking at a map and having average income data by blocs, one can come up with the best specific system for each individual case. These systems are not really predictive, but they can explain existing specific urban situations.

Specific Elements When carefully looking at these maps, one should also consider how people behave as they move around in a given city.

First, there are obstacles like rivers or highways that people tend to refrain from crossing to go shopping, even if a store or mall is closer than one on the same riverbank. In Hong Kong, a resident of Hong Kong island has a mind-set that makes it difficult to go shopping on the Kowloon side, although he can take the subway to cross the channel. In Paris, people living in the Left Bank have a tendency to go shopping there, while people living in the Right Bank do not readily cross the Seine for shopping. They would obviously do it to go to work or to go to school, but less for shopping. Why? There is no easy explanation for this.

Railway lines are also considered a psychological obstacle, particularly if they are not underground. But railway stations, as we have seen in the case of Japan, not only work as magnets to passengers, they also attract those who never take the train.

Which are the best sides of a street? In the northern hemisphere for a street going east to west, the north side is always preferred because it has more sunlight when the south side is shadowed. Of course, when the street is very narrow and the buildings very high, the difference disappears somewhat. But in Paris, in the Champs Elysées, there are three times more passersby using the northern pavement than people using the southern pavement. Is the rent three times cheaper on the south side? Not quite, but real estate agencies say that south side rents are on average 30 percent cheaper than those on the north side. This can be an interesting alternative for destination shopping brand stores, but would certainly make no economic sense for convenience stores that must take advantage of the number of potential customers passing by their stores.

In streets going north to south, the east side is preferred because it receives more light in the afternoon when people do most of their shopping.

What about cities like Madrid or Singapore, where the climate is very hot? In that case people prefer to walk in the shadow, but to a lesser extent because the sun lights the northern stores the same way it does in London or in Tokyo, making them more attractive.

Does that make a difference? Obviously yes on the Champs Elysées in Paris, as there are three times more passersby walking on the north pavement than on the south one; if the store on the south side carries a brand that is not a strong destination one, that store risks attracting three times fewer customers than if it had been on the north side. And this point is not insignificant, because, as we just mentioned, the rent on the south side of the Champs Elysées is not three times cheaper than on the north.

Cluster Analysis As one considers a given city, the trade areas will result in a sum of clusters that will be defined as a function of economic analysis and trade analysis. In a small city, the trade areas of two supermarkets overlap, but if there is only one jeweler he will have the advantage of most of the people going to both of the supermarkets.

Every time a customer makes a purchase, it is interesting to know where he or she lives. If they pay by bank check, it is very simple to register the address. If they pay by credit card and an ID card is not required, then the information is a bit more difficult to obtain. Alternatively, it can be obtained by a market research survey done from a sample of people walking out of the store. Regardless of how this information is collected, it is interesting for a given brand to know the percentage of volume done with consumers who can reach the store in 5, 10, 20, 30 minutes or more: This can give very precious indications on how to promote the store and on which territory, and can also be very useful when considering a second location in the same city.

Reilly's Laws

William J. Reilly's laws date back to 1929 and are still considered to be the only way to assess the pulling power of two similar stores in two cities, or the impact of several competitive stores in the same trade area.

The First Reilly's Law This was developed to define which point between two cities, A or B, people prefer to go.
    The first Reilly's formula states:

$$\text{Point of equal probability} = \frac{\text{Distance (in km) between A and B}}{1 + \sqrt{\dfrac{\text{population of A}}{\text{population of B}}}}$$

Reilly in fact measured the attractiveness of each city as a function of its population.
    If we assume that the distance between A and B is 100 kilometers and that city A has 40,000 inhabitants and city B 10,000, it becomes:

$$\text{Point of equal probability} = \frac{100}{1 + \sqrt{\dfrac{40,000}{10,000}}} = 33.3 \text{ kilometers}$$

This means that someone 65 miles away from city A, which is four times larger than city B, would prefer to go shopping in city A. Only those people living less than 33.3 miles from city B would go shopping there.

This law is still valid today. It has been modified slightly to take into account not distance but driving time and to take into consideration the different obstacles previously defined. It has also been adapted so that in some cases it does not compare the populations of the two cities, but the volume of retail sales in those cities.

Retail sales are a very good measure of the attractiveness of two cities, but very often people prefer to use as criteria the square meters devoted to fashion goods or to a given type of goods.

The Second Reilly's Law The second Reilly's law deals with the presence of similar stores in the same location, as is often the case for luxury goods. Are brands helping each other or hurting? We discussed earlier the case of Chinese real estate operators being ready to decrease their rents for top brands. This is an indication that the market believes strong brands can attract customers who might in the end also buy other less "attractive" brands.

It is obvious that some retail activities are antithetical. For example, a bridal shop would not be well located next to a gas station or a shady nightclub. The problem is not only the difference in standing or positioning, but also the mood of the consumer when he or she decides to enter a store or look for another one. In the same way, a fast-food chain restaurant next to a Gucci store would have a negative impact on the consumer mood and the way he or she might feel before entering the Gucci store. Is it located in the best and most prestigious location in the city?

William Reilly states that the presence of two stores in the same area will have a positive or a negative impact as a function of three criteria.

The volumes of store A and store B: This is slightly reminiscent of the size of the two cities in the first Reilly's law. Obviously, the bigger the store volume, the greater its attractiveness. Actually, rather than volume, it may be more interesting to look at the number of purchase receipts generated by each store. A jewelry store, with very high sales levels but very few customers per day, will not attract the number of customers a retailer of ties or gloves needs to make its daily volume. But the relative volume concept is appropriate if the two stores are selling the same product types.

A concept of purposeful purchasing, which boils down to the idea of the pulling power of each brand. For brands A and B, one will record the ratio of customers making a purchase divided by the consumers planning a purchase. If the purposeful purchasing ratio is high, this means that the brand is clearly a destination one and that it is a strong business generator for others. When the purposeful purchasing ratio is low, we are clearly in front of a brand generating little volume on its own and relying very much on others to make its sales volume, piggybacking, so to speak, on the customers brought in by other brands.

Using the case of the Chinese luxury shopping mall real estate developer, we could advise him to apply a purposeful purchasing ratio to each of the luxury brands he wants to deal with, and adjust his store rents accordingly. It would still give a big advantage to the strong volume generator brands, but it would certainly be fair.

A degree of customer interchange giving a positive coefficient if the two brands are highly compatible (10 to 20 percent customer interchange), moderately compatible (5 to 10 percent customer interchange), or slightly compatible (1 to 5 percent customer interchange). There is also a negative value if the stores are incompatible, or even detrimental.

William J. Reilly's idea was to say that the increase in sales due to the proximity of two competitive stores is:

• Directly proportionate to customer interchange.
• But inversely proportionate to the ratio of their volume.
• And proportionate to the sum of purposeful purchasing. We can write it:

$$V = I(V_L + V_S) \times \frac{V_S}{V_L} \times (P_L + P_S)$$

With V_L and V_S being the volumes of the large and small stores, I being the degree of customer interchange, and P_L and P_S being the ratio of purposeful purchasing of the large store and the small store.

To take an example, this would be:

V_L = volume of large store: 5,000,000 euros
P_L = purposeful purchasing of large store: 90 percent
V_S = volume of small store: 3,000,000 euros

P_S = purposeful purchasing of small store: 30 percent
I = degree of customer interchange: 25 percent

We can write:

$$I(V_L + V_S) = 0.25(5,000,000 + 3,000,000) = 2,000,000 \text{ €}$$

This is inversely proportionate to the ratio of their volume:

$$I(V_L + V_S) \times \frac{V_S}{V_L} = 2,000,000 \times \frac{3,000,000}{5,000,000} = 1,200,000 \text{ €}$$

And

$$I(V_L + V_S) \times \frac{V_S}{V_L} \times V_S \times (P_L + P_S) = 1,200,000 \times 1.2 = 1,440,000 \text{ €}$$

This amount of additional business (18 percent of the total) should be divided between the two brands, as an inverse function of their purposeful purchasing.

Application to Luxury Goods

These concepts of pulling power, customer generation, and additional benefits from brands that help each other in the same location, certainly ring a bell in the luxury field where some brands like Loewe or Bottega Veneta have been taking advantage of the strong support they were getting for their Asian location by Louis Vuitton and Gucci. But the gathering of many competitive brands in the same location provides another advantage—it makes shopping a diversified and pleasant experience.

Dealing with Different Types of Customers

Two different kinds of customers visit stores:

1. *The purchasers:* They are interested in a brand or a product and want to be provided efficient and knowledgeable service.
2. *The browsers:* They visit the store for their own entertainment and their enlightenment. They are not planning to purchase anything and probably

will not, but they might do it next time. They are looking for a sensory experience and even if they never buy, they can act as opinion leaders and convey positive or negative messages about different brands.

The idea here is that purchasers and browsers expect more from a store visit than just finding a tie or a silk scarf. They want to be part of a strong experience. They have to be entertained and surprised. This entertainment requirement is dealt with in different ways:

- Japanese department stores have generally one floor or part of a floor dedicated to restaurants: a French restaurant, an Italian one, a Chinese one, and obviously a Japanese one. Sometimes they also organize art exhibitions in their premises. They want to be more than a department store and act as a cultural magnet in the cities where they are located. Sometimes individual luxury brands organize their own museum in some of their largest stores. The Louis Vuitton Champs Elysées store in Paris has its own gallery of modern art on the top floor (unfortunately, using a different side entrance) in which several exhibitions per year are presented. In the Hermès flagship store in Seoul, the basement functions as an extremely well-decorated museum with a collection of traditional Hermès historical pieces.
- Each luxury store, through its own design, should provide some added aesthetic values and interesting elements that the typical browser would love to see.
- Temporary (pop-up) stores are a good tool for giving this entertainment dimension to browsers and purchasers alike.

Some U.S. shopping malls have a good grasp on the concept of atmosphere and entertainment. In the Mall of America, the West Market was developed to provide a European atmosphere, while South Avenue was an attempt to look like a replica of Rodeo Drive and East Broadway was designed as a kind of lotus shape. Of course, at first it might look very cheap or artificial, but the objective is to surprise people and give them something new and different.

As he was developing a new commercial zone in Singapore Inc., Lee Moch Suan, the minister of industry, explained this new development in these terms: "The essence is to brand the 'product' so that people's expectations are met, so that they can experience that branded identity. We have to create an image in this development to provide a sense of unity." Purchasers or browsers alike would likely say that this is what they expect of a new shopping area.

Adjusting the Location to the Luxury Characteristics

As they develop a brief for the definition of a new store concept, retail managers should answer the following questions:

- Is the expected store atmosphere appropriate?
- Is the overall image of the store in line with its price positioning?
- Will it attract people who have already entered the area or is the brand itself a strong one for destination shopping? In each case, the atmosphere of the store might be different.
- How wide and deep is the merchandise assortment, and what does it change in terms of product presentation?
- How many customers can be in the store at the same time?
- How can we facilitate sales staff and consumer interactions in the store?
- What are the additional services needed (alterations or after sales)?

The answer will depend very much on the expected store location, its environment, and its primary target customers.

The Example of London

In his book on retailing, Emanuele Sacerdote[2] gives the example of a study by Management Horizons Europe on the positioning of different London streets for the implantation of a luxury store. Table 5.6 gives an example of this analysis.

The idea is that on top of its effectiveness at generating sales for a given brand, a store's location tends to make a distinct statement of what the brand stands for and what it is: A store location is a strong communication tool. It is an investment in image, and the characteristics it communicates must be understood at the very beginning of the location search analysis.

---

[2]Emanuele Sacerdote, *La strategia retail nella mode e nel lusso* (Milan: Franco Angeli, 2007).

Table 5.6 Positioning of Different London Streets in Terms of Brand Communication

	Classic	Moderately Progressive	Progressive	Trendy
Covent Garden		x	x	
King's Road		x		
Brick Lane			x	x
Regent Street	x			
Bond Street	x	x		
Carnaby Street			x	x
Sloane Street	x	x		
Knightsbridge	x	x		

SOURCE: Management Horizons Europe Project 2006, in Emanuele Sacerdote: *La strategia retail nella mode e nel lusso* (Milan: Franco Angeli, 2007).

The Different Leasing Systems

We will now explain the different leasing systems that exist around the world as well as their business implications. We will then provide some examples of rental costs in different locations in the world.

The Three Major Leasing Systems

To secure a top location in a major luxury target city, it is generally necessary to pay some form of *key money* on top of the standard rent. There are three different setups.

The Japanese Way In Japan, leases are generally signed for a period of nine years, but with a possibility for the lessee to move out every three years. The rental amount is clearly defined in the rental contact with possible escalation clauses, which are stated.

As the lessee signs the rental contract, he must give the lessor an amount of key money equal to the rent for the duration of the lease. For example, for a nine-year lease, he will have to give a check with an amount corresponding to nine years of rent. The lessor can cash the check and give the amount back to the lessee at the end of the renting period. If after nine years the two parties decide to sign another nine-year lease, at a higher rental cost, the lessee would have to write an additional check for this difference for the next nine years.

At the end of the lease, if the lessee wants to get out, he will get his key money back, with no bank interest of any type.

This system is very interesting for the lessor, as, in a way, during the term of the lease he gets almost a double rent in cash. The day he rents out a store, he can bring to the bank the equivalent of nine years of rent payments. In general, 10 to 15 years of rent is the cost of buying or building a store. In fact, the lessor can pay back most of his purchase investment when he leases out his property. He can then buy another store and start again.

For the lessee, the system is extremely costly and renting and opening a new store is a very heavy investment. Renting 10 to 20 stores in Japan would require an almost impossible investment for a luxury brand, even a major one. It would therefore rent one or two stores and develop a network of shop-in-shops with department stores: This is the reason why most of the luxury brands in Japan are in department stores.

On a second level, the luxury brands that were successful decided to start a retail store from scratch. They purchased a piece of land, if possible in a very good location, then built their own store, to their own specifications. Many of them ended up being either megastores or at least impressive flagship stores.

The Japanese key money system was probably at the beginning a system of protection against the development of too many imported foreign brands stores. Over time, it gave an incredible premium to department stores and was a strong incentive to the development of fully owned stores.

The American Way In the American system the lease is signed for a very long duration: 9 to 10 years. There may be some sort of key money paid to the former lessee, officially to cover some decoration costs, but they would remain minimal.

Rent increases are specified at the start of the process and mentioned in the contract. There are no end-of-lease benefits for the lessee and the contract starts as soon at it is signed.

It is important to note that there are no exit clauses in American contracts. That means that if, after three to four months, the lessee realizes that the location was really not that good or that they would never break even with their brand and merchandise in that location, they must still continue to pay the rent for the duration of the lease without any type of possible negotiation. It is, for example, impossible when facing below-budget sales, to ask for a rent decrease. If the decision is made to close the store, then the rent must still be paid. The only way out is to find someone else who will sublet the place, generally for a lower rent, and still pay the difference.

Many people have lived through this difficult situation and have discovered over time the way to beat the system. A foreign luxury firm can create an individual subsidiary that only deals with a given city or even a given store. The day that store really does not perform and must be closed, the solution to escape the financial commitment with the lessor is to file bankruptcy and forget about everything.

Lessors have naturally found a way to prevent that from happening. They sometimes ask for a warranty from headquarters in Milan or in Paris. If the location appears to be very good and desirable, some brand managers may accept such clauses. In other situations they would probably refuse.

The American system is the standard lease system in China, Hong Kong, and most other parts of Southeast Asia, but with much shorter leases (generally three years) so that the financial commitment (and risk) is more acceptable.

The French Way Unlike the Japanese or the American systems that are tilted to the advantage of the lessor, the French system, also used in Southern Europe, works to the advantage of the lessee.

Under the French system (called Fonds de Commerce), once the lessor has signed a lease with a lessee, he receives a monthly rent, but has no other advantage. Every three years, the lessee has the opportunity to move out, but the lessor is committed to rent the property for nine years. Rental leases cannot define rent increases: There is an official national index of building cost increases that defines them.

At the end of a period of nine years, the lessor still cannot get rid of the lessee who wants to stay. He must start a new contract for a new period of nine years with a minimal rent increase.

The lessee can, at any time, find someone who would be interested in renting and ask for a large amount of key money to pass on the lease to this new lessee. He then sends a registered letter to the lessor to tell him he has passed on the store to another person. The lessor cannot take advantage of this change to increase the rent. He may know that a large amount of key money has been negotiated, but it does not affect him in any way.

The only case in which the lessor can have a say in the transfer is if the original lessee had a very limited retail objective for the store, like ready-to-wear or optical. If the second lessee wants his store to be a different kind of retail destination (for example, fast food or mobile phones), then the lessor has the possibility to negotiate this modification of the original lease for something like a rental increase.

The idea of this Fonds de Commerce system is that as a retailer stops his activities and passes on his store, often including its fixtures, merchandise, and customer base, he can move out with a reasonable amount of money. This was very useful at a time when independent retailers had no retirement plans. The Fonds de Commerce key money could give him enough cash to organize a new life. But things change, and now, in Paris, some store locations are presented with "American leases" with no key money and a duration of 10 years.

In France, for top locations, rents are sometimes very old and have never been significantly raised. The adjustment to market price is then done by the amount of key money that has to be paid to the previous lessee. An advantage for a new tenant is that this key money appears on the balance sheet as a company asset and can be financed by a bank loan, with the bank taking a warranty on this asset.

Whatever the system, for top locations that everybody would like to acquire, the best offer will sometimes be higher rent, or a very large amount of key money—or both.

Example of Rents for Top Locations

Specialists frequently publish examples of rental costs for different cities in the world. To make sure data can really be compared, they should include some kind of adjustments based on different key money systems. Figure 5.4 provides an example of these calculations.

One can see that New York and Hong Kong are the most expensive places in the world. In New York, a store of 200 square feet would cost

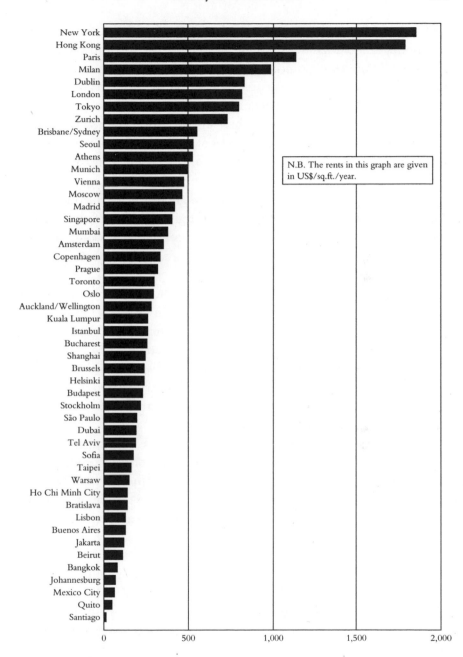

N.B. The rents in this graph are given in US$/sq.ft./year.

Figure 5.4   Rental Costs of the Best Locations in the World

$3.4 million a year. In Tokyo, it would cost half that, but the financing key money amount has not been integrated into the calculations.

Some interesting points: Munich or Madrid rents are basically half the price of those in Paris or Milan. This may explain why we said earlier that many global retailers have stores in those cities. Also, Shanghai is three times cheaper than Tokyo: Specialists consider that the sales per square foot of a luxury retail store in China is three times lower than in Tokyo. The rental costs seems to have been adjusted for that situation.

In fact, on a global level, with all things being equal, one might think that rental costs are basically adjusted to the average expected sales per square foot. The different stores' profitability would also be affected by the average cost of an experienced sales staff in different parts of the world.

Another consideration is the number of hours a store should be open in different parts of the world. In Japan or in China, luxury stores are generally open seven days a week and from 10 A.M. to 10 P.M., that is to say 84 hours a week. In Europe, stores are open six days a week from 10 A.M. to 8 P.M., or 60 hours a week. This 40 percent difference must also be taken into account in the store budget forecast.

Tables 5.7, 5.8, and 5.9 provide examples of the rental costs of top locations in different parts of the world.

Also, as one studies different alternatives, one is confronted with stores that have 100 percent of the floor space on the ground floor and others that have a part in the basement or others that have some space on the second floor. What is the effectiveness of different floors in terms of retail sales? What is a given is that even when there is an escalator, it is difficult be bring customers to the second or the third floor of a store.

An old study, even if it is outdated, has the advantage of answering some of these questions. William Davidson was able to find a document belonging to an American department store to analyze the different levels of rental cost as a function of the floor level. The results are shown in Table 5.10.

What can be seen is that from the ground floor to the second floor, accountants from this Ohio department store considered the space was 50 percent less effective. On the third and fourth floors the discount

Table 5.7 Rents of Top Locations for European Countries (2009)

City	Location	€/sq.m/yr
Paris	Avenue des Champs Elysées	7.732
Milan	Via Montenapoleone	6.800
Rome	Via Condotti	6.500
London	New Bond Street	5.885
Zurich	Bahnofstrasse	5.246
Paris	Rue du Faubourg St Honoré	4.787
Paris	Avenue Montaigne	4.787
Milan	Via della Spiga	4.700
Milan	Corso Vittorio Emanuele	4.600
Dublin	Grafton Street	4.350

Table 5.8 Top Locations in the Americas (2009)

City	Location	€/sq.m/yr
New York	5th Avenue	11.983
New York	Madison Avenue	9.586
New York	East 57th Street	7.190
Los Angeles	Rodeo Drive (Beverly Hills)	4.793
Chicago	North Michigan Avenue	3.395
San Francisco	Union Square	3.195
San Francisco	Post Street	2.796
Chicago	East Oak Street	2.796
Sao Paulo	Iguatemi Shopping	1.596
Vancouver	Robson Street	1.584

was 64 percent in the first case and 72 percent in the second. This is probably an indication of the percentage of people entering a store and moving up to the second, third, or fourth floor.

For the basement, the figure is extremely low: 14 percent. In Europe, people seem to have found ways to make the basement floor and basement merchandising more attractive than in the United States, where it was traditionally seen as a discount and overstock selling place.

Table 5.9 Top Locations in Asia and Australia (2009)

City	Location	€/sq.m/yr
Hong Kong	Causeway Bay	11.687
Hong Kong	Central	9.278
Hong Kong	Tsim Sha Tsui	8.543
Tokyo	Ginza	5.950
Tokyo	Omotesando	5.409
Tokyo	Shibuya	3.516
Sydney	Pitt Street Mail	3.410
Seoul	Myeongdong	2.796
Brisbane	Queen Street Mall	2.864
Seoul	Gangnam Station	2.806

Table 5.10 Rent Allocation per Floor in an Ohio Department Store

	Percentage of Total	Index Compared to Ground Floor
Basement	5.1	14
Ground floor	36.1	100
2	18.2	50
3	13.1	36
4	10.3	28
5	9.3	26
6	3.5	10
Office space	4.4	
	100%	

SOURCE: William Davidson, *Retailing Management* (New York: John Wiley & Sons, 1999).

In fact, the purpose of different store levels has been clearly explained by Ellen Diamond.[3]

• The first floor is generally assigned to impulse products with lower price points than other products sold in the same store, so that

---

[3]William Davidson, *Retailing Management* (New York: John Wiley & Sons, 1999).

they bring people into the store and induce them to purchase a product they would not have on their shopping list. Perfumes and cosmetics are a perfect example of this category. Also, because the space is expensive and a prime location, it is better adapted to high margin items.

- The second floor should present the most profitable products, and generally, ladies' fashion and accessories.
- The third floor could have ladies' designer fashion. These items have a higher ticket price, so it is better if they are sold in a more secluded area of the store, where there is less traffic. It is also a good idea to have the costliest merchandise in a relatively exclusive location.

In conclusion, we have clearly seen that prime locations are expensive and for a global brand, the total fixed costs of rents for 50 to 100 stores can have a huge impact on the yearly profit and loss account. This is why, in some cases, franchising may be an interesting alternative.

As a rule of thumb, there is a ratio that can help an average brand work out what a reasonable amount of rent would be as a percentage of budgeted sales. In Europe it should be around 10 to 20 percent of sales. In Asia the figure is considerably higher, being between 20 and 30 percent of expected sales.

It is often said in retailing that the decisive factor for success is location, location, and location. But opening too many stores at the same time can endanger the financial balance of a company. Also, a new store may need more than two years to reach its first expected sales plateau: During that time and before breakeven can be achieved, new stores require cash and financial support. Therefore, the "company operated stores" strategy is only valid when the products presented in the stores are extremely attractive and can lure local customers easily.

Sometimes, when a luxury brand is working on a relaunch, there is a tendency to open new stores before the new generation of products has been completely finalized. One should not forget that the name of the game is to sell products. How attractive is the present merchandise? And is it adapted to, for example, Asia or the United States? We could mention many brands that had opened beautiful stores in Hong Kong, only to close them 18 months or two years later and at a great cost, since sometimes the rental contract was still running and only a part of the decoration had been depreciated. The same has happened in the United States; after New York and Los Angeles store openings, the American staff of many European brands may push to opening Chicago, Miami, Boston, and San Francisco before the products have been completely tuned in to the American customer.

There's no doubt that location, location, location is very important. But the right merchandise needs to be available in that location, location, location. When this is achieved, you're retailing on easy street.

Chapter 6

Luxury Store Concept and Design

Threshold resistance is what keeps your customer from opening your door and coming in over your threshold. I think we can reduce that with a better design.

—*A. Alfred Traubman*

L uxury brands reinvented themselves the day they decided that they had to sell through company-owned stores and not just through wholesale. This has led them to develop completely new skills—one of which is store concept and store design. To address this critical issue in luxury brand retailing we will examine three major topics:

1. The store concept: Store concepts are the realization of the brand vision. We therefore have to understand the role of the brand vision before we look at the specifics of store design.
2. The store design: This gives us an understanding of both the store format and the importance of store windows.
3. Visual merchandising: This is an art that luxury brands have mastered, as it gives customers the feel of the brand.

Turning Around a Brand: The Store Concept Urgency

When Domenico De Sole became CEO of Gucci in May 1994, one of his very first moves was to redesign the stores: "In December 1994, within six weeks, all stores worldwide had been 'milanized,' that is, redesigned on the model of the Milan store. Small changes, not expensive but which made major impact."[1]

When Gucci bought Yves Saint Laurent in November 1999, the very first thing they did was develop the store network and redesign the standard store format. The model of the new YSL store, designed by Tom Ford and architect William Sofield, was opened in December 2000 at the Bellagio in Las Vegas, the second being the New York Madison Avenue flagship store in September 2001. The number of stores, which was 15 when the brand was bought, grew to 30 a year later and to 40 two years later. In 2010 YSL had 78 stores worldwide.

When Gucci bought Bottega Veneta in February 2001, the brand owned 19 stores. The first new-look flagship store was opened in December 2001 on Madison Avenue. Six more stores—in Paris, Milan, London, San José, Costa Mesa, and Chicago (a move to a more prestigious place in the Hyatt)—and eight stores in Japan were planned for 2002, together with the complete refurbishment of existing stores, all within one year. This means that within two years of its takeover, Bottega Veneta renewed all its stores and doubled their number! In 2010—nine years later—the brand had 148 stores.

---

[1]Les Echos Conference, March 14, 2000.

Stores are where the brand meets the customer. This is where the vision and the style of the brand are expressed. This is where a luxury brand has to invest in CAPEX if it wants to increase its visibility. Brands that do not have the money to do this, or brands that do not appreciate that in-store is where it all happens and stubbornly keep old concepts going, will face serious problems.[2]

All luxury brands revolve around a vision—a *Weltanschauung*. What vision of the world, what meaning, does the brand convey? What makes its statements unique?

How the Giorgio Armani "Vision of the World" Informs Its Store Concept

"My own fashion is in sync with our world. I view my job as a mission: I must not produce anything superfluous, I must show the way, create references."[3]

"It is essential to me to eliminate uselessness, at work, at home, even in my social life. Everything needs to have a purpose and to exist in harmony with its environment. The woman who wears Armani is a subtle individual whose elegance comes from her inner self rather than from showing her breast; she evolves gracefully in a man's suit jacket."[4]

There are three fundamental elements in Giorgio Armani's vision of the world:

1. **Mixing:** Mixing realities: "Fashion today has different realities—women dress in many different ways. Therefore there

(continued)

---

[2]This is the case for Bally, the Swiss brand that Texas Pacific Group bought in October 1999. Having decided to turn it into a luxury brand, they have not had this sense of urgency. After closing down most of the second-rate stores, they were left with 179 stores in July 2001, out of which *two* had the new concept (in Berlin and Singapore) and only 15 had been refurbished along softer and much less luxurious lines!

[3]*Elle*, November 18, 1991.

[4]Ibid.

can't be just one trend, but many can be mixed together."[5] Mixing fashions: "You no longer have one single fashion but a mix of fashions."[6]

2. **Contrast:** Contrasting sensitivities within a single person: "I think that today the most attractive man is that man who accepts ironically a certain sense of insecurity, not being afraid of showing it. . . . I also love imagining him tender, free to express his feelings, his emotions, being shy, as a vital and precious part of his personality."[7] Contrasts between sexes in fashion: "She wanted a men's jacket with the silk satin T-shirt underneath—a very strange mixture at the time."[8] "An elegant woman knows how to play with opposites, associate contrasts. . . ."

3. **Harmony:** "Luxury, today, is no more showing one's power to others. It is more like a harmonious life. Being in harmony with oneself, with one's clothes; harmony must exist in one's home and in those places where we enjoy ourselves. Yes, harmony must link everything, it is my philosophy of life."[9]

Giorgio Armani contrasts the-woman-who-is-herself to the-woman-who-shows-off. Favoring the first, he considers that the clothes he designs must enhance that woman's personality, helping her be harmonious. Her colors should express serenity. Her body being on the move, her clothes should be made to move with her. He wants to dress people who are actors of their own lives and consider themselves as free and autonomous. As Giorgio Armani himself says in one of the articles quoted on the previous page: "Imposing any fashion means having no respect for the person who wears your creations. Personally, I do the opposite.

---

[5] *Harper's Bazaar*, September 1996.
[6] *Elle Décoration*, 1989.
[7] Launch Eau de Toilette, 1984.
[8] *Harper's Bazaar*, September 1996.
[9] *Elle Germany*, September 1991.

My goal is simple: helping people refine their own style through my clothes and avoid turning them into fashion victims."

He applies this philosophy by mixing materials: ("I have invented no shapes, but only the way to mix cloth with shape in some very special combinations: leather and georgette, white silk and coarse tweed"[10]); using neutral colors ("Marrying two beiges seems subtle to me"[11]); eliminating all that is superfluous ("less is more"); mixing shopping interests within his shops ("I wanted a corner for music, newspapers and a small restaurant. I also would have liked to have an art gallery. It must be a meeting point."[12]); and a concept of space ("A part of town dedicated to fashion only is the worst of things"[13]).

This explains why Armani stores are a mixture of beige and grey hues, why the Armani Casa stores are harmonies of brown and beige, and why the Emporio Armani store in Paris was one of the first to sport a restaurant, the Armani Café, which now has an independent entrance. All the brand's store concepts are consistent with the brand vision.

The Store Concept: Implementing the Brand Vision

The number one issue for luxury brands is making sure that their vision is implemented everywhere—and in a consistent manner. (See the Four-Pole Brand Vision in Figure 6.1.) To understand how this impacts the visual merchandising strategy of the brand, we suggest breaking down a luxury brand's activity into four major components:

1. **Production of the Brand Vision:** This is where the ongoing flux of ideas and images that embody the brand vision (or the

---

[10]Madame Figaro, September 19, 1992.
[11]Elle, April 24, 1995.
[12]Marie Claire, February 1998.
[13]Ibid.

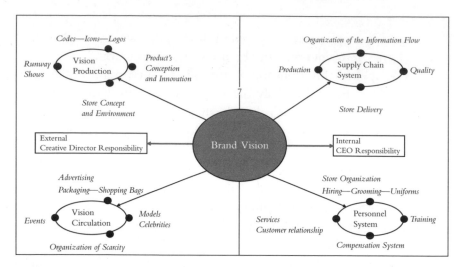

Figure 6.1 The Four-Pole Brand Vision Consistency Model
Source: Michel Gutsatz "Luxe Populi," op.cit.

creator's vision, if he is still at the helm) are created. Major examples are found in runway shows, in products themselves, in the store concept, and, of course, in the codes and icons of the brand (its logo, its iconic products, its corporate color). This explains the critical importance of the store concept itself, because this is where the brand meets the customer on a daily basis.

2. **Circulation of the Brand Vision:** Once the brand vision is created, it has to be transferred, transmitted, and circulated. Key to this circulation is advertising, of course, but also packaging, shopping bags, the use of a "face" (someone who is consistent with the brand, not chosen because she is the person of the moment!), the major events organized by the brand—an anniversary, a product launch, an exhibition. We think, for example, of the diverse strategies used by luxury brands to educate Chinese customers about their heritage, like Louis Vuitton's retrospective exhibition in Shanghai in 2010 or artisan shows that encapsulate the know-how and the quality of the brand (see the case study on luxury and craft displayed in stores in China).

   Both vision production and vision circulation are the direct responsibility of the brand's creative director and are implemented at the store level by the visual merchandisers who are part of the retail image department (see the case study showing the Bally organizational chart). Creative control is maintained by this team at the brand's corporate headquarters, thus developing standardized merchandise presentation and providing visual displays for the windows. They may even design signature music to be used in the stores (see the case study describing the Bally Visual Development Study).

3. **The Supply Chain System:** Once the brand vision exists and is circulated, the complete supply chain system has to be organized consistently and in line with the brand vision. This means, for instance, that new products advertised should be delivered to the stores *before* the advertisements hit the public, not after, in which case sales are lost and the brand's image is impacted negatively.

   One of the authors was witness to such brand damage when he was HR director at Bally. At a meeting of the executive committee, the creative director flew into a rage: "Where are the shopping bags? We have redesigned all the brand identity. We have a new store concept. We have new packaging but the new shopping bags are *not* in the stores! Where are they?"

   No one knew.

   A few days later he was visiting the warehouse and on the floor were huge packages. "What are these?" he asked the logistics manager. "The shopping bags." "But we are looking for them everywhere! Why are they not in the stores?" "Because I have no code for them—you know I can't ship anything without a code! And the IT department tells me they have such a backlog that they have no time to generate a code for *free* items!" (Meet the daily management issues that complicate brand consistency.)

4. **The Personnel System:** All this needs people. Building a luxury brand consistently needs people with the right competencies, a store organization in line with the brand image, and a precise definition of the sort of customer relationship the brand wants to tap into. We examine all these issues in Chapters 10 and 11.

   These last two topics are the direct responsibility of the CEO and his functional teams.

**Case Study: Luxury and Craft Displayed
in Stores in China**

In partnership with the French Chamber of Commerce, Hong
Kong hosted the 2010 edition of "Boutique Boulevard: So Lush, So
Central"—the rendezvous event for luxury brands in Hong Kong.

From May 14 to May 23, the most famous brands organized a
series of meetings with luxury professionals who were able to display their savoir-faire to their numerous fans in Hong Kong, and
share their exceptional universe with them.

The event that opened with an evening reserved for the
happy few took place in the most dynamic sector of Hong Kong,
the Central District. The itinerary ran through the district, link-
ing the various malls dedicated to luxury brands and allowing
people to wander from one boutique to the other and watch various demonstrations:

- A workshop (Scents & Sensibility) proposed by Guerlain and
  conducted by one of the creators of L'Instant by Guerlain,
  Ms. Sylvaine Delacourte, who showed why and how to wear
  a fragrance.
- A workshop dedicated to the art of shaving (twice), presented by
  the barber of the prestigious Mandarin Oriental, Angel Gonzales.
- Advice from the esteemed French sommelier, Pierre Legrandois.
- A number of brands, from Dunhill and Tiffany to Armani,
  Cartier, and Gucci, along with Louis Vuitton, offered workshops in dressmaking and presentation with tips on fashion
  and etiquette.

This event also echoed the Savoir Faire Exhibition held from
April 30 to May 2 by Dior in Hong Kong for its new Rosewood
jewelry collection. Held for the first time in Paris the previous
year, the Dior Savoir Faire exhibition helped to firmly establish
its unique jewelry pieces as an expression of the expertise and the
creative passion of Dior.

Encouraged by the success of the Paris event, three jewelry
craftsmen made the trip to Hong Kong in order to demonstrate

their expertise and display the new Rosewood collection. This collection, designed by Victoire de Castellane, consists of 13 items and paid tribute to Christian Dior's favorite flowers: the roses from his garden at Milly-la-Forêt.

Where does this obsession for luxury brands to organize this type of event stem from? What advantage do they gain?

This type of "seduction operation" that presents the savoir-faire of the most prestigious brands is very popular and highly appreciated in Asia. Indeed, with the increasing numbers of Chinese nouveaux riches, luxury brands try to teach their current and future clients about the values on which their reputation in Europe is based. These values, crafts, expertise, and the demonstrations of the meticulous gestures of skilled workers validate their legitimacy and the prices established by the famous houses.

This display of manufacturing procedures, the immersion in the history, and the discovery of the universe of the brand go hand in hand. Once the client has been convinced that the product is well made and of quality, he or she has to be persuaded to adhere to the image of the brand and to what it projects. This process takes more time than a simple act of seduction, but if it is successful, customer loyalty will follow and they will be convinced that they have placed their trust in a quality brand that closely reflects their own personal values.

Furthermore, organizing commercial operations of this caliber in a group can also attract considerable media coverage and turn Hong Kong into a meeting point for luxury in Asia. In fact, China and Hong Kong are generally very fond of spectacular promotional events that create a buzz. In an environment where one-upmanship is always present, luxury brands in Asia usually try to be more imaginative than their neighbors and will consistently strive to raise the bar of their events.

Even though luxury brands do not always attract customers in the immediate aftermath of these events, they will still have initiated a few of them. The visitors who turn up out of curiosity, and who might not correspond to the core clientele targeted by the brands, are nonetheless likely to be fascinated by the universe of a brand and become its customers as soon as they are able. This preliminary approach to a clientele that is less aware also helps to demystify access to some of these famous luxury brands, which is often seen as intimidating.

Store Formats: Closed or Open?

The traditional luxury brand store is a closed store, which is to be entered through a glass door. There are, however, different formats possible, ranging from closed to very closed format, all based on the window concept:

- A closed window, with no view of the inside of the store, and a door that opens only on request: This is the traditional format for all jewelry and watch stores—like the green jewelry format that Cartier used to display in most of its stores.
- An open window, displaying products, with a removable back that gives only a partial view of the inside of the store. This is now the standard for luxury stores in fashion and leather goods. It can also be used by jewelry brands—as seen with the Cartier slate display format in Faubourg Saint Honoré in Paris.
- An open see-through window that allows the customer to envision the whole store when standing outside: This is the case for the Versace store on Fifth Avenue in New York.

Each of these formats will generate a different relationship between the customer and the brand, which will very much depend on the familiarity of the customer with the brand (see Table 6.1).

Democratization of luxury means also that potential customers, not familiar with the brand, must be able to access it without feeling rejected or intimidated. The open window format is, therefore, much more suited to new customers. There exists a fourth store concept, the open store, which is the ultimate in welcoming unfamiliar customers: No door and no windows hinder the entrance. There are two examples of such stores:

1. Almost all the travel retail stores in airports have this format: People can come in without having to push a door open. All studies show that this facilitates access to luxury brands for nontraditional customers. Even jewelers like Cartier and Bulgari adopt these open stores in their airport locations.

Table 6.1   Store Format and Brand–Customer Relationship

	Familiar Customers	**Nonfamiliar Customers**
Closed window	They will feel at ease and sheltered from the rest of the world in a very exclusive environment.	They will feel totally unwelcome and will not even push the door open.
Open window		A good compromise to entice nonfamiliar customers to enter.
Open see-through window		They will feel more comfortable and can anticipate what will happen inside.

2. Sephora, the perfume and cosmetics distributor, has adopted this format. Their Paris Champs Elysées flagship is a perfect example and warrants comparison with the traditional Guerlain *parfumerie* that is 50 meters down the avenue. Both occupy approximately the same width but entering the Guerlain store can be trying: First comes a very heavy door behind which is a guard; this is flanked by two traditional windows through which the customer can see that it is a small store in which there are up to four salespeople (see Figure 6.2). The whole effect is very intimidating.

Sephora, on the other hand, is an open portal on the avenue, with a soft slope that draws you into the store. The guard is very discreetly placed and there is a constant flow of visitors from the street into the store and out: There is no barrier to entry (see Figure 6.3). As a result you will see customers inside who would never enter the Guerlain store next door. And they will likely buy their Guerlain perfumes and cosmetics at Sephora!

Store Customization and Flagships

A major credo of all luxury brands is that they have to have similar stores worldwide, so as to create a unique brand image that customers will immediately recognize. Prada is a perfect example: The control

Figure 6.2   The Guerlain Store
SOURCE: Photo by Michel Gutsatz.

Figure 6.3   The Sephora Store
SOURCE: Photo by Michel Gutsatz.

syndrome developed by the brand has led it to not only have similar formats for their stores (mint green paint and ice color carpets), but also similar formats for their offices.

This strategy was fine-tuned in the early years of this century. Brands that considered themselves to be strong decided to move forward, Prada being, as it often is, a pioneer in this field. In 1999 it commissioned Rem Koolhaas on three projects: a new 22,680-square-foot store in the former Guggenheim Soho space in New York; a redesigned 20,520-square-foot Los Angeles store, and the 43,200-square-foot San Francisco store. Other architects, Herzog & de Meuron, who gained fame for the Tate Modern project in London, redesigned the Tokyo store, as well as Prada's New York offices and the Tuscan factory headquarters.

"This is an exceptional project," Miuccia Prada said in a *WWD* interview "We believe that many brands now have stores that look alike—and that's just boring. We wanted to develop an experimental store. We wanted to ask, 'What does shopping mean?' We understand that customers today enjoy shopping, that it's become a way to socialize and communicate."

Prada introduced a new concept here, which they called epicenter stores—and which has now been generalized throughout all luxury brands as flagship stores. They are those stores that will be used to help define the brand and show customers the ostentation, the space, the lavishness a luxury brand is capable of. As Rem Koolhaas said: "The danger of the large number is repetition. Each additional store reduces the aura and contributes to a sense of familiarity. The danger of the larger scale is the Flagship syndrome: a megalomaniac accumulation of the obvious that eliminates the last elements of surprise and mystery that cling to the brand, imprisoning it in a 'definitive' identity. But expansion can also be used for a redefinition of the brand. By introducing two kinds of stores—the typical and the unique—the epicenter store becomes a device that renews the brand by counteracting and destabilizing any received notion of what Prada is, does, or will become. The epicenter store functions as a conceptual window: a medium to broadcast future directions that positively charges the larger mass of typical stores."[14]

---

[14]Projects for Prada, Part 1.

Typically, flagship stores can be five to eight times larger than standard stores, can extend over much more than the traditional one floor, and can include more than just a store. The Chanel Ginza flagship in Tokyo, which opened in 2005, has 10 floors. As *Architectural Record* mentions: "Functioning as a 21st-century branding billboard, the building is a conceptual rendering of a classic Chanel tweed," says principal architect Peter Marino. "The design team's primary objective was to create a contemporary, iconic architectural expression of the Chanel ethos. At 215 feet, the building is the tallest in the upscale Ginza shopping district. The 10-story building comprises a three-level Chanel retail boutique, a fourth-floor exhibition and concert space, rental offices on the upper floors, a gourmet restaurant on the penthouse level, and a multifunction rooftop garden terrace."[15]

A marketing director who was interviewed about flagships once said, "The rules of luxury retailing are clear. Space, and what we call 'the extravagant use of the empty space,' defines a luxury experience. By having commercially inactive space we signal exclusivity, luxury and an extravagance that is at the heart of luxury."[16]

These distinctive spaces can also help the brand build its reputation through a unique mix:

• Historical buildings: This allows part of the history of the building to embed itself in the brand's own history. The foremost example, and the first of its kind, was the acquisition by Ralph Lauren of the Rhinelander Mansion in 1986. This 20,000-square-foot flagship was owned by a major New York aristocratic family in the early twentieth century. Turning it into a store, complete with original fixtures, paintings, and furniture, gives the brand unmistakable cachet that proves its legitimacy— that of the WASP lifestyle. Ralph Lauren's headquarters on Madison Avenue prove it further: The lobby in mahogany is (as the commissioned architects said) "redolent of the first class lounge on the *Normandy*."

---

[15]http://archrecord.construction.com/projects/lighting/archives/0511chanel.asp.
[16]C. Moore et al., "Flagship Stores as a Market Entry Method: The Perspective of Luxury Fashion Retailing," *European Journal of Marketing* 44, no. 1/2 (2010), 139–161.

- Working with famous architects: "Luxury brands are the new patrons of architecture—we have taken over from the popes and royalty!"[17] Since the early 2000s, all major luxury brands have been working with big-name architects—both because it has a positive impact on the brand's image and because it gives them a strong innovative push as they tap into the architects' creativity.

Developing the brand's image means having excellent relationships with the press, and the fashion press specifically. Flagship stores have a role there, which can be best understood with this fascinating counter-example: One retailer explained that when their London flagship was closed (due to untenable operating costs), the British fashion press abandoned all coverage of the brand and, according to the company, sales in their other outlets were adversely affected: "The press need a place to connect with the brand. When we closed our store, it was as if we were wiped from the journalists' memories. It was incredible. It did not matter what we tried to do, we just did not matter to them anymore. We had to quickly reverse the decision because no press coverage is just terrible for luxury brand sales."[18]

These flagship stores have yet another role: They support the relationship that the brand has with its other distributors. The existence of a new store concept—created by a famous architect—can provide leverage when a brand wishes its license partners or distributors to upgrade their stores and can be used as a showcase to recruit and retain wholesale customers: "It is very clear to us that the flagship store has an important role to play in the development of a wholesale business. When we opened a flagship in Shanghai, the impact upon our wholesale business was incredible. If we refurbish the flagships we also know that we will attract more than one hundred new wholesale customers as a result."[19] The flagship is where the brand trains its franchisees and informs them about new collections and about the launch of new product ranges; it is where it exhibits the new merchandising strategy that wholesalers will have to adopt at some point.

---

[17]Ibid.
[18]Ibid.
[19]Ibid.

Flagship stores and new store concepts are therefore at the heart of the very complex relationships that are built between a brand, its customers, its distributors, and the press. It is a very costly decision to launch a new store concept and invest in a flagship store, but the returns are there: One should never evaluate such an investment by its sales figures only!

Store Windows

As Scott Fellows, former creative director of Bally, once said to one of the authors: "Why do you think I display blue and red shoes in the men's windows? Because this will draw customers inside the store and they will leave with a pair of black or brown shoes!"

In the art of selling, store windows play a very important role: This is the first visual contact the customer has with the brand and its products. Windows can stop passersby in their tracks and draw them into the store. One day one of the authors was walking in Soho in New York, when his eyes were drawn to . . . a blank window. Across the street from where he stood was a shop with a blank windowpane. This was contrary to everything he had in mind concerning visual merchandising, so he crossed the street. As he came nearer the window he started seeing what was inside, and when in front of it he had the full view of the interior of the store! This is a fascinating example of how a brand in the early 2000s mastered the intricacies of the relationship a window can establish with a passerby: Issey Miyake's Pleats Please had used a new glass technology to astonish and draw attention to its brand and products.

A few years later (late 2005) Abercrombie & Fitch once again reinvented the absence of a window: Its new Fifth Avenue flagship sported closed windows. No product was shown. More than 10 windows— a precious asset at such an expensive location—were blacked out. Instead, customers were drawn to the entrance of the store with blaring music.

The window is where emotion starts.

How many luxury brands—outside their flagship stores—develop windows that reinforce the brand image and strengthen the emotional bond with their customers? Too few.

How many brands use their store windows to inform the customers and to instill in them the knowledge of the brand? One of the authors was recently quite surprised when, in the window of the

Bally New Bond Street store, he saw pictures of nineteenth- and early twentieth-century shoe models that the brand created. Within a few seconds the message had been conveyed.

How many luxury brands do what Bonwit Teller department stores did in the 1930s: commission artists to design their windows—with Salvador Dali, Man Ray, and Marcel Duchamp among others? And going on in the 1950s, Andy Warhol?

Most brands just use store windows as product displays. Luxury brands have more to tell their customers and all passersby. They should use these windows to prove their uniqueness and build an emotional relationship. This is exactly what Hermès has been doing with Leila Menchari's extraordinary creations and what Paul Smith does with most of his stores: create emotion. Making the viewer wish he or she could enter and be part of the story.

Visual Merchandising and the Corporate Brand Image

Store windows are an important part of the visual merchandising of the brand. Luxury brands have transformed what was once one of the major traits of department stores into a key constituent of their corporate brand image. They have learned that every detail is important and that specific teams—the visual merchandisers—are required to implement, at store level, the artistic directions decided at the corporate level. The very best way to understand this is to examine a case one of the authors experienced in the Bally organization as it was implemented in 2000, strongly influenced by U.S. department stores.

The Bally Retail Image Management Organizational Chart

The retail image management team included both a global team and regional teams, who implemented the corporate image directions in each store.

(continued)

The global team was directly under the supervision of the creative director and was named Retail Image Management (see Figure 6.4). It consisted of:

- A global visual merchandiser coordinator.
- Four corporate visual merchandisers for fully owned stores.
- One corporate window dresser for fully owned stores.
- One VM coordinator for wholesale and duty-free stores.

We immediately understand the importance given to window dressing, as a specific visual merchandiser's work is dedicated to windows.

- Four visual merchandisers/window dressers for Europe.
- Four visual merchandisers/window dressers for Asia and the United States.

When in a store, visual merchandisers have to verify how their directions are implemented by the store managers. They therefore need specific documents. The document shown in

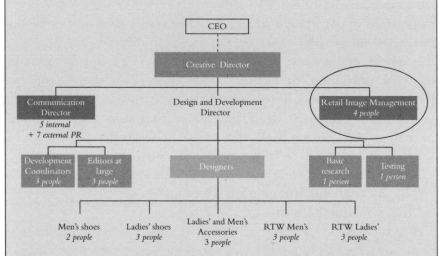

Figure 6.4   Bally Retail Image Management Organizational Chart

SOURCE: Michel Chevalier and Gerald Mazzalovo, *Luxury Brand Management, a World of Privilege* (Hoboken, NJ: John Wiley & Sons, 2008).

Figure 6.5 is an example of a form filled in by the corporate visual merchandiser after visiting a store.

COUNTRY	**FRANCE**	CITY	**PARIS**
BRANCH NAME	**ETOILE**	DATE	**14.03.01**
BRANCH MANAGER		IN STORE VM	
REGIONAL MANAGER		CLUSTER MANAGER	
VM REPRESENTATIVE			

PILOT STORE ☑   NON PILOT STORE ☐

	1	2	3	4	5
	v.poor	poor	acceptable	good	excellent
General Status of the Branch:	☐	☐	☑	☐	☐
Windows:	☐	☐	☑	☐	☐
Impact:	☐	☐	☑	☐	☐
Men's Dept:	☐	☐	☑	☐	☐
Ladies' Dept:	☐	☐	☑	☐	☐
Maintenance:	☐	☐	☑	☐	☐
Staff Presentation:	☐	☐	☐	☑	☐
Staff Support:	☐	☐	☐	☐	☑

TOTAL SCORE: 27/40

Manager feedback on current status of the branch (if applicable):

Stock level:	v.poor	poor	acceptable	good	excellent
	☐	☐	☑	☐	☐
Pictures Taken:	Before ☐		After ☐	Before & After ☑	

Figure 6.5   Bally Visual Development Study Document

(continued)

A month later, the visual merchandiser came back and his comments proved the local team had understood the visual directions:

VM Comments

The store is in good condition.

The blocks that we ordered during our previous visit have been delivered.

We renewed the layout, which will increase the number of options on display.

X has been very helpful and we would like her to be the in-store Visual Merchandiser.

Conclusion

Prada epicenter stores and every branded flagship store are templates of "wow" stores. But are they anything other than examples of brands trying to impress other brands? Can they not be viewed simply as part of the escalating battle for customers' dwindling attention? Koolhaas versus Gehry, or Droog versus Future Systems may be just an expensive version of brands fighting each other. Is the customer merely a hostage to "a spiraling upwards of grooviness which tends to take the customer out of the equation—it is art director talking to art directors and designers to designers. The customer has increasingly become a spectator of the circus rather than the focus."[20] Our contention here is that the attention that luxury brands lavish on store concepts and visual merchandising—however important, as we have seen—is not the be-all and end-all. Whenever service is not the main focus, the customer will be excused from the frame, except to be asked how impressed she or he is by a store which is, ultimately, nothing but décor.

[20]Simon Doonan, former creative director of Barneys New York, in www.salon.com/life/style/2001/06/25/retail_redesign.

Chapter 7

Luxury Store Economics

Marketing managers are increasingly being held accountable
for their investment.

—*Philip Kotler*

L ike any corporation, a store must be organized, budgeted, run, and controlled. We explained earlier that for good reason, many stores in the United States were run by a separate subsidiary of a foreign group, created only to manage each outlet in an independent way. This may be the way people think about their stores in general: individual businesses with original investments, inventories, employees, and daily operations. This is why budgeting is so important: There is a fundamental requirement to analyze at the outset the viability of a project and to follow it regularly.

The aspect of control is also very important. When a brand owns and operates from 100 to 500 stores in the world, it must make sure it knows where the cash is, where the inventories are, and how the sales are recorded, if possible, with the right margin.

To run a group of stores, it is necessary to look at major operating criteria.

In a study conducted in 2010 by the A.T. Kearney consulting group,[1] executives of 53 major U.S. retailers were asked what customer information they were diligently gathering and analyzing for the running of their stores.

Figure 7.1 shows the major findings of the study. Not surprisingly, the number of transactions per store (also called the number of cash register tickets) is the most common operations criterion, followed by the average size of the transactions (also called the average ticket). After the total amount of sales, this a clear indication of a store's activity: How many people made a purchase yesterday?

The third criterion is the number of store visits: How many people have entered the store? How attractive is it to people passing by? This is an indication of the pulling power of the store and of the

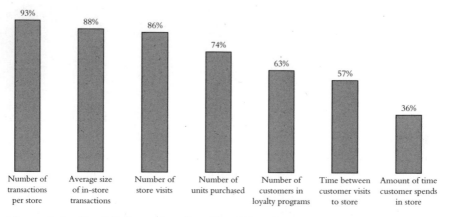

Figure 7.1 Retail Information Considered Very Important
SOURCE: A. T. Kearney, "Achieving Excellence in Retail Operations," study, 2010.

---

[1] A. T. Kearney, "Achieving Excellence in Retail Operations," study, 2010.

appropriateness of its location. These three criteria are clearly followed by every retail executive, which is no surprise.

The fourth criterion, also followed by almost everybody in the trade, is the number of units purchased. This measure deals with the effectiveness of the sales staff (are they able to sell an additional complementary item?) and of the merchandising setup (are socks and shoe polish items attractive enough, so that everyone buying a pair of shoes is also tempted to purchase some socks?).

None of these four criteria is surprising, and they are described at length in this chapter: They are the main variable of retail economics and merchandising control. But the following criteria are somewhat of a surprise.

Sixty-three percent of retail executives look carefully at the number of customers in loyalty programs. This indicates that most of these executives have implemented loyalty programs in their stores and that they view them as a very important part of their business. The lesson for those who do not have a loyalty program may be to see how one can be implemented, even in a luxury environment where products are supposed to play hard to get.

The last two criteria, the least important, relate to consumer behavior. The time between customer visits to the store is considered "very important" by 57 percent of the respondents: They want to see how often their stores are visited (and by whom? regular customers, average customers, or lapsed customers, for example?) which will help define the most logical duration of merchandising programs. Should the store bring new products, new presentations, or new show windows every week, every month, or six to eight times a year? The frequency of client visits will define the most adequate program.

The last criterion also relates to customer behavior in the store: How long do they stay? Do they feel comfortable? Are they happy to be there? How long can they stay in line for the cash register before becoming uncomfortable? All these issues are discussed in this chapter.

In the first section, we present the basic retail business model and the basic retail ratios, then we look at stock purchases and margin control to discuss the basic information systems required, and we finally present a useful follow-up system.

The Retail Business Model

In this section, we describe break-even analysis, the concept of margin, and then the cash flow needs for different retail systems and we finish with an example of store performance.

The Break-Even Analysis

Figure 7.2 provides an example of break-even analysis. One can say that breakeven is reached when gross margin resulting from sales is equal to the sum of all fixed costs necessary to make those sales.

In this illustration the fixed costs (shop rent plus sales staff salaries plus fixed miscellaneous costs) are represented on a horizontal line. They do not vary with the level of sales. A first line indicates the level of sale. A second line indicates the gross margin. In the example shown, we have assumed that the gross margin is 50 percent of sales. At one point, S1, the gross margin line resulting from sales, crosses the horizontal line of fixed costs. At that point the gross margin is equal to the fixed costs. Up to that level of sales, the store is losing money and

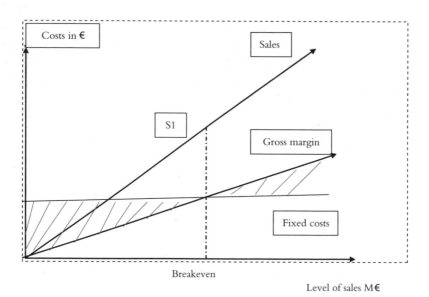

Figure 7.2   Break-Even Analysis

for different levels of sales the losses can be identified by the triangle between the horizontal line of fixed costs and the gross margin line. Above the S1 level of sales, the gross margin is the triangle above the line of fixed costs below the line of gross margin.

There is, therefore, a simple relationship between the projected level of sales for a given retail location and the fixed costs associated with this location. The following scenario illustrates this clearly. Every brand would like to have a very large store in a prime retail location—for example, a 3,000-square-foot store on avenue Montaigne in Paris. But in that location, the rent is probably around 1,000 euros per square foor per year. The rent would therefore be 3 million euros per year. Sales staff cost, for eight people, would be around 400,000 euros per year including miscellaneous fixed costs. This store would therefore have fixed costs around 3.4 million euros per year. Using a gross margin of 50 percent, this store would break even at a level of sales of 6.8 million euros. Can a given brand reach that level of sales easily? If not, can it afford to open a store in that location? Yet one could argue that the very best locations and the most expensive ones provide better levels of sales than a small street in a Paris suburb, where the rental cost for a store of the same size would probably be 180,000 euros per year. Perhaps the solution is to shoot for a smaller store, say an 800-square-foot one, on avenue Montaigne: Then the rent would be 800,000 euros, a smaller staff would cost 200,000 euros and the breakeven could be around 1 million euros. It may be easier to reach this level of sales, but it is still a lot. Another option may be to use this small avenue Montaigne store as a flagship store, with sales around 1 million euros to break even, and to have two shop-in-shops at Printemps and Bon Marché where the brand would have only variable costs and would be able to bring a net margin above 500,000 euros. The set of the three locations (one flagship freestanding store on avenue Montaigne and two shop-in–shops) could then break even and the brand would be able to develop a strong profitable presence in Paris. But let's not forget that in Bon Marché and Printemps the brand would not have its full margin. It would have to share it with the department store operators, so the level of sales in these two locations would have to be relatively high in order for the total to reach break-even.

Setting up retail stores is in fact a trade-off between rental costs and expected sales. Very few brands can afford to be in the very best locations with very large stores. All brands have to look at what makes sense for them at a given time. For each store, aside from the necessary break-even analysis, three elements can be considered the key performances indicators:

1. Sales per square foot
2. Number of stock-keeping units per square foot
3. Sales per full-time sales staff equivalent

These criteria allow a brand to roughly compare one of their retail outlets to another.

Margin Analysis

Retailers are always discussing gross margin, which is the difference between the retail price and the product cost. But it could be expressed in different ways.

It could be a markdown, that is to say, a percentage of the profit divided by the retail price, as it appears in Table 7.1—30 percent. It could also be a markup, or a percentage of the profit divided by the cost of the product, or 42.8 percent as shown in the same table. In retailing, people use the markdown exclusively as it is easier to follow and to compare with the level of sales.

The Concept of Coefficient

Sometimes retailers do not speak of gross margins, but of coefficients instead. A retail coefficient is the retail price divided by the cost of the product sold. In luxury fashion, a retailer will generally work with a

Table 7.1 Margin Analysis

	Markdown	Markup
Retail price	100 percent	100 percent
Cost	70 percent	70 percent
Margin	30 percent	42.8 percent

coefficient of 2.4 or 2.6. This could be directly translated in gross margin percentage, as it is done in Table 7.2.

In fact, coefficients of 2.4 and 2.6 correspond to gross margins of 58.3 percent and 61.5 percent, quite similar to the 60 percent we used previously.

Inventory Turnover

In describing the direct cost of operating a store, we haven't yet mentioned the cold hard fact that the merchandise found in a given store has to be purchased and financed.

The inventory turnover is the ratio of yearly sales to average inventory during the year. Table 7.3 gives examples of types of inventory turnover for different businesses.

Supermarkets have merchandise that goes rapidly out the door and in some product categories it is delivered almost every day. Their inventory can turn around 12 times a year. In addition, because they

Table 7.2 Retail Coefficients and Gross Margins

	Coefficients of	
	2.4	2.6
Retail price	240	260
Purchase price	100	100
Absolute margin	140	160
Gross margin in %	58.3%	61.5%

Table 7.3 Examples of Inventory Turnover

	Supermarket	Fashion Store	Jewelry Store
Yearly sales	1,000,000	1,000,000	1,000,000
Average inventory at cost	83,000	250,000	1,000,000
Inventory turnover	12	4	1
Accounts receivable	90 days	90 days	90 days
Inventory financing needs	(+333,000)	(−187,500)	(−750,000)

have 90-day terms of payment, at the end of the year they could still owe one of their suppliers three months of inventory.

- With this system, the supermarket inventory is more than paid entirely by the suppliers, as the store has a positive cash flow situation of 333,000 euros, as indicated in Table 7.3.
- On the contrary, a jewelry store requires a full year of inventory at any time to be able to offer a large enough selection of jewels to make a sale. Their suppliers help them a bit in their financing, but they still need to permanently invest 750,000 euros to make sales of 1 million euros.
- A fashion store would be somewhat in between. With an inventory that turns four times a year, they have to finance 187,500 euros to make yearly sales of 1 million euros.
- This is obviously an additional cost of operating retail stores when the merchandise is sold at wholesale to a multi-brand retailer or to a department store; the retail inventory financing is paid by them at no cost for the brand. When the brand deals mainly with its own retail stores, it must take into account this situation and finance it. This investment is extremely heavy for jewelers and has to be taken into account in the development of a retailing strategy.

What should the mix therefore be of fully owned retail stores, shop-in-shops, corners, or wholesale activities? This is obviously a crucial strategic decision and economic constraints are a very important part of that decision.

When we speak of a mix of systems, people sometimes have difficulties understanding what this generally means. The feeling that all luxury brands are sold in company-operated freestanding stores is so strong that people have a tendency to forget the real situation: Most luxury fashion products are sold outside of freestanding stores. In Table 7.4, we present the situation of three different brands, with different strength and attractiveness: Chanel, Givenchy, and Pierre Balmain.

At first sight, the three brands have a relatively similar number of points of sales, going from 155 to 286, but of course the volume is quite different and the setups are completely different.

With 135 freestanding stores, the largest number of them in Europe, Chanel has a strong presence. As can be seen in Table 7.5, two countries,

Table 7.4   Fashion Retail Setup for Three Different Brands (number of stores)

	Freestanding Stores	Shop-in-Shops	Multi-Brand Stores	Total
Chanel	135	151	0	286
Givenchy	23	70	123	216
Balmain	1	17	137	155

SOURCE: Websites, 2011.

Table 7.5   Chanel Fashion Retail Setup

	Freestanding Stores	Shop-in-Shops	Total
Americas			
United States	22	85	107
Other	6	4	10
Asia and Oceania			
Korea	16	0	16
Japan	9	31	40
China	6	0	6
Others in Asia	21	9	30
Oceania	6	0	6
Europe	40	18	58
Middle East	9	4	13
	135	151	286

SOURCE: Company website, 2011.

the United States and Japan, rely heavily on shop-in-shops in department stores (116 of a total of 151, or 77 percent). They are much stronger in other Asian countries than in China and have probably decided to grow in this new territory.

Givenchy, as shown in Table 7.6, is basically a strong department store brand with only 23 freestanding stores (some of them probably franchised) and more than half of its points of sale in multi-brand stores.

Pierre Balmain, with only one freestanding store, in Paris, remains basically a multi-brand store brand.

Table 7.6 Givenchy Fashion Retail Setup

	Freestanding Stores	Shop-in-Shops	Multi-Brand Stores	Total
Europe				
France	3	8	16	7
Rest of Europe	1	7	38	6
United States	—	28	32	60
Japan	1	5	14	20
China	8	6	1	15
Other	10	16	22	48
Total	23	70	123	216

SOURCE: Company website, 2011.

In each case, the retail emphasis is completely different:

- For Chanel, the emphasis must be on keeping the balance between freestanding and shop-in-shop locations, developing sales in department stores and managing the brand attractiveness.
- For Givenchy, the emphasis is obviously in the development of shop-in-shop businesses and increasing the number of freestanding stores.
- For Pierre Balmain, the story is different; the emphasis is on the slow translation of activities from multi-brand points-of-sale to shop-in-shops and in the creation of some freestanding stores.

The point here is that there is not one single retail strategy, but a business plan adapted to the strength and the cash availability of different brands.

Comparing the Performances of Different Stores

What makes some stores profitable when others are losing money can be attributed to many factors. To go from a profitable store to an unprofitable one, one must move only two or three variables that seem secondary—but the final result can be quite different. In Table 7.7, we give an example of this.

Table 7.7 High Performers versus Low Performers

	A	B
	Strong Performer	**Poor Performer**
Size of the store	2,000 sq. ft.	2,000 sq. ft.
Sales	1.600,000 €	800,000 €
Sales per square foot	800 €	400 €
Gross margin	€ 50%	€ 40%
Rental cost per year	300,000 €	400,000 €
Sales staff cost	300,000 €	350,000 €
Operating margin	200,000 €	−430,000 €

Store B is losing 53.75 percent on sales, which is an awful situation. What are the reasons for such a bad performance?

- The sales per square foot, which are much too low and are responsible for most of the problem.
- The gross margin, which is 10 percent lower than in store A. Actually, when sales are not being made, the staff is generally frustrated; they do whatever they can to make sure the cash register rings and they have a tendency to grant price discounts. Also, if the store is poorly located, customers may be stingy and buy the cheap, low margin products rather than the most profitable ones.
- Obviously, the rent is too high relative to the sales productivity of location B.
- Sales staff costs not being controlled and are not in line with the level of sales.

This example serves to illustrate how difficult it is to make money when everything is not aligned. Store B is quite certainly a mistake. It should be closed. But the store manager has good explanations for his or her performance: There was major street work in front of the store, making it difficult for customers to enter, and the merchandise was not adapted to the customer base of this location. Next year the street work will be finished, product assortment mistakes will be corrected, and we will break even.

Should you believe that? Retailing decisions boil down to this kind of problem. Should you trust everybody? When should you call the end of the game? When everything goes fine, retailing is very easy. When things start to get out of balance, that's another story.

The Basic Retail Ratios

Let's look at some general concepts and then at sales forecasting systems.

General Retailing Concepts

The attraction coefficient is the percentage of people passing on the street, in front of the store, and entering the store.

This coefficient is very useful in a shopping mall, as it represents the immediate pulling power of the brand among potential shoppers. It is less meaningful for strong destination brands if they are freestanding, although a very strong brand may be interested in measuring the percentage of people entering a luxury mall and visiting its store. Measuring the attraction coefficient for other brands in the same site is also quite useful.

How large is this figure? It depends on the location and the type of brand. Before opening their flagship store at the very top of Champs Elysées in Paris, Montblanc people counted 80,000 people passing the store on a weekday. How many are just looking straight at the Arc de Triomphe, trying to find a way to the underpass entry? But even if, given the make up of that crowd and the brand positioning, they have an attraction coefficient of 0.1 percent or 0.3 percent, that still amounts to 80 to 240 customers entering the store each day. Not bad!

The beauty of the attraction coefficient is that for a given brand in a similar neighborhood and shopping environment, this attraction coefficient should be more or less stable: By counting the number of people walking past a potential location, you can have a general indication of the number of customers that may end up walking through the door.

The conversion ratio is the percentage of customers buying something over the number of people entering the store. This ratio is obtained by counting the number of people entering a store and comparing it to the number of sales receipts recorded by the cash register.

The conversion rate can never be 100 percent, as one counts the number of people entering a store and people often go shopping together—a man and a woman, or a couple with kids, or two friends—but they will make only one purchase. Therefore, a supermarket has a conversion ratio around 80 percent. But an art gallery has a probable conversion ratio of less than 1 percent.

Counting people as they enter a store is sometimes done by security people, who have counters in their pockets. In mass-market stores, there is sometimes an individual light linked to a mechanical counter at the entrance door. If not, it is possible to have the cashier record the information as he or she sees people entering the store.

For luxury goods, the conversion rate should be rather high for destination stores and lower for others. A ratio of 60 percent would be excellent and 30 percent would probably be on the low side.

This conversion ratio is very useful for forecasting sales for a new store in a country or a city in which the brand already operates. Also, by combining the attraction coefficient and the conversion rate, it is possible to predict how many customers would buy in a new prospective location.

If one store has a conversion ratio that is much lower than the other stores of the same brand, this would probably indicate that the new location is not optimal for the brand or to its type of merchandise: Perhaps the prices are wrong or the merchandise is not adapted to the type of shoppers.

The average ticket is self-explanatory. Multiplying by the number of receipts provides your daily sales figure and can also include other indications like the average number of purchased items. As one records the average ticket per individual sales staff, it is also possible to compare the efficiency of different individuals on the shop floor.

The percent of repeat customers can also be obtained through a customer database and is an indication of the quality of services in a given store or the strength of the merchandising mix.

The Use of These Concepts

Counting the number of people entering a store (which can be done from a car parked across the street or a bench in a shopping center) and multiplying it, first by the conversion ratio then by the average ticket, provides an indication of how many sales a given store can make in a day or in a week. Is it easy to assess the conversion ratio? Yes, if we assume most people having made a purchase would be proud to come out with a visible luxury shopping bag. Assessing the average sales ticket is a bit more complicated, but in a tracking study it may be possible to send 10 research staff to look at 10 separate amounts appearing on the cash register at different times of the day and during different days of the week: These 100 pieces of information can be used to roughly work out the average ticket of a competitor in a given location, and therefore its most probable sales level. Not only can these ratios help a brand understand the economics of one competitor or predict which kind of sales level it should expect in a given location, it can also help compare the performances of different stores of the same luxury brand.

Figure 7.3 presents a consumer performance matrix that we have developed to collect data from different stores. It focuses on change over time of the number of tickets and the average ticket amount.

As one compares different stores' performances on an annual basis, some stores may be seen to increase their number of tickets and the average ticket amount: This is a "virtuous" phase. But if the store's average ticket is decreasing, it may not necessarily be an indicator of bad performance if, at the same time, the number of tickets is growing. We call this a "recruitment" phase. And if the average ticket is growing but the number of tickets is decreasing, this is known as the "loyalty" phase. The only phase to avoid is, obviously, the decline phase. A store in any one of the first three phases can be seen as growing, albeit growing for different reasons. It's worth mentioning that each of the different phases requires different promotional programs.

| | | Average Ticket | |
		Growing	Decreasing
Number of Tickets	Growing	Virtuous Phase	Recruitment Phase
	Decreasing	Loyalty Phase	Decline Phase

Figure 7.3   Consumer Performance Matrix

In the case of a new luxury ladies' ready-to-wear collection, following the conversion ratio during the first two weeks of a new spring-summer collection and comparing it with the same ratios for the previous two or three years lets you know immediately whether the collection is strong, average, or weak.

Sales Forecasting

To estimate the sales potential of a new location, it is necessary to use the brand's average values for the attraction coefficient, the conversion ratio, and the ticket. With this information at hand, adjusted to take into account specific characteristics of a given location—for example, the level of income of the average customer, or the style of those people passing by (are they on a shopping trip or not?)—it is possible to assess, by merely counting the number of people passing by, what would be an expected level of sales.

In general, this level of sales (and in this case, both the conversion ratio and the average ticket) is also dependent on the expected size of the store.

In fact, the way retailers look at their sales performances and compare different stores of the same brand is often done by dividing total sales by store size: This is the traditional *sales per square foot* measure.

Department store groups tend to use this measure of sales per square foot to assess the effectiveness of their different retail locations. Looking at square feet is also a way to take into account the initial investment or the rental costs of the different stores they manage. On top of that, we can assume that the larger the store, the bigger the merchandising inventory and therefore the greater the investment in products necessary to obtain a given sales level.

But the same department store will also use the criterion of sales per square foot to compare the effectiveness of different product categories: ladies' ready-to-wear compared to men's ready-to-wear or home decoration or perfumes and cosmetics activities.

The criterion has also been modified for stores that present products on shelves, like perfumes and cosmetics stores: They speak of *sales per linear foot* of shelves and they use this ratio to compare different stores of the same chain. They also use it to look at the profitability they obtain with different brands or when they compare the efficiency of their perfumes versus their makeup or their skin care setup or the mix of these three major product categories in different store locations.

But all product categories do not provide the same level of profitability. This is why another criterion is also widely used: the *gross margin per square foot.* This is a second tool of retail efficiency analysis, and widely used.

Figure 7.4 shows an example of sales curves as a function of the size of the store. There is no direct relationship between total sales and square feet: The lines indicate, for example, that brand A starts slowly (if the store is too small, its products cannot be attractive to the consumer, but then as store size increases it develops very fast) and then reaches a plateau.

Brand B, on the contrary, has products that do not sell well until the store is larger. At the beginning, its sales per square foot are almost half of those of brand A; but with a large store, its total sales performance becomes almost similar to that of brand A.

Brand C is doing quite well in a smaller store and its performance does not increase significantly as the store size increases.

This pattern depends on the brand standing: The sales per square foot of Cartier are significantly higher than the sales per square foot of Bulgari in similar locations. But obviously, the smaller the merchandising assortment, the less effective a very big store: Having 5,000 square feet to present exclusively top-quality ladies' handbags and luggage may not be the most effective way to use floor space.

It is difficult to give optimal figures for sales per square foot as they depend very much on the environment, the brand standing, and the

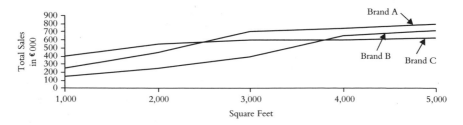

Figure 7.4   Sales as a Percentage of Store Size

type of merchandise. But as a rule of thumb, in 2010, one might have said that in a month:

- For a Southeast Asian multi-brand store, the target would be 120 euros per square foot.
- An average mall in the United States should have reached 200 euros per square foot. The Mall of America would do 410 euros per square foot.
- The Museum of Modern Art in New York, in its bookshop, was supposed to do 1,400 euros per square foot per month.

This ratio of sales per square foot is a very important criterion of retail effectiveness. When they can gather this information on their competitors, luxury goods retail managers can compare their level of sales per square foot to those of such competitors: If the level is lower, this in an indication that either the brand attractiveness is limited or the product is not adapted to the sizes of the stores.

Let's take a look at a brand that had a level of sales per square foot consistently 40 percent below its major competitor and the leader of the sector. The number one company objective was to close this gap through a more effective advertising program designed to increase awareness and attractiveness. It also deployed a change in the product merchandising selection.

In Table 7.8, we present the analysis of Tiffany's stores in the United States. We can see that the number of American stores changed from 70 in 2007 to 96 in 2010, an increase of 37 percent. During the same period, sales decreased, due to the 2008 economic crisis that

Table 7.8 Analysis of Tiffany's U.S. Retail Stores

	2010	2009	2008	2007
Number of stores	96	91	86	70
Square feet	598,100	584,400	558,000	493,000
Average store size in square feet	6,230	6,422	6,488	7,043
Total U.S. sales (billion US$)	1.574	1.410	1.586	1.759
Yearly sales per square foot	2,630	2,414	2,843	3,570

SOURCE: Annual reports.

Table 7.9 Trends in Coach North America Retail Stores

	2010	2009	2008	2007	2006
Number of stores	342	330	297	259	218
Square footage	929,530	893,037	795,226	627,737	562,553
Average store size	2,718	2,706	2,677	2,597	2,580

SOURCE: Annual reports.

affected the American market and in particular, the jewelry sector. But only by looking at the sales per square foot measure can we have a clear picture of the situation: a drop of 27 percent over the period.

This analysis of square footage is not always possible, as the data is seldom available. In Table 7.9, we have, for example, data on the North American retail stores of Coach, but we cannot find in their annual reports an indication of the sales trends as the result of the opening of so many stores.

In this respect, an analysis of Gucci data, unfortunately old but available for the period 1996 to 2001, paints an interesting picture. During that period, Gucci decided to grow its total company-operated square feet from 151,800 to 422,490—a multiplication of three—in a period of six years. The impact of this move was a dramatic decrease in sales per square foot, from $3,400 to $2,817, or a drop of 17 percent.

The picture is revealed in Figure 7.5. As a company opens new stores, it takes some time for it to pick up additional volume. But it is very important to follow its progress in order to be able to react and take the necessary measures to correct the situation. The drop in sales per square meter that we see here can be explained in several different ways:

- Figures of 2001 were impacted by the September 11 drama, in particular in the United States.
- When a new store opens, it takes generally two years for its sales to reach their full potential.
- As one brand expands its number of stores, the new stores are logically in second-choice locations with less potential than the first stores.
- As the selling space for a given brand is increased, it is necessary to increase the number of items available for sale. It sometimes takes time for the merchandising staff to recognize that they also have to change the product selection.

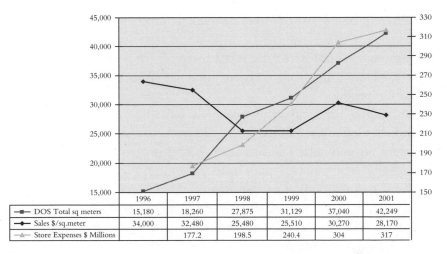

	1996	1997	1998	1999	2000	2001
DOS Total sq meters	15,180	18,260	27,875	31,129	37,040	42,249
Sales $/sq.meter	34,000	32,480	25,480	25,510	30,270	28,170
Store Expenses $ Millions		177.2	198.5	240.4	304	317

Figure 7.5   Gucci Sales per Square Meter as a Result of New Store Openings

Stock Purchases and Margin Control

We begin this next section by looking at the purchasing budget, then at inventory and margin controls.

The Purchasing Budget   For any given season a store should purchase what it can sell. Therefore, the purchasing budget exercise starts with a sales forecast. It is then divided by months and transformed into purchases, at purchasing costs.

The open to buy (OTB) concept was invented by American department stores. Each department manager makes a sales budget by brand and then an "open to buy": This is an amount that the department manager is allowed to buy for Brand X for the next year.

If Brand X's performance for the past two or three years has been good, the sales budget for next year would probably be increased and then the OTB would satisfy demand for that brand. If, on the contrary, Brand X performances have been lackluster, then next year's OTB would be lower than this year's. Many luxury brand managers have had to fight over this fact in their discussions with purchasing managers from department stores that had low OTB for their brand.

But the system of OTB is now used (by one name or another) by almost all luxury retail store operators. The purchasing budget (OTB) by brand and by season forms the basis of every purchasing system.

Different brands use different systems, as in the following:

- Sometimes the store or the retail manager for a given country can buy whatever he or she feels are adequate from a very large collection of products.
- Sometimes the local store managers have no say in the decision and headquarters automatically delivers the merchandise, based solely on centralized information based on past sales (colors and sizes, for example) and types of merchandise.
- More frequently, part of the assortment is automatically delivered to a given store and store managers can select 40 percent or 60 percent of the assortment according to what seems most appropriate for their specific stores.
- Sometimes the purchasing budget is divided into three groups: One part is centralized at headquarters, a small part is allocated for a given country, and a third part is the sole responsibility of the store manager.

In this respect, each brand must define its own policy and procedure. Prada, in 2005, had a policy of 0 percent autonomy given to the store managers or the country retail managers in the selection of merchandise for their stores: shipments were automatic, with no flexibility at all. Louis Vuitton is considered to have a relatively rigid selection policy too, but with computer system adjustments and a lot of special, intelligent autonomy as part of the process. It would therefore appear that the stronger the brand, the less autonomy given to the store managers.

This is, however, not that simple, as it is well known that a Japanese and a Chinese store selling the same brand sell completely different products. Even in China, the people in the northern part of the country purchase different colors and shapes than those living in the southern part. If the brand is very well organized and can rely on complete and well-selected historical data, it can decide, from their headquarters in Paris or in Milan, how the Tianjin store should be stocked. If this historical data does not exist, or if it is not well integrated into a foolproof system, there is no other way than to ask the sales staff to make their own subjective selection.

In the purchasing phase, there are trade-offs that are not easy to assess. For leather goods, customers generally buy black, brown, and beige, but for a display to be lively and attractive, it is better to also have white, yellow, and red items on the shelf. Headquarters might require the stores to offer a full variety, but a store manager with short-term vision may want to forget those products that may well end up with their prices deeply cut at bargain sales.

Watches provide a similar example: To make a sale, it is much more effective to present a full collection, but generally the most expensive gold watches sell much less than the more accessible and relatively cheaper items. Store managers may be tempted to purchase the lowest priced watches, at the expense of a full presentation of a complete line required to communicate the sophistication of the brand. Headquarters will undoubtedly insist on the purchase of the full line, but later on, they might evaluate store managers on their inventory turnover.

So far, we have spoken almost exclusively of the system of two collections a year: spring-summer and fall-winter. This system is in fact now changing with "croisière" lines, which increase the deliveries to four times a year.

Retailers have also discovered that if they bring in all the merchandise, say in September, for the full winter collection, some loyal customers will enter the store at the end of October or November and ask whether they have anything new. Therefore, they often divide the seasonal collection into several themes and keep some merchandise in the warehouse, bringing some into the store in October and the rest in November. At their own initiative, they are changing the system.

Finally, everybody in the industry looks at Zara with their 26 collections a year. Zara works on a different business model, but luxury companies can learn something from them. Some have already implemented a similar model, as is the case of Tous, the Spanish middle-range luxury jewelry company, that now works on 26 jewelry collections a year.

The Inventory Turnover Inventory turnover is the ratio of the number of unit sales in a given year to the average inventory in the store during that year. Generally, as the units of products are heterogeneous for a luxury store, one will compute the ratio of sales (at cost value) to the average inventory of the store.

$$\bullet \text{ Stock turnover rates } = \frac{\text{Number of units sold}}{\text{Average inventory}}$$

U.S. Department Store—Sales Volume

	Small	Average	High
Men's clothing	2.0	2.2	2.4
Furniture and bedding	2.1	2.4	2.8
Boy's clothing	2.5	2.6	3.4
Books	2.8	2.8	3.1
Major appliances	3.2	3.1	3.9
Womens' hosiery	3.5	3.1	3.4
Womens' ready-to-wear	4.3	4.5	5.4

Figure 7.6   Inventory Turnover as a Function of Store Size

Source: William Davidson, *Retailing Management* (New York: John Wiley & Sons, 1999).

Figure 7.6 shows an example of standard turnover ratios in an American department store.

One can see here that in a department store, the ladies' ready-to-wear inventory turns 4.3 to 5.4 times a year, more than twice the rotation of men's clothing. The seasonal aspect of ladies' ready-to-wear bargain sales probably has a positive impact on the turnover. On the contrary, men's clothing, perceived as less seasonal, ends up remaining in the store much longer.

Out of Stocks and Stock Transfers Nothing irritates the customer more than out of stock items. For example, if a woman sees a product one day, waits two or three days before deciding to purchase it, goes back to the store to buy it but is told that the product has already been sold, she will be frustrated. So imagine the absurdity of this not uncommon scenario, when another customer sees and likes a dress displayed in the show window of a store. She enters and cannot find her size or, even worse, finds out the dress is completely sold out in every size except the unit in the show window, which happens to be size 4, not her size. She may complain to the clerk, asking why they promote a product that they are unable to sell, right there in the show window, only to be told that headquarters decides which products must be in the show windows, irrespective of what is in stock in the store.

How is it possible to prevent out of stocks? One could very simply buy too much merchandise and make sure that until the very last day of full price selling, the seasonal collection is still in the store in all sizes and all colors. But this would be too expensive. As for restocking, very often the fashion products that have been prepared for a given season were manufactured in one shot, very far away. It may take two to three months to start a new order and get a given item back to a store.

One solution is to organize transfers between stores. Many companies have two or three deliveries a week to all their stores and can therefore organize returns and shipments within two days. The customer can be told to come back to get the merchandise she wants. She may actually not come back, but at least the service would have been provided.

Retailers with more than six stores in a given trade area have traditionally been accustomed to checking the inventory situation every night in each store and to organize additional deliveries and transfers for the next morning. Today, this can be done automatically by computer: All stores are linked to a central IT system that records sales and can organize the necessary transfers. One such system is called "Sterling Always In Stock" and can deal with this issue effectively. But innovations are still needed in this field. For example, once an item of a desired size has been located, it should be possible to deliver it to the customer's home address the following day. A mix of in-store selling and direct delivery should be developed.

Another disadvantage to having too much inventory at the end of the season is that customers can often sense overstock as they enter the store and may decide to wait for bargain sales. There is no denying that if a woman enters a store on December 12th and tries on a piece that she likes very much and she sees three or four identical items hanging in the store, she may wait until January to buy in the bargain sales. If, however, she is told, "You are lucky, this is the only size that is left in this style!" she will most probably buy it at full price.

After the large drop in sales that American department stores suffered during the last quarter of 2008, bargain sales in January 2009 were huge, and at distress prices. So in order to make sure customers would come back to the stores in October and November 2009 and buy the fall-winter collection at full price, Saks Fifth Avenue, Neiman Marcus, and Nordstrom all implemented a policy of double-digit decreases in inventory purchases on their collections, to convince consumers that they had to buy at full price.

Margin Control As previously discussed, the margin is the difference between retail price and cost, expressed in percentage of retail. Since cash registers are linked to a central computer system, it is possible to follow the margin online for every store and every transaction.

This is not as simple as it seems, as different product categories might use a different retail coefficient. But the information can flash every time the expected margin has not been obtained.

According to the retail policy of each brand, different policies can be set regarding the discounts available for sales staff to use in order increase sales, and in particular, to increase the number of customers buying a second item. The policy for some brands is to give sales staff the freedom to give up to a 5 percent discount and to leave open the possibility, in some extreme cases, to go up to 10 percent, provided the country retail manager has approved the special discount. This should appear daily on the fact sheet and be listed by individual sales staff for each store.

Other special prices include staff purchases (which must be limited to a monthly or seasonal maximum amount) or journalist purchases.

Pilferage can only be identifiable if missing pieces are identified after a physical inventory of a store. This inventory was traditionally done three times a year, at the end of the fiscal year (generally January 1st) and at the end of the two bargain sales (February 28th and August 30th). It seems advisable to do it also at the end of June, before the start of the spring-summer bargain sale, and also in the middle of each season, say, at the end of October and the end of April.

Special sales return procedures should also be implemented so that any anomaly can be detected.

Analysis of the Return on Investment

In any business, people speak of return on investment. In a retail situation, assuming we forget about key money and store decoration costs, this is a function of the size of the average inventory.

We can therefore speak of a gross margin return on inventory investment. The formula is as follows:

$$\text{GMROI} = \frac{\text{Gross margin dollars}}{\text{Total sales}} \times \frac{\text{Total sales}}{\text{Average inventory investment}}$$

This ratio is in fact the multiplication of two well-known ratios:

$$\text{Gross margin} = \frac{\text{Gross margin dollars}}{\text{Total sales}}$$

$$\text{Inventory turnover} = \frac{\text{Total sales}}{\text{Average inventory investment}}$$

The return on investment is therefore the multiplication of two basic retail ratios: the gross margin percentage and the inventory turnover ratio. Table 7.10 shows different structures with identical returns on investment.

In each of the three cases, the return on investment is the same and therefore the financial performances are identical. But in the first case, one manages to turn over the inventory eight times a year, so the store has the equivalent of all products sold during a period of six weeks. It is possible in this case to take only a 25 percent margin and still do quite well. In the second case, the priority being the gross margin, this time set as 40 percent, at the expense of the inventory turnover. In the third case, there is a relative balance between the two criteria.

Table 7.10 Retail Strategies

	Gross Margin in %	Inventory Turnover	GMROI
Priority to sale objectives	25.0	8	200%
Priority to margin objectives	40.0	5	200%
Priority to balanced strategies	33.3	6	200%

The lesson here is that it is possible to make money, even with a low margin, provided the stock moves rapidly. In Chapter 1, we described this situation, comparing the financial structure of a supermarket, a fashion store, and a jewelry store. The point is that if the stock turns over rapidly enough, the margin can be significantly reduced, without affecting the overall return on investment.

Basic Information Systems

The system starts with all cash registers linked to a central computer so that sales, inventory, and margin can be controlled online for each store, each sales staff, and with analysis of different types of merchandise.

Retailing is a field in which it is necessary to react immediately if sales are growing faster than expected (the stores will be out of stock) or growing more slowly (orders may need to be cut immediately, or else there will be a cash squeeze).

Following monthly sales is not as easy as it seems because some months have five Saturdays (the biggest selling day in the week) while most have four, making comparisons difficult. Some IT systems correct this by an index. Many retailing companies in the United States do not use monthly statistics at all, but prefer to work with 13 periods of four weeks each. For luxury goods companies, this is seldom the case, as retail is only one part of the activities, with all others working on a monthly basis.

Computer systems can analyze real out of stocks and expected out of stocks and product transfers. They can compute theoretical OTB and analyze the forecast delivery schedules to see if they are in line with expected sales.

They can also work on theoretical margins, theoretical inventories, and theoretical prices to analyze actual variations from their data. And they can do that by store or even by sales individual.

At the end of the day, in luxury retailing, the top unit of observation is the retail store and when talking to the general manager of Salvatore Ferragamo, or of Hugo Boss, it is always surprising to hear them describe the performance to date of their main Chicago store or their Shanghai outlet: This simply means that they read those figures almost every day so that they can react very fast.

The RFID (Radio Frequency Identification)

The Radio Frequency Identification (RFID) was created in the United States in the 1970s. The idea was to attach tags to different objects for identification and tracking purposes.

RFID tags can be read several meters away. Contrary to bar codes, it is possible to add additional information to the tag several times as it passes close to an RFID reader.

This system was first used for retail activities in 2005 by the Freedom Shopping, Inc. retail chain in North Carolina. A passive RFID tag can be included in a product label (at an individual cost of five cents) and can record, for example, the date on which the product went through quality control and was sent to a warehouse, the date on which the product was displayed in the store (identify the store/give the retail price), the date on which it was sold, and eventually the date on which the item was returned.

Using this system, a brand can follow the progress of each item from production to its presence at a point of sale and the precise number of days it has stayed in the store. It is also possible to localize the product and eventually organize transfers from one store to another.

This type of analysis is not new, as any good electronic system can already identify how many stock-keeping units (SKUs) have been sent to a store, how many have been sold, and therefore how many remain in inventory. The difference with RFID is that the computer information flow can be double-checked by the individual presence of each item on the retail floor. It can verify whether the SKUs that arrived first in the store were the first to be sold on the retail floor.

In 2005, Walmart asked 100 top suppliers to apply RFID labels on each product shipped to them. The retail chain uses the system to monitor promotional activities: It can indicate how many products left the factory with a special discount deal (valid for a limited period of time) and how many items were sold at discount during that period, how many items were sold at discount outside of that period, and how many items that may have been prepared for a special promotional sale ended up being sold at full price.

For luxury goods, the RFID system can locate each individual item over time, identifying the store where the merchandise was last seen. If it disappears from the inventory, the system can also help identify possible pilferage. What's more, it can actually identify the origin of a product found in a gray market location, making it more difficult for gray market operators to hide their friendly merchandise suppliers. But RFID labels can be erased using a microwave oven.

The RFID is not the only way to manage a merchandising information system, but it is the only way to look at individual items as units of retail information.

The Follow-Up Grid

Figure 7.7 shows an example of a typical follow-up grid for each individual store in a group. A similar page can appear for any single store. It gives monthly sales and cumulative sales for the past two years as well as forecast sales for the year to come. It also analyzes monthly margins so that its trends can be followed. It provides monthly starting and ending inventory with an indication of expected delivery of merchandise already purchased. The last column on the right indicates the inventory in the number of months of sales.

This table comes from a confidential business case written on a fashion retail store chain in Hong Kong (Stradivarius Fashion Store) and looks at the purchases and sales of a confidential brand, called for the purpose of the case Paolo Bencini.

The case was written in 1998, just after the handover of Hong Kong to China. As can be seen in column 6, cumulative sales were doing very poorly as 1997 to 1996 registered a drop of more than 20 percent in cumulative sales.

The two following columns make it possible to follow the margin, by an indication of the cost of goods, of the merchandise sold for each month. This figure relates to the products purchased and delivered.

The next three columns give for 1996 and 1997 the inventory level at the beginning of each month, and for 1998 the forecast beginning inventory if 1998 sales happen to end up as forecast.

Luxury Retailing: Stradivarious Fashion Stores
Sales & Purchasing Forecast 1998: Paolo Bencinl Brand

Unit: 000 HK$ Exchange Rate US$ = 7.8   HK$

Month	Sales (Actual) 96	(Actual) 97	(Cumulative) 96	(Cumulative) 97	97/96	CGS 96	CGS 97	Purchase 96	Purchase 97	Beginning Inventory 96	Beg. Inv. 97	Beg. Inv. 98	Purchase 98 Committed	Purchase 98 Modified	1998 Forecast Sales (Forecast)(Actual) % of A/F	CGS	Ending Inventory	Inventory turnover
Jan	7,000	5,000	7,000	5,000	71%	3,675	2,940	19,500	17,160	12,000	19,430	28,742	19,500		4,000	2,352	26,3900	13.9
Feb	6,000	4,000	13,000	9,000	69%	3,150	2,352			8,325	16,490	26,390		9,750	3,200	1,882	34,258	13.6
Mar	8,000	6,000	21,000	15,000	71%	3,040	2,220			24,675	31,298	34,258			4,800	1,776	32,482	17.2
Apr	7,000	5,000	28,000	20,000	71%	2,660	1,850			21,635	29,078	32,482			4,000	1,480	31,002	17.2
May	6,000	4,500	34,000	24,500	72%	2,280	1,665			18,975	27,228	31,002			3,600	1,332	29,670	16.8
Jun	5,000	4,000	39,000	28,500	73%	1,900	1,480			16,695	25,563	29,670			3,200	1,184	28,486	16.3
Jul	7,000	6,500	46,000	35,000	76%	3,675	3,822			14,795	24,083	28,486			5,200	3,058	25,429	15.1
Aug	6,000	5,500	52,000	40,500	78%	3,150	3,234			11,120	20,261	25,429			4,400	2,587	22,842	14.0
Sep	5,000	3,500	57,000	44,000	77%	1,900	1,295	17,160	15,600	7,970	17,027	22,842	18,036	9,018	2,800	1,036	30,824	19.2
Oct	4,000	2,800	61,000	46,800	77%	1,520	1,036			23,230	31,332	30,824			2,240	829	29,995	18.9
Nov	3,000	2,100	64,000	48,900	76%	1,140	777			21,710	30,296	29,995			1,680	622	29,373	18.6
Dec	3,000	2,100	67,000	51,000	76%	1,140	777			20,570	29,519	29,373			1,680	622	28,752	18.4
Total	67,000	51,000				29,230	23,448	36,660	32,760					18,768	40,800	18,758		
Jan-99															4,000	2,352	26,400	16.9
Feb-99														7,000	3,200	1,882	31,518	10.1

Notes: Average margin

1996	Standard	62.0%	
	Bargain	47.5%	Jan, Feb, Jul, Aug
1997	Standard	63.0%	41.2% Jan, Feb, Jul, Aug
	Bargain		
1998	Standard	63.0%	same as 1997
	Bargain		
	Average	54.0%	
1999	Bargain	41.2%	same as 1997

1998 Sales forecast is 20% less than the actual sales of 1997.
1999 Sales forecast is identical to the 1998 sales.

Annual purchase was modified based on sales forecast and average margin. Accordingly 50% of 1998 spring-summer order shall be canceled. Inventory turnover = Ending inventory/past 12 month CGS × 12.

If by chance, the 98 purchases had not been modified and were maintained at full speed (19,500 in February and 18,036 in September), inventory of December 31st, 1998 would have reached 37,536 or 24 months.

Figure 7.7   Follow-Up Grid

The last five columns deal with an on going forecast: the sales forecast and the actual sales for each month, with the corresponding cost of goods, plus the last forecast ending inventory.

By looking at the last columns—the monthly forecast ending inventory turnover, in number of months—one can see that even at a lower level, the modified purchases were much too high, given the present sales level: Unless the Stradivarius Fashion Store was to take more drastic measures and cut its purchase budget even more, it would clearly end up in a cash crunch.

This follow-up grid has several advantages:

- It enables a systematic control of sales levels, as compared to forecast.
- It makes strong margin controls possible.
- It puts the inventory situation and the inventory forecast and the planned committed fashion forecast on the same sheet.
- It is an instrument for following monthly store performances.

Both general retail and luxury retail involve fields of details, data, analysis, and follow-ups. At any time, things can get out of control. Follow-up must occur on an almost daily basis and management must be prepared to react rapidly.

Chapter 8

Luxury Retail Pricing

Many marketers neglect their pricing strategies and the effect they can have on the market.

—*Philip Kotler*

It was said earlier that pricing had no place in the retail marketing mix because it was inherently integrated with the product offering. Within the realm of luxury retailing, pricing decisions are generally centralized and are not the responsibility of the store manager or even the retailing manager. Pricing is therefore perceived as secondary in the context of retailing. But pricing remains a very important part of running a store: Even in luxury retail, price comparisons with competitors, decisions about bargain sales pricing, and assessments of the level of price reduction required to significantly increase sales should not be neglected.

Even if pricing decisions are centralized for fully owned stores, franchisees may have some autonomy in that matter. They will be told by the brand headquarters what the retail price should be, but top management cannot legally impose it, as in most countries price fixing is prohibited. Also, department stores cannot decide on prices for shop-in-shops or corners, but they have full control of their own counters. So pricing remains an issue and deserves special discussion here. In the first section, we discuss regular pricing decisions. In the second section, we look at discounting prices to increase sales.

Regular Pricing Decisions

First, let us discuss the worldwide price system to identify the different selling variables. We finish with a look at margins.

Worldwide Pricing

The same price cannot be set everywhere in the world. In many countries, products that are imported are subject to customs duties that can sometimes reach 100 percent of the export price. In some cases, there are value-added taxes (included in the retail price) and local taxes (generally not included in the retail price and added at the cash register). There are also very different costs of operating a store. Opening a store in Tokyo and paying sales staff can cost two to three times more than doing the same thing in Madrid: All this must somehow be reflected in the final retail prices.

In general, luxury brands don't set up a single worldwide retail price, but work on the basis of three zones, as shown in Table 8.1.

For Europe and what is generally the home city of the brand, price is fixed at an index of 100. For New York, one generally tries to have a retail price slightly above that of Europe, as illustrated in the table, at

Table 8.1   Retail Price Zones for Luxury Fashion

	Paris/Milan	New York	Tokyo
Domestic market	100	105–110	145
Duty free	80	84–88	116

105 or 110. But if the dollar is weak against the euro, then New York prices could go down to 90 or 95 and be cheaper than those in Paris. The trend would then be to increase the retail prices in the United States as well, but this can be done only two or three times a year (when a new catalog is printed, for example). If American brands don't need to increase their prices, European brands will be cautious about raising their prices too rapidly to remain competitive. The New York price will then be used in the United States and will serve as a reference for the zone. For example, if Argentina has a 30 percent customs duty, the domestic Argentinean price would theoretically be 105×1.3 or $110 \times 1.3 = 136.5$ or 145, and may be fixed at 130. In Mexico, with a 10 percent customs duty the retail price could be at 120.

In Asia, the retail price reference is based on a Tokyo price of 145. This higher level is due to Japanese (or Chinese) customs duties, plus the high cost of operating in the area.

We just said that when the U.S. dollar decreases it is not easy to increase retail prices because it can only be done at certain times and when no special printed promotional activity has been planned and organized involving a final retail price. Therefore, the lead time before one can act is generally a few months, or even quarters.

Decreasing retail prices is not that simple either. A brand that directly owns 100 percent of its retail setup can do it relatively easily, given the operational lead times previously mentioned. But things get complicated if some of the merchandise is sold through independent stores, by franchisees, or at department store counters. If asked to reduce retail prices on existing inventory, an independent retailer will insist on retaining their full margin percentage at the lower retail price. So, if the retailer bought the product at 50 to sell at 100 and the decision is made to reduce the retail price to 90, the retailer will ask that their cost for the product be reduced to 45 so that the percentage margin they make remains at 50 percent. Since they are likely to have already paid for their inventory, they will want to be reimbursed or given a credit. Therefore, when a brand organizes a retail price reduction, it would need to send sales representatives to all the points of sale to physically count the number of products in existing inventory in order to give the independent retailer the equivalent credit for each product. This is sometimes done, but it is complicated and expensive, which is why when a price decrease is needed because of a currency valuation, the tendency is to wait and forgo future price increases, so that the needed retail price reduction only materializes in two or three years.

In the three price zones, the duty-free prices will generally be set at 20 percent below domestic prices. In Table 8.1, we can see that the prices become 80, 84–88, and 116, and it is generally more expensive to buy fashion, accessories, or perfumes at Tokyo Narita airport duty free or Shanghai Pudong airport duty free than in Paris domestic stores. So, even though the market is globalized, there are still differences in retail price.

Over time these differences may be reduced. In Japan, for example, the METI (the Ministry of Economy) tries to force luxury brands to reduce these disparities by regularly publishing the Milan, New York, and Tokyo retail prices of certain iconic luxury items. But as long as there are differences in customs duties and operating costs, regional price variations will remain.

Sell In, Sell Out, and Sell Through

When we speak of pricing and see the impact that a price has on an item in a given country (in line with competitive price levels, of course) we should also look at the concept of sell through, which is a handy indicator of price validity.

Let's start by assuming that a brand doesn't work exclusively with directly owned stores, but also works with franchisees, department stores, and wholesalers.

Sell in is the number of units that the brand has sold to a retail partner, for example a franchisee. Let us assume that the brand has delivered 100 units of a given stock-keeping unit to a franchised store in Moscow.

Sell out is the number of units that the Russian partner (the franchised retail store) has sold during a given period of time: This is the exact number of products that have been purchased by final consumers at the tail end of the distribution system. Let us say, for example, that the sell out in Moscow, after four months of full price sale, is 60. That means that 40 products are still in inventory at the end of the full price season period.

Sell through is the percentage of units that have been sold by the retailer during a given period of time. To continue with our Moscow example, let's say that the sell through was 40 percent during the first two months, 52 percent after three months, and (as you may have guessed) 60 percent after four months.

A strong fashion product for a strong brand should have sell through of 65 percent to 85 percent during the full price period before the bargain sales period starts.

Sell through can also be followed—and should be followed—every month. In the same example, the sell through might have been 25 percent during the first month and 60 percent at the end of the period of four months.

Looking at specific products, if a new leather handbag has a sell through of 10 percent during the first month of sales (for example, as part of a winter collection during the month of September), we know there is a problem. Either the product is not very attractive to the consumer or the price is too high. On October 15, it might be wise to decrease its retail price by 20 percent and eventually give the franchisee a credit on the wholesale price so that he or she is able to keep a full margin at this lower retail price.

Looking Again at Margin

As explained earlier, the margin is the percentage of profit (retail price minus product cost) divided by the retail price. Sometimes margins are just 4 percent, but they can also be of 50 percent, and in this case journalists may write articles explaining that retailers make more money than manufacturers.

This gross margin percentage is in fact quite misleading. It is by definition a "gross" margin and doesn't take into account the retail operating costs, which can be very high. Next to the gross margin, it is sometimes interesting to look at an operating margin, including a normal ratio of the store fixed costs. If rental cost plus sales staff costs represent 30 percent of forecasted sales, this operations margin becomes 10 percent or 20 percent, which is not the same thing.

Should all the products in a given monobrand store work on the same gross margin ratio? This would be the simplest way: In order to calculate his retail price, the store manager would simply take the purchasing prices and multiply them by the same retail coefficient. But this is not always the case. If a brand tries to use the same retail coefficient for its core products (e.g., ready-to-wear) it may have to work with a lower coefficient (and therefore a lower margin) for new product categories that are not produced in the same cost-reducing volumes of their standard lines. You are therefore likely to find two or three different margin levels in a monobrand retail store.

In fact, for different product categories and different types of stores, the overall pricing and cost structure can differ considerably, as was indicated by William Davidson in his book on retailing management. He distinguished between high fashion retail stores, standard department stores, and supermarkets. Figure 8.1 reproduces his figure.

This table shows that fashion brands require a higher margin to deal with retail markdowns, which we will discuss in the next section, and that even with a standard margin of 60 percent, they end up with an actual gross margin of 50 percent and just 7 percent net profit. Department stores have fewer markdowns and supermarkets work on a 20 percent gross margin to end up with 2 percent net profit.

But even in a department store, margins vary from one product category to another. This is what appears in Table 8.2.

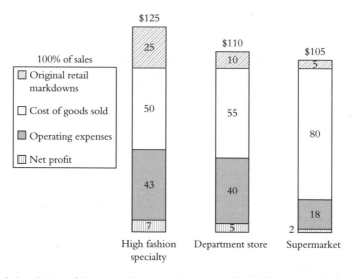

Figure 8.1 Original Pricing, Cost, and Margins for Different Retail Sectors
SOURCE: William R. Davidson, Daniel J. Sweeney, and Ronald W. Stampfl, *Retailing Management* (New York: John Wiley & Sons, 1988).

Table 8.2   Department Store Margins by Product Category

Jewelry	70%
Women's Apparel	65%
Fashion Accessories	65%
Women's Shoes	65%
Menswear	55%
Men's Shoes	55%
Home Furnishings	55%
Children's Clothing	50%
Electronics	35%

SOURCE: Ellen Diamond, *Fashion Retailing* (Pearson Prentice Hall, 2006).

Table 8.3   Impact of Percentage of Bargain Sales on Total Sales and Amount of Bargain Discount on Total Margin (Assuming a Gross Margin of 40 Percent)

		Final Total Margin on Full Sales Percentage of Products Sold at Bargain Sales				
		10%	20%	30%	40%	50%
Percentage price cut during bargain sales	30%	38.1%	36.2%	34.1%	31.8%	29.4%
	40%	37.5%	34.8%	31.8%	28.5%	25.0%
	50%	36.8%	33.3%	29.4%	25.0%	20.0%

The Special Case of Fashion Retailing

What is the acceptable gross margin a fashion store needs to make money? It all depends on its sell through. If sell through is good and only 10 to 20 percent of the merchandise must be sold at bargain sales, then life is easy. But if a line does not sell and 40 or 50 percent of it must be sold at a bargain price, the economics of retailing become quite difficult. In Table 8.3, we consider a store with a standard gross margin of 40 percent. If, for some reason, its seasonal collection does not sell, 40 to 50 percent of the total purchased stock (or the sell in) may need to be sold at a bargain price—and the more they need to unload, the deeper the percentage of discount needed to get rid of the merchandise. In that example we have used 30, 40, and 50 percent as the most probable discount required. But with a 40 percent gross margin, cutting prices by 50 percent means incurring a loss on any unit sold at that price. The gross margin for the total season is therefore not 40 percent, but around 20 or 25 percent—not an easy way to make money.

The lesson from this table is clear: The theoretical fashion gross margin at full price is one thing. The average gross margin, once all of the merchandise has been unloaded one way or another, is quite another.

In fashion retailing, it is possible to speak of making a profit only when all merchandise that was purchased has been sold.

In Table 8.4, we compare three different brands that have a very different sell through. Brand A sold 90 percent through and must get rid of only 10 percent of its volume at bargain sale prices. Brand B sold through 70 percent at full price and must unload 30 percent during bargain sales. Brand C has a low sell through (40 percent) and must sell 60 percent at bargain prices. We have assumed that the full gross margin was 60 percent and bargain sales were at a discount of 40 percent, therefore providing a 33 percent gross margin at bargain prices.

In each of those three cases, the brand's financial performance is quite different. In the first case, for Brand A, the total margin is very close to the theoretical one: 57.3 percent. For Brand C, the final margin is only 43.8 percent. This is a 13 percent difference. For a retail

Table 8.4 Retail Margins for Three Brands with Different Levels of Bargain Sales

	Brand A	**Brand B**	**Brand C**
Theoretical margin	60%	60%	60%
Percentage sold at full price	90%	70%	40%
Margin index	54	42	24
Percentage sold at bargain price	10%	30%	60%
Margin at bargain price	33%	33%	33%
Margin index	3.3	9.9	19.8
Actual season's margin	57.3%	51.9%	43.8%

store operator, carrying brands with a strong sell through or brands with a weak sell through makes a lot of economic difference.

Pilferage also affects gross margin. Merchandise may be stolen by customers, but also by sales staff. In fact, it is generally believed that a third of pilferage comes from clients and two-thirds from staff. The methods of stealing can vary too. The most obvious would be for someone to pick up a product and rush out of the store without going to the cash register, but it's not always that simple: Most products, especially ready-to-wear pieces, have a security system that must be removed at the cash register. Also, many stores have security guards at the door.

Other systems are less visible and perhaps more effective. A salesperson, for example, may sell an expensive dress to a friend but key into the cash register the code of a different and cheaper item. Or, if a customer fails to take the cash register slip with their purchase, a sales staff might keep that document for few days and then put this slip in the cash register as a return, taking the corresponding cash from the cash register while pretending the product was put back into store inventory. When the piece appears as missing, during a physical inventory at the end of the season, people may overlook the fact that some missing pieces can correspond to earlier returns.

Shoplifting is another issue related to pricing, as it affects the store's gross margin. It can be evaluated by doing inventory control and recording the pieces that are still part of the theoretical inventory but are missing on the sales floor and in the stockroom.

To prevent customer theft, the most effective system is the Electronic Article Surveillance (EAS) system. It is in fact a tag and alarm system. The tag contains a device that is inserted into the price tag. It must be deactivated at the cash register. If the article has not been processed at the cash register, a sensor located close to the exit door sounds an alarm and alerts the personnel.

Another system, used generally in Europe, is an electromagnetic (EM) system that can also be deactivated or reactivated if the merchandise is returned.

But in a luxury environment, it is not easy to insert strange-looking labels or put electronic portals close to the exit doors. Live closed-circuit televisions and security guards may appear less intrusive and still be just as effective.

To deal with employee theft, things are a bit more complicated, as store staff do not necessarily need to come out of the store with a piece of merchandise; methods described earlier in this chapter virtually ensure that a product will never be found when an inventory is conducted and managers may be unable to associate a missing item with a "theoretical" return.

The best system for reducing staff shoplifting seems to be the very careful selection of new applicants to a sales floor job.

Price Discounts and Bargain Prices

What is the best way to get rid of excess merchandise? Let's look at standard discounts and special sales events before looking specifically at bargain sales.

Standard Discounts

In a store, the theoretical gross margin very seldom materializes. Even for very strong brands and a highly sellable seasonal collection, things are never that easy.

In certain cases, sales staff has the authority to give a discount to their best customers or to those buying two or three products during the same shopping visit. This is absolutely forbidden for very top brands, but for less exclusive brands, a 5 percent discount may be possible. Sales staff is given strict guidelines for what they can and cannot do.

The only exception that the strongest brands make to their strict no-discount policy is for press people and staff. This can have an impact on the gross margin.

Should there be some form of loyalty card? The idea of a loyalty card may seem too down-market to fit the luxury retail environment. And in truth, cards aren't really necessary: Why give a Chanel VIP card to someone who already has several privilege credit cards in her designer wallet? Instead, it is much more sophisticated and exclusive to tell a regular client that if she buys in a given store, she will receive a 10 percent discount. This will be stated and keyed into the CRM cash register. Chanel used to give a 10 percent discount to its top Hong Kong customers for merchandise purchased there. Telling a customer is much more impressive than handing her a plastic card.

Another nice way to give a top regular customer preferential treatment is to tell her she will have "the same advantage as press people" including a 10 percent or 20 percent discount.

Although this can be done for top customers, special treatment for a broader base of regular customers is much more difficult to organize. As soon as a mechanism is organized, it can look systematic and less sophisticated, which can lower the prestige of the brand. A common practice is to invite some selected customers to bargain sale previews, one or two weeks before the official date. The real wording of the invitation must be carefully reviewed because in many countries there is a restricted official date for bargain sales and any special sale occurring before that date must be given a completely different name.

The last situation is the case of tourists and major tourist cities. There is a rule in Paris, Hong Kong, and elsewhere that guides who recommend that crowds of tourists enter a specific downtown duty-free store receive one or two euros per person who enter the store, plus a commission on sales. This is naturally unacceptable for monobrand stores or flagship stores, since those busloads tend to carry little prestige.

Does this mean that flagship stores cannot give commissions to tour guides? In truth, they sometimes do, but in a more sophisticated way. Jewelry stores, for example, may receive a visit from a guide who says she might come back to the store with a princess from the Middle East and would recommend that she make a purchase above 20,000 euros. The guide may ask for a 5 percent commission on the side. If the answer is no, the guide will not come back to the store. If the answer is yes and the guide is serious, she will probably come back with the princess, and advise her to buy expensive pieces. The following day the guide will come back to the store, alone, to pick up her commission.

Special Events

In some cases, it may advisable to run a special event with price reductions before the bargain sales begin. This type of event can have several kinds of objectives:

- *Stimulate the sale* of the regular merchandise and provide an opportunity for customers to visit the store an additional time.
- Provide the opportunity to sell *items that have been specially made* for this event and that can provide a full margin while still giving the consumer the feeling he or she is getting a good deal.
- Provide some extra push to products that had a *low sell through* at the beginning of the season and could end up in overstock in a few months.
- Attract *new customers* to the store.

All this can be done, but it must be very carefully planned and organized. For example, the selection of merchandise for this event must be very subtle: Products should have a high degree of selling potential (which conflicts with the idea of selling slow-moving items) and have an impulse buying characteristic.

This is not a simple matter. Retail specialists always believe that price promotions done out of phase with traditional timing do not work, unless huge discounts are involved.

So the rationale for a special event must be carefully thought out. It can be:

- A trunk show and the presence of an exceptional quantity of merchandise.
- A special factory sale, but at very deep price cuts—much below traditional bargain sales.
- A collection of items not sold in the brand store on a regular basis, but existing in other stores (not in the same city) or from other countries.
- A new product category, not yet in town, for which the brand wishes to test customer reactions.

Even if the idea of getting a good deal is ever-present, it should never be the thrust of the occasion or the official reason for such events.

Who should be invited? If it is a large event, almost everybody from the mailing list. If it is a more exclusive sales event, invitations should go only to those people who have been carefully selected during a very long process.

Bargain Sales

For fashion products, it is necessary to unload the end-of-season collection in order to create room and generate cash to bring the new collection in. It could be done in or out of the store, with big discounts or not, with or without advertising, and for varying durations.

Bargain Sales On or Off the Premises? Bargain sales can be run in the store itself or outside. Both systems have their own requirements.

The advantage of running it in the store is that there is no rent to pay for an additional location and it is easier to organize. It does not need to be advertised, as people tend to know when bargain sales begin, and will go from one store to the next looking for deals.

The disadvantage of doing it in the store is that it disorganizes the selling floor and, during the bargain sales period, almost no full price sales are recorded. This may be acceptable for standard brands, but it is a real shame for those brands that do a large part of business with tourists. Tourists would be visiting the store anyway and are ready to purchase the products on their shopping lists at full price. If the product on the list is on sale, they will buy it at the discount but probably not take advantage of the opportunity to buy a second piece, which means that the store would not optimize its gross margin.

In Paris, for example, all the very major brands like Hermès, Louis Vuitton, and Yves Saint Laurent organize their bargain sales off the premises. They rent a space for three or four days and conduct their sales in such locations.

The advantage of this system is that the bargain sales can be concentrated in only a few days and during that period the stores can go on with their normal selling activities and provide the service expected by tourists. Also, it is easier off the premises to give those bargain sales a very special character and attract more people than would have visited the stores.

The disadvantage of the off-premises bargain sale is that it can only work for a very strong brand with strong pulling power that can attract a large number of visitors. If Courreges was doing an off-premises sale 20 kilometers away from Paris, one couldn't guarantee that many customers would make the effort.

However, for prominent brands with the strength to draw bargain hunters to random locations, off-site bargain sales means that they can clear old stock out of their shops in just a few days, and run their retail store activities in January and July as any normal month.

When the bargain sales are organized off premises, there is, of course, a need for some advertising (often in a newspaper) or a mailing campaign, but the costs of these must be limited to reflect the total volume of merchandise to unload.

Which Price Level? The answer to this question is quite simple. If the objective is to unload excess merchandise and improve cash flow, the markdown should be significant and attractive.

Retail managers are often tempted to try to sell at a bargain discount of 20 percent or 30 percent for one week, marking the merchandise down to 40 percent and 50 percent during the second week, finally reaching 70 percent during week three. However, retailing managers who have managed many bargain sale operations say that the first markdown is the least costly: It is better to start the sale well, with a 45 percent discount, than wind up with lots of stock to sell after three weeks at 70 percent.

There are those retail managers who think that starting with a small 20 percent discount helps the brand maintain their strong identity by communicating the idea that its merchandise is hard to get. But a customer may think otherwise; he or she may think the offer is not attractive enough or downright deceptive. He or she will probably not come back the second or third week.

Who Should Be Invited? For bargain sales to be effective, almost everybody should be invited. When a sale is run in the retail store, this is obviously the case. In another location, bargain sales are first restricted to staff members and journalists for a few hours, are then extended to the very best customers, and finally opened to the public on the second day.

When bargain sales are held in the store, the top regular customers should be invited to a preview a few days before the sale, where they can purchase their preferred products.

Invitations can be mailed, and for some types of off-premises sales, the event should be advertised in newspapers.

How Long Should the Sale Last? The sooner it's over, the better, so that the store can get back to its normal activities. Outside of the store, bargain sales last three or four days. In the store, it tends to last three weeks. If most of the excess inventory is sold in a week and half, it is much better. Then whatever merchandise is still around can be gotten rid of another way.

Distressed Merchandise

If the brand has its own factory outlets, it can send the remaining merchandise there. Sometimes it can be sold to overstock experts with the labels removed, but this is rarely effective because products end up being promoted in shabby outlets with billboards proclaiming: "Original X brand, with labels removed." The most prestigious brands sometimes end up burning their leftover merchandise (although it would be wiser to sell it at 80 percent discount during bargain sales and make at least some customers very happy).

Throughout this discussion on pricing, we have described what should be done about price in a retail environment, notwithstanding the fact that the regular price was a given—not a negotiable—element. The job of the retail manager is therefore to manage special prices for different price-promotional events. In this case, one should always look for a meaningful differential threshold, or, to put it another way, find the price difference, the price discount, or the bargain sale price level that would be significant for the customer and generate a purchase. This threshold differs from one brand to another, but the general principle is that it does not make sense to cut corners: Discounts or bargain prices should be clear and generous. They should be perceived by the customer as providing a major purchasing opportunity. It is in this way that the brand will keep its status, prestige, and attractiveness.

Chapter 9

Customer In-Store Behavior

Go into a store and watch what people do.

—*Paco Underhill*

R etail is fundamentally a hands-on business. Nothing will ever replace the observation of customers and their interactions with the products, how sales assistants behave, and how customers and sales assistants interact. Retail is about what happens on the floor, which has us convinced that effective training is only achieved in the store. In addition, luxury brands must recognize that customers are not merely in awe of the brand and its products: They are full actors in the relationship (which we will discuss in the next chapters). Consequently, observing how customers behave in a store is critical to luxury retail.

Unfortunately, no studies on luxury store behavior have ever been published. They certainly exist, but are closely guarded as part of the confidential knowledge base that each major luxury group maintains for internal purposes. However, if we look at mass-market studies, and in particular fashion mass-market studies, we can reach general conclusions about how consumers behave in a store.

In-Store Behavior

The best in-store behavior research has been described by Paco Underhill[1] in his book *Why We Buy.* In this section we will present some of the findings he describes and discuss projects on which he has worked.

The Tracking Studies

Paco Underhill's company, Envirosell Inc., has developed a system of tracking studies. The idea is to use a team of 3 to 10 trackers, armed with the floor plan of a given store or shopping center, and tasked with writing down how consumers move into and within a store: Which way do they really go? What do they touch? How do they behave? How long do they stay in a given place? What do they look at? What do they buy? How do they pay? What do they do after they have paid? Not to mention the very precise places they have been.

A tracking study would, for example, say that a man:

3:25	Enters the store
3:27	Reaches the Brand X perfume counter, looks at perfume Y, picks up a tester, sprays and smells it, then puts it back; looks at another perfume of Brand X
3:31	Salesgirls coming to speak; man walks away
3:33	Looks at ladies shoes, looks at the prices of three styles
3:36	Walks to the belt rack; touches five products, selects one, tries it around his waist
3:40	Goes to the cash register; pays by credit card
3:45	Walks out

---

[1]Paco Underhill, *Why We Buy: The Science of Shopping* (New York: Simon & Schuster, 1999).

On a given day, each tracker can follow 20 to 50 customers, depending on the specific questions being asked and the size of the store. Within two to three days it is possible to gather a relevant sample of 200 to 500 precise customer behaviors and measure the likes of:

- The parts of the store that are seldom visited (what can be done to attract more customers to those areas?).
- The major points of destination.
- How the way people look at the products and the duration of the normal shopping process differs between product categories.
- Which product locations enable the best multiple purchase behavior.

Simple answers like conversion rates by apparent demographic criteria can also be given, as well as the behavior of people according to their looks or their shopping style.

How Do People Behave?

As people enter a store, the first thing they do is to walk straight in, rapidly. So, the exact entry point of a store is certainly not the most effective selling place. People also tend to use the entrance as a meeting point, which means that it may not be very welcoming for others. Also, as customers walk into a given store, they find themselves moving from one environment (the street or the mall) to another one (the shop), which requires a moment of sensory adjustment before they can take in what they now have around them. This transition location is therefore not a good selling place, contrary to popular belief. It's only once they get past the transition location that customers will slow their pace and be ready to look at what the store has to offer.

As they enter the store, they have a tendency not to go straight but to move imperceptibly to the right. This is why in most supermarkets the entrance door is not at the center, but slightly to the right. People will therefore walk to the right, find a wall after a few meters and bounce back, covering on average a larger portion of the store than they would have if the door had been in the center or on the left.

Table 9.1   Average Time Spent in a Home Design Store

A woman with a woman	8 minutes 15 seconds
A woman with a child	7 minutes 19 seconds
A woman alone	5 minutes 20 seconds
A woman with a man	4 minutes 41 seconds

SOURCE: Paco Underhill, *Why We Buy: The Science of Shopping* (New York: Simon & Schuster, 1999).

As they walk around the store, customers tend to touch products, and they often do it with their right hand. Even in supermarkets in countries where people drive their cars on the left side of the road, they push their shopping carts on the right side of the aisle in order to have an easier contact with the products.

Will they read a complicated sign? Probably not, since they tend to look ahead and don't stop to take in details.

Do they want to be seen from the street? It depends on the type of products the store is selling. For fashion and luxury, people generally prefer not to be seen by friends who happen to be walking past on the street while they try on a dress or look at an expensive watch. This is why luxury stores often have blind show windows and fashion stores often have internal corners or hidden places; dressing rooms are usually in a hidden place at the end of the store (generally on the left side).

What can increase the conversion rate in a given store? By conversion rate we mean the percentage of people entering a store and coming out with a purchase. Strangely enough, the longer they stay, the higher the conversion rate, so it is in the interest of store management to make sure people are welcome and feel comfortable, so they stay a little bit longer than in a competitor's store.

Paco Underhill measured the average time people stay in a home design store. Results are provided in Table 9.1.

In-Store Expectations and Perceptions

Table 9.2 summarizes what people expect—and resent—in a given store. For example, customers want to touch products, but some brands, like Louis Vuitton and Hermès, make sure customers have no

Table 9.2   In-Store Expectations and Perceptions

They want	They do not want
To touch products	To line up
To look at themselves in the mirror	To have too many mirrors
To find things on their own	To be obliged to ask silly questions
To speak	To find unreadable labels or inexplicit codes
To be respected	To be told the product they want is out of stock
To make a good deal	To face intimidating sales staff

SOURCE: Paco Underhill, *Why We Buy: The Science of Shopping* (New York: Simon & Schuster, 1999).

direct contact with the products and have to ask: This is their way of engendering a sense of scarcity or at least to give the feeling that each product is very special.

People also want to look at themselves in a mirror, but they don't want to be surrounded by mirrors like those found in American supermarkets or drugstores, that are set up at a 45 degree angle from the ceiling so that the cashier can see what people are doing in the store: They don't want to be spied on, but they do like to catch a glimpse of themselves here or there as they walk along in the store.

A similar situation arises when we look at interaction with sales staff. People say that they like to speak but they don't want to be intimidated by the sales staff. They are looking for a pleasant and supportive environment where they will not feel they are pressed to do this or that.

In the last line of Table 9.2, customers say they want to get a good deal. This does not necessarily mean that they are looking for a bargain and are interested in a deep discount. They simply do not want to be cheated and want to feel like they have purchased at the right price and in a pleasant and rewarding environment.

Paco Underhill identifies many other specific behaviors. For example, he mentions that when they visit a supermarket, 90 percent of women have a list, but only 25 percent of men have one. Yet in 60 percent of the cases, both end up with purchases that were unplanned.

How do consumers react to *waiting time*? To assess this, one can measure the precise time people have had to wait for something, and then ask them how long they thought they waited. Interestingly enough, there are no discrepancies between 90 seconds of actual time and perceived time. However, two minutes seems like three or four, three minutes seems like five, and four minutes seems way too long.

This is a problem because we know that waiting time is the number one criterion for assessing quality of services: Any person waiting more than three minutes in a store may feel frustrated and unhappy.

How can this be handled? By showing customers that you care. Customers feel much better as soon as they have a chance to interact with someone. At one major luxury brand flagship store in Hong Kong, management was concerned by the long lines of Japanese and Chinese customers waiting to enter. So they rented an apartment in the building next door and the security guards would hand everybody a little card saying: "We are very sorry that you have to wait to enter our store, but it is too small to handle so many customers at the same time. To make sure you can be served as soon as possible we have rented an apartment next door, on the 21st floor, and if you go now, you will be served immediately by one of our staff."[2] Most of the people would read that card, nod their head, and stay in line. They appreciated the sentiment, but preferred to stay in line to have the full service in the real store.

Aside from interaction and care to relieve time anxiety, other techniques can be deployed to make the waiting more pleasant. In a bank or post office, orderly lines and systems that ensure a service on a "first come, first served" basis make people feel more at ease. To this end, individual lines leading to four or five counters is the ideal system whereas a very long line leading to 20 counters (such as those that can be found in railroad stations) is not ideal. With so many people standing in one line, people tend to become frustrated, even if the flow is handled very fast. It is much more effective to manage three lines of six or seven people each: Customers will be given the choice to wait here or there. The flow probably will be handled just as rapidly in each line, and most people will feel happy with their individual choice.

---

[2]As told by a sales assistant of a luxury brand to one of the authors.

Another easy way to relieve the tension of waiting is to create a diversion: Some banks use television sets tuned in to a news channel to make sure people have something to do while they wait in line. This seems to be a very effective way to alleviate the problem.

Supermarket Merchandising Rules of Thumb

Turning now from individual specialty stores to supermarkets, you might think that we are drifting rather far from the specifics of luxury retailing. Yet among the aisles and vertiginous displays are a wealth of carefully identified customer behaviors from which professionals in *all* retail sectors can learn.

A first research area deals with *facings* and facing extensions. A "facing" is the face of a product standing on the shelf that can be seen by the consumer. Facings are independent from the number of products on the shelf behind: They are what the consumer sees as he or she moves around in the store. What happens is that, depending on store size, product brand awareness, and loyalty, doubling the facing of a product increases sales by around 30 percent. So, in a given product category and with a limited amount of space allocated on the shelf, there is a way to optimize sales or profit for the category by increasing facings for fast moving or more profitable items and decreasing facings for slow moving or less profitable items. This practice is called "product category management" and it is a very important part of supermarket merchandising. This is, however, not a simple task, since it varies as a function of price changes for one product or another or of advertising and promotional activities.

Does this apply for luxury retail? Naturally, not as much as in a supermarket, but the concept of product category management certainly works to define how much space should be allocated to different product categories and to each individual item. In a perfume and cosmetics store, one doesn't give each product exactly the same amount of space on the shelf. Some brands should be given more space and some others less space in order to provide a more effective retail environment.

Product *height* is another important dimension: the lower shelf, at floor level, is less effective than the shelf at eye level. In a supermarket, merchandisers representing different brands fight to make sure that their products are not at floor level; they try to convince store operators to put their products on higher shelves.

A study called the Colonial Study was conducted many years ago and has apparently never been replicated. It studied sales of 400 different products as they moved from the higher shelf (eye level), to the middle shelf (hand level), to the floor level.

Results can be found in Table 9.3.

Strangely enough, when products are raised, sales increase slightly more than they decrease when they are lowered. But the basic lesson, as indicated in the index, is that when one product is raised from hand to eye level, its sales increase by around 50 percent and when they go from hand level to floor level, their sales decrease by 30 to 40 percent, which is a lot. And from floor level to eye level one can see that the volume is slightly more than doubled. This is a very important part of managing product presence in a store.

Given what is at stake, product category management systems provide optimization rules at any given point in time.

How effective are *displays*? In fact, several studies have indicated that irrespective of its market share, a product on display (end-of-aisle display) sells between four and five times more than it does on the shelf. Displays are therefore more effective for high volume products than for slow movers on the shelf. But slow movers, when on display, recruit more new consumers than they do on the shelf, therefore increasing their market share. The fact that in their larger stores Sephora uses display areas where products are piled high to attract new customers indicates that what happens in a supermarket can also happen in a perfume store, probably with similar impact.

Table 9.3   Changes in Volume as a Function of Shelf Height

	Increases When Products Go Up	Decreases When Products Go Down	Index
Eye level	218	100	148
Hand level	134	80	100
Floor level	100	48	70

SOURCE: Colonial Study.

An important finding in supermarket merchandising studies is that new products have a tendency to be less effective in stand-alone displays than existing products. If we extend this to the perfume business, this probably means that displays in Sephora stores of new perfumes would also be less effective than displays for older products, except when, in addition to the display, the new product is being promoted by in-store demonstrations or special promotional programs.

All these tools from outside the luxury arena provide very interesting insights into what can happen in a luxury store and how luxury store operators can act in order to manage their stores more efficiently and profitably. The products might be very different, but the consumers happen to be the same, and will have similar reactions in a sophisticated brand environment, in a standard textiles store, or in a supermarket.

The bottom line is that just like any other store, a luxury one must understand the expectations of its consumer and make sure nothing is done by chance: Everything must be thought out, planned, and implemented in the most effective way. This is very clear to anyone interested in luxury retail activities.

Chapter 10

The Importance of Stores in Customer Relationship Building

So many designers forget that the customers are, in the end, the VIPs.

—*Paul Smith*

L uxury brands face a major issue: In a very competitive environment they have to retain their customers. Most internal studies show that about 20 percent of customers generate approximately 60 percent of the brand's revenues: This means that a brand has to find ways and means to build customer loyalty. Keeping a customer loyal and evolving new customers into loyal customers is critical for the brand. The store is where it all happens. This is where the brand meets all its customers. This is where the relationship is built.

Two aspects are essential here, which we will analyze one after the other:

1. Store management is a very specific discipline that needs specific competencies and tools. We will describe most of them and provide you with detailed tools on job descriptions, hiring, compensation, and career development in the Appendix.
2. Long-lasting relationships with customers should be built based on the development of personalized service (a topic that will be developed in Chapter 11).

Why Sales Assistants Must Know All about the Brand

It was September 2008, at the Paul Smith boutique in Paris. It is a surprising place, reflecting the philosophy of the creator: "classic with a twist." The walls are covered with framed objects, paintings, and books. It's a shop that stuns in the high-veneered universe of luxury brands.

One of the authors was looking for a purse as a gift to a friend. The sales assistant showed him several styles and from among the articles carrying the emblematic multicolored stripes of the brand, one purse caught his eye. On one side was the facsimile of a letter addressed to Mr. Paul Smith in a feminine hand, perhaps that of a child. On the other side of the clasp were five enigmatic letters, in the same hand: S.W.A.L.K.

He questioned the sales assistant, asking why this model was so different from the others. Pointing to the wall next to her, she said that Paul Smith collects the letters that are sent to him and the most beautiful among them are displayed in the stores. He then asked her the meaning of the five mysterious letters. Silence. She did not know.

On returning home, he attempted to solve the mystery himself: Those letters had to mean something; they were not there by chance! And in fact, they actually did have a meaning, a real story behind them: During the war, British soldiers and their wives, not able to write their feelings and their desires freely in their letters, invented acronyms to thwart censorship:

B.U.R.M.A.: Be Upstairs Ready My Angel
M.A.L.A.Y.A.: My Ardent Lips Await Your Arrival

B.O.L.T.O.P.: Better On Lips Than On Paper
H.O.L.L.A.N.D.: Hope Our Love Lasts And Never Dies

And S.W.A.L.K.? Sealed With A Loving Kiss. What an admirable, moving symbol: On this purse, an object of feminine intimacy, in which women keep countless precious and frivolous items, this acronym, a message of love, acquires a real meaning. Paul Smith, in creating this object, charged it with a world of emotion, referring not just to his own letters (although who is the woman or child who writes to him in this way?) but also to the immortality of any amorous correspondence. For the woman who acquires this object, it will become an article more precious than all others.

One day Paul Smith said, "So many designers forget that the customers are, in the end, the VIPs." He is absolutely right, but what the author experienced here shows that this message is not applied in his own boutiques. This example is only an illustration of the fact that luxury brands are still far from realizing the importance of making their vendors the living story-keepers of their brands. The very special and emotional relationship that forms between a consumer and a brand has to be constantly nurtured: The stories and the storytelling are an essential part of it. When he was human resources director at Bally, one of the authors made requalification and upgrading of the sales staff an essential feature of his guidelines: We must never forget that they play a key role in the relationship that exists between the brand and its customers. Salespeople are the carriers of the uniqueness of the brand and its communication; they are its first ambassadors — well before "the people."

They should be better paid, better trained, and better managed: This is a price that luxury brands should be willing to pay.

The Retail Issue: Retaining Customers

If you have recently entered a luxury brand store, as the authors did in preparation for writing this book, you must have had similar, mostly appalling, experiences. Negative situations range from not being welcomed by salespeople who look bored to death, to arrogant attitudes that make you feel you are totally out of place in the store. There have been occasions when the salesperson did not take any sort of interest in us; their only concern seemed to be in getting the deal done, making us feel like little more than a walking credit card. In one store visit, we witnessed the extreme case of a salesperson spending 20 minutes with an elderly gentleman, telling us after he had left that the man is a very good customer of the brand who was looking for a specific product his usual store did not have. He had come out of his way to the flagship store and "would come back." When we asked if he had taken down this gentleman's name and address to keep in touch with him, surprise was our only answer. We have taken entire groups of trainees to visit luxury brand stores and they always came back with the same comments:

- The stores are dirty, sometimes unkempt, not the luxury idea they had in mind.
- The personnel are arrogant or don't care.

Whenever they came back with a satisfactory experience they would rave about it. Putting these trainees in the most difficult situation there is, that of not buying a single thing, is an excellent benchmark of the sort of service a brand is ready to give to their prospective customers. The real question is: Do they really consider them as prospective customers or just as a nuisance, wasting the time of salespeople who are paid a percentage of the sales?

A 2001 study by French marketing company Euromap is even more fascinating.[1] The study involved a panel of 600 affluent European women (noted as "the leaders") who were familiar with luxury and luxury brands. In fact, they were experts in the field. Nevertheless, 20 percent of them found the luxury brand store where they shopped intimidating! 22 percent found them not welcoming! 20 percent had the feeling of disturbing the sales staff! And 20 percent thought salespeople did not listen to what they were telling them!

Luxury brands are like spoiled children: They are so accustomed to seeing customers lining up to buy the products that they rarely

---

[1]Study made in France, Germany, and Italy. Figures were unchanged since the previous study in 1997.

consider them to be worthy of interest. Two extreme cases are worth mentioning here:

1. A few years ago a French brand, faced with hordes of Japanese customers, was trying to give their European customers better treatment. Stores were then organized in such a manner that the Japanese customers were lined up on one side and treated like cattle, while any non-Japanese entering the store were given a red-carpet treatment. Luckily, this did not last long.

2. When questioned about the existence of a customer database, the managing director of an Italian fashion brand told us: "Of course not. This gentleman you see here buying a dress for the lady with him? Maybe it is his mistress. It would be totally inconvenient to ask him who he is and maybe then send information to his home that may bring trouble to him."

The reasons for not considering customers as individuals are numerous. Companies like Tiffany have been developing IT-based clienteling techniques for more than 40 years, but mostly with regard to tracking each customer's purchases.[2] This is a very imperfect approach to knowing the customer: What that person buys is the complex result of the interaction between their wishes, the salesperson's attitude, the current background of the customer, and the product offering of the brand. All of this can and should be monitored.

---

[2]Before anyone invented the term CRM, very high-end retailers such as Tiffany & Co. had been collecting individual purchase data and marketing to a segment of well-heeled customers. The technique is called "clienteling," and Tiffany can even cull microfilm- and microfiche-based customer sales records back to 1956. In 2000 it introduced a customer data application to match customers to specific store locations and purchase patterns. But it's an inexact science, admits Bill Haines, group director of systems development at Tiffany, in Parsippany, New Jersey. "Matching retail transactions to specific customers, accurately and consistently, is a challenge," he says. "And even if you do that, what people buy and what people tell you they like are often two different things." Clinton Wilder, "No Time for Gloating," Informationweek.com, September 17, 2001.

Minding the Store: A Specific Business

When most luxury brand executives visit one of their stores they are concerned with visible things: the merchandise ("has it been delivered on time?"), the display ("this doesn't look right"), and the sales ("how much did you do last Saturday?"). Their only interaction with the sales staff is through the store manager, if at all. Very few luxury brands see each of their stores as bona fide business units that need a professional at its head and motivated, trained salespeople on the team. Louis Vuitton is one of the rare ones that does. They hire store managers with business degrees, they develop extensive training programs for the sales staff, and they have redesigned their compensation system accordingly.

Viewing a store as a business unit requires an understanding of the major responsibilities that are undertaken there (see Appendix Tool 3: Defining Staff In-Store Responsibilities and Figure 10.1).

For luxury brands, everything that concerns merchandising and image is centralized (like grooming standards—See Appendix Tool 8). The only domain left as the direct responsibility of the store team is sales itself: managing customers, managing the store team, and managing the relationship with the store's environment. This is where a significant difference can be made (see Appendix Tool 6: Setting Sales Targets).

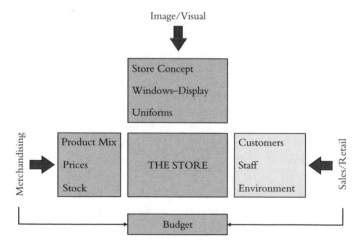

Figure 10.1   Store Responsibilities

Store managers and sales assistants must be viewed as professionals and, as such, special attention should be granted to them. This means ensuring that employee performance supports the company business objectives and drives their achievement. This means simultaneously considering the following four issues:

1. **Hiring**: Luxury brands must come to recognize that their traditional hiring pool (the other luxury brands) is just one of their recruitment sources. *Talent* is what they should look for and talent can be found in service—critical sectors like luxury hospitality and private banking. Store managers must be regarded as business unit managers and their business skills must be ascertained. Traditionally, they were successful salespeople who have gone through the ranks. In today's environment, this can be catastrophic because their management skills may be scant and their business skills nonexistent. Hiring business school graduates as store managers is very innovative and can be a very successful move, provided they are given long-term career incentives (see Appendix Tool 2: Managing Retail Recruitment).

2. **Compensation**: In traditional terms, compensating the sales force has two major characteristics. It is low and its structure varies from region to region. Europe will have a significant fixed component and a low individual variable one; the United States will have almost all the compensation linked to individual sales and Japan will have a fixed component and a collective variable one.

   Both problems should be addressed: Global compensation levels should be raised[3] and a unique global compensation system that includes a fixed component (for salespeople to feel secure), an individual variable component (to reward personal achievements), and a collective variable component (to reward team efforts)[4] should be applied (see Case Study: A European Comparison of Retail Staff Salaries and Appendix Tool 7: Designing a Fair Retail Compensation System).

---

[3]The marketing director of an Italian luxury brand told us recently, when asked to cut costs, "Of course, it was on the store personnel that it was done. Who would think of cutting costs on the products or on advertising and PR?"

[4]Each region will then adapt the system to its local traditions and constraints, but stay within the margins decided by the brand.

3. **Developing competencies**: To be an efficient sales assistant or store manager one has to have specific competencies that the brand must continuously enhance. Brand education, product knowledge, clientele building techniques, store management techniques, and team management techniques are essential. Training is necessary to set standards and transmit knowledge. However, it will only begin to change behavior if it includes real activities and experiences for people to learn from (not just notes and presentations) and is followed up with ongoing on-the-job coaching. Managers must manage their employees' performance, as opposed to sending their people off to training classes and expecting miracles. They must therefore be aware of the factors that affect performance and be capable of influencing them. They must themselves be trainers.

   Senior managers have a critical role here: They must sponsor training initiatives by being present during implementation and follow-up in order to send out a clear message. The brand trainer's role is, in fact, to train the store managers by supplying them with the skills, tools, and support necessary to manage their employees' performance. They are performance consultants and must develop a true working partnership with business managers in order to both assess the behavior necessary for good performance and instill that behavior. (See Appendix Tool 1: A Standard Retail Organization and Tool 4: Job Descriptions and Competencies.)

4. **Career planning**: Traditionally, salespeople go on being salespeople. The most successful will move on to assistant store manager and store manager positions, or will be poached by the competition. Strange ballets are thus seen around Place Vendôme in Paris: People will move from brand to brand, with a salary increase at each move, to finally come back "home." The raise they would never have received by staying in one store will have been gained by moving around. Salespeople and managers must be given clear career incentives. There are at least four career tracks open to them, and each of them should be considered (see Appendix Tool 5: Defining Career Opportunities and Employee Development).

   1. Move from store to store or from category to category to develop the salesperson's competencies.

2. Move up from salesperson to assistant store manager to store manager.

3. Move to buyer positions regionally or centrally (depending on the brand's organization): Their expertise about local sales is an asset here.

4. Move to training positions.

Case Study: A European Comparison of Retail Staff Salaries

In 2001 one of the authors—then the HR director for a luxury brand—commissioned a European study to understand the differences in compensation luxury brands were paying to their retail staff. Two staff categories were studied: store managers and sales assistants. The results were enlightening, and led the author to completely redefine the compensation system of the brand's retail staff.

The results of this study are presented here. The figures are obsolete, but the major findings are still significant. The three key ones are:

1. Salary levels vary from city to city. Because of differences in purchasing power, this is the case everywhere.

2. Salary levels will vary very much by brand. For instance, when the study was done, sales assistants within a given city could earn approximately 50 percent more at Gucci or Chanel than at Bally or Hermès.

3. Compensation systems vary greatly with each brand *and* within each brand. Let us take the example of Brand X. Store managers were paid:
   - Paris / Milan / London / Munich: fixed salary + individual variable
   - Geneva / Brussels / Madrid: fixed salary + collective variable

(continued)

Brand Y was a different story:
- London/Geneva/Brussels /Madrid/Milan: fixed salary
- Munich: fixed salary + individual variable
- Paris: fixed salary + collective variable

This means that these compensation structures are not driven by local culture (since they varied from brand to brand) but by the brand's local history, and the sad fact that no clear European compensation strategy was devised at the time. This is confirmed by the retail staff compensation structure in 2001 in the author's company:

Country—Region	Fixed	Collective Variable	Individual Variable
Japan	100%		
Asia Pacific	85%	15%	
United States before 6/01			7.5% to 8.5% of net sales
United States since 6/01	Guaranteed minimum of $8–$10 per hour		7.5% to 8.5% of net sales
Europe Switzerland	Fixed	Different percent for different product groups	
Germany	Fixed		Different percent for different product groups

As we know, a compensation system has a significant impact on customer relationship building. This means that luxury brands, if they consider customer relationship building as strategic, should first and foremost redesign their retail compensation systems.

Building Client Relationships:
The Challenge of Personal Service

The challenge that luxury brands increasingly face is growing customer loyalty. This can only be achieved at the store level by developing service.

Twenty-first century consumers want to be thought of as individuals, not as anonymous credit card holders who may, in the very best cases, be sent an offer based on their latest buy at (for example) Tesco, because Tesco has implemented transaction data analysis. Or when connecting at Amazon.com, the screen has a message for you: "Hello, Mr. X. We have recommendations for you." They have the technology to recommend books in line with your latest purchases and ask you to improve these recommendations by giving them additional information on how you rate the books you have bought.

Tesco and Amazon consider the people who shop there as *customers* and not just *anonymous consumers*, which is at least a step in the right direction.

But twenty-first century customers want to be considered as *clients*: They want to be recognized, treated as unique, pampered, and reassured. And they know the difference between a computer-generated offer and a personal offer.

The challenge for luxury brands is to build on one of the myths that accompany them: They care for their customers. They must learn to develop personal relationships with *all* their clients to satisfy them and make them want to come back into any of the brand's stores. *They must become luxury service companies.*

Three objectives are critical here:

1. **Develop clienteling**: Each client must be recognized as such and all his or her personal information treasured. Clienteling means establishing a personal relationship between a salesperson and a client. This can only be achieved through specific attitudes and with the help of tools.

    Salespeople must be client-focused: Each person entering the store is to be considered as a future client, be it today or in a year's time, be it in this store or in any other of the brand's stores. Each client should be assessed and profiled, his or her motivations and expectations determined, and each piece of information hoarded. Clients constantly reveal information about themselves to the alert observer: in conversation, when shipping or receiving packages (business, vacation, and related addresses), when selecting gifts (names, tastes, addresses, and significant events in the lives of family, friends, and associates), from conversations among clients, and from their business cards. The objective for each salesperson is to be trusted by their clients, who will only then consider them as competent advisors.

Tools can range from the simplest to the most sophisticated. The client book is a basic tool each salesperson should have. It helps salespeople develop an intimate knowledge of their clients, become a trusted advisor of each client, and plan the selling season.[5] An IT solution such as CRM software and a database are an alternative, as long as it includes all qualitative information salespeople acquire on the clients and not just figures.

2. **Make service the cornerstone of the client relationship**: Shopping by appointment, personal merchandise presentations, wardrobing, delivering purchases (or grouping purchases in a department store), sending handwritten notes of thanks, informing tourists of the name of the closest store manager in their country; these are but a few of all the services a client can receive in a luxury brand store.[6] Financial rewards can also be developed, as

---

[5]With an intimate knowledge of his clientele and a thorough grounding in the collection and the buy for the store, a proactive salesman can plan his business through the selling season. By charting what to sell to a specific group of key clients, he further increases management's ability to predict business and manage stock flow. The salesperson identifies core clients, analyzes their past purchases, and compares them against the buy set for the store. Building around specifics in the collection, she or he plans which items to sell, when, and how best to introduce them to the client. This requires a steady, meaningful dialogue with clients and a true understanding of the entire collection.

[6]"Holt Renfrew has introduced a complimentary concierge service for shoppers. Services rendered include restaurant reservations, 'unobtainable' tickets for shows and events, sending gifts and sourcing services such as babysitting and pet sitting. At the same time the shop has launched a complimentary personal shopping service specializing in wardrobe-building, image consulting and special occasion dressing, sourcing from every department in the store." (*Luxury Briefing*, February 2002.)

Neiman Marcus (InCircle program) and Saks Fifth Avenue (Saks First) have been doing successfully since the 1980s. Levels of services are to be determined at the brand level and implementation at the store level then is critical.

3. **Recognize the central role of the sales staff**: Each salesperson has an essential role to play in identifying the client, in caring for his or her needs, and in delivering the very best service. As Russell Reynolds Associates recently said in their brochure: "Information doesn't build companies; science doesn't build companies; intuition doesn't build companies; promises don't build companies; volume doesn't build companies; boundaries don't build companies; people do." This refers us back to hiring, compensating, training, and providing career incentives. This also reminds us of the relative roles that sales staff and clients have in the relationship. In most cases these roles are asymmetrical: Either the salesperson considers the client as a nuisance (arrogant attitude) or considers the client as some sort of a superior being who can spend in five minutes what she or he doesn't earn in a month's time (inferiority attitude). A regular relationship should be built on the acknowledgment that salespeople and clients are on a par, engaged in a business transaction. Ritz-Carlton has thus coined an exceptional motto all luxury brands should ponder: "We are Ladies and Gentlemen Serving Ladies and Gentlemen."

Case Study: The Four Different Sales Assistant Profiles[7]

The annual Wharton Retail Customer Dissatisfaction Study has determined that customer dissatisfaction is mostly caused by

(continued)

---

[7]"Are Your Customers Dissatisfied? Try Checking Your Salespeople," Knowledge@ Wharton, May 16, 2007.

employee–related issues, and not by store or brand-specific issues. This led the authors of the study to identify the essential characteristics to be found in ideal sales associates. They found four:

The most important is being an "engager." Associates fitting this description smile and interrupt whatever they are doing to help a shopper. Problems associated with not finding an engager are most prevalent overall, and across all store types.

The second most important type of salesperson is the "educator." This employee is able to explain products, make recommendations, and tell customers where products can be found. Does the salesperson help you find what you need, inform you, and educate you?

Another type of ideal sales associate is the "expeditor." This employee is sensitive to customers' time and helps speed them through long checkout lines. This sales person recognizes that, with their intervention, things can keep moving forward. Someone has to notice the problem and go out of their way to alleviate it.

Finally, the research indicates that customers want "authentic" sales help. These associates let customers browse on their own, and appear genuinely interested in helping regardless of whether a sale is made or not.

Successful sales assistants blend all four of these "archetypes."

The reader will find in the Appendix all of the tools necessary to tackle the questions raised in this chapter. It is a toolbox for successful implementation of a consistent retail store management strategy, intended to develop the strength of the brand customer relationship.

Chapter 11

Building Loyalty in Luxury Brands

When people walk into a Louis Vuitton store, they should get the best service in the world.

—*Bernard Arnault*[1]

Delivering unique service and personalizing the relationship with the customer is the major issue facing luxury brands today. How can this be achieved?

We suggest six essential steps for brands to follow:

1. Focus on the customer, by putting him or her at the center.

2. Turn repeat customers into brand advocates.

---

[1]"Retail Optimization Is Luxury's New Buzz," *WWD*, May 25, 2010.

3. Deliver a unique brand experience—and implement it.
4. Define the brand contract with customers and adopt specific tools for retail optimization (client segmentation, CRM, etc.).
5. Define customer journeys.
6. Use customer experience design.

Introduction

The luxury industry is now faced with four major issues that concern customers and will shape its future:

1. Luxury customers globally seek more than the product: They expect experience and personalization of the relationship. They look for a level of service that is far beyond the standards that luxury brands deliver today. This will require new competencies—especially at the retail level—and a new way of relating to customers.
2. The luxury industry is entering new markets (like India and China) that will be the levers of its future growth, but at the same time they must find ways to grow mature markets: *They therefore have to adapt to different customer cultures and face the mature market's changing customer expectations.* This means achieving the right balance between new markets and new customers and driving short-term revenue in these regions while maximizing long-term revenues from existing customers in more mature markets.
3. *Retailing is a profession that luxury brands do not traditionally master.* As we discussed in Chapter 10, brands face critical business issues in their stores because this is where the brand meets its customers. They must therefore hire store managers, develop sales experts, and rebuild compensation systems.
4. Building long-lasting customer relationships requires that luxury brands must *define real customer relationship strategies.*

This means that, at long last, the customer is king for luxury brands. Brands that have built their growth on a strictly top-down model for attracting new customers (more products in more stores in more countries) have to instead imagine how they can develop their business by having customers come back and build loyalty (thus driving revenue and profitability). They have to ensure that the customer is firmly at the center of all their activities and become truly customer-centric in their approach. Unfortunately, many brands have difficulty accepting this sort of customer empowerment because they believe it is necessary for them to have complete control.

Step 1: Focus on the Customer

Luxury brands have spent lots of money developing new products, opening new stores, and sending messages to their customers using traditional communication channels—advertising and communications can represent up to 15 percent of annual sales. But none of the money spent is as valuable as meeting their customers. When customers flock to the store, why is it necessary to bother about who that customer is and what his or her expectations are? We can therefore understand the flight to emerging markets (Louis Vuitton and Zegna just opened stores in the Mongolian capital and Gucci has opened stores in Azerbaijan and in Yekaterinburg in Central Russia) and the expectations linked to the Chinese market: Bain in a recent report expects China to become the world's number-two luxury market.[3] Many brands will therefore prefer to open new stores in new markets.

> *None of us are in the business of selling necessities; luxury is the business of creating and satisfying desires.*
> —Belinda Earl,
> CEO, Jaeger[2]

Let's face it: Luxury brands are in danger of trivialization. Too many stores kill the necessary exclusivity a luxury brand must have in order to develop its image—there was only one Hermès store, in Paris, until 2010; now there are two in Las Vegas! Luxury brands seem unaware of this. Moreover, they are faced with another issue: the decline in sales per square foot in existing stores.

Four major factors have contributed to this decline in sales:

1. The economic crisis.
2. The rise of the Internet, which develops consumer empowerment.
3. The new consumer mega trends, among them the rising importance of "green" attitudes and of sustainable development.

---

[2]"Managing Luxury Brand Growth," KPMG, 2006.
[3]"China Luxury Market Study," Bain, November 2010.

4. The situation in Japan. This is a very important luxury market, where, convinced of the endless luxury hunger of consumers for their products, brands have been opening store after store (Burberry has 75 stores in Japan and only 32 in the United States, Hermes 64 against 30, Prada 15 against 35, and Bulgari 31 against 17; in other words, twice as many shops in Japan as in the United States, even though the markets are roughly the same size) even though sales have been in decline since 2006.

As a consequence, luxury brands are slowly realizing that markets are maturing faster than they thought. Focusing on their current customer has become an issue and retail optimization has risen to the top of the agenda.[4] They are now concentrating on becoming better retailers to grow sales per square foot and must therefore gather in-depth knowledge about their customers and their expectations.

Companies have an increased interest on improving results and are under greater pressure to deliver and be measured on results (both ROI and marketing spend). This focus on data gathering, measurement, and bottom line has been the case for some years now in both the beauty and wine & spirits sectors, where luxury brands have always battled directly against mass brands in the same distribution channels. Fashion, watches, and jewelry, mainly distributed in very selective channels, all are now facing similar issues.

Traditional luxury brand marketing strategies are ineffective here: Above the line/sponsorship/celebrity endorsement/product placement/advertising do little to help build personalized customer relationships.

Case Study: The Traffic Issue
Luxury stores do not all deal with the same levels of traffic. Here are some examples:

French fashion brand flagship (Paris): 800 clients a day (and 3,000 on a day during the bargain sales)

---

[4]"Retail Optimization Is Luxury's New Buzz," *WWD*, May 25, 2010.

Italian fashion brand flagship (Paris): 600 clients a day and 1,000 on a Saturday

French leather goods brand (Paris stores): flagship, 4,000 clients a day; secondary store, 500 clients a day (and 1,000 on a Saturday)

French jewelry brand flagship (Paris): 25 clients a day

European durable goods luxury brand flagship (Paris): 100 clients a day

Perfume and cosmetics at a selective retailer flagship (Paris): 15,000 clients per day (30,000 on a Saturday)

Needless to say, there is a big difference between dealing with 25 or 30,000 customers a day. For the sake of this chapter, given that perfume and cosmetics open-space retailers is a very different category, let us focus on more traditional luxury brand stores. We suggest that different luxury models are at work here:

Model 1: Private Sales Model In stores with less than 100 customers a day, the typical number of sales staff is around 7, which means less than 10 customers per sales assistant per day. The brand will organize sales on a one-to-one basis: Each customer will be given the time and attention necessary to finalize the sale.

Model 2: Luxury Sales Model Stores with around 500 to 800 customers a day will typically have 35 to 50 sales staff, which translates to approximately 15 customers per sales assistant per day. The brand will constantly strive to find the right balance between the luxury experience and the pressure from the number of customers.

Model 3: Professional Process Model Stores with over 1,000 customers a day will tend to have 200 sales staff, which means up to 20 customers per sales assistant per day. The brand has professionalized the complete sales process, but has to deal with a major issue in not compromising the luxury experience.

Step 2: The Loyalty Effect—Turning Repeat Customers into Brand Advocates

Luxury brands, which have always focused on traditional marketing techniques, are now entering the customer relationship era.

Benchmarks show the positive commercial impact of loyalty marketing strategies. They will grow the average spend per customer by 7 percent and will increase the frequency of shop visits by 10 percent. The benchmarks also show the importance of word of mouth:

- Propensity of positive word-of-mouth spread by members is 1.7 times bigger than by non members.[5]
- Word-of-mouth drives sales revenue growth.[6]
- "Over the course of a typical week, the average American consumer participates in 121 word-of-mouth conversations, in which specific brand names are mentioned 92 times. Looked at another way, Americans participate in 3.5 billion word-of-mouth conversations every single day! Brands are discussed 2.3 billion times per day. Brands, it is fair to say, are a major currency of conversation in America."[7]

But luxury brands should beware of the ubiquity of the words "loyalty" and "customer satisfaction." It is interesting to go back to a seminal paper from the *Harvard Business Review* in 2003[8] that shows that "a single survey question can serve as a useful predictor of growth . . . customers' willingness to recommend a product or service to someone else." The precise wording of the question was: "How likely is it that you would recommend (brand X) to a friend or a colleague?" This led to the construction of a unique scale separating "brand promoters"— those customers with the highest rates of repurchase and referral, who

---

[5]Colloquy.com, 2009.
[6]LSE London, 2008.
[7]Ed Keller, "Unleashing the Power of Word of Mouth: Creating Brand Advocacy to Drive Growth," Word of Mouth Marketing, ARF, September 2007.
[8]Frederick F. Reichheld, "The One Number You Need to Grow," *Harvard Business Review* (December 2003).

gave ratings of 9 or 10, from "brand detractors," who gave answers from 0 to 6, and from "passively satisfied" with ratings of 7 and 8. Moving a step further, the paper recommends plotting the brand's revenue growth against its "net promoter score," that is, the percentage of promoters minus the percentage of detractors. This fascinating study (followed by many others) shows that:

- Word of mouth is critical to a brand.
- Detractors can be dangerous.
- Promoters are real brand advocates.
- A brand's major issue should be to convert customers into promoters.

Other major studies confirmed that advocacy drives growth in all categories, with brands and companies with high net-promoter scores and low negative word-of-mouth rates growing four times as fast as companies with low net-promoter scores and high negative word of mouth.[9]

Most retailers struggle when it comes to building strong relationships with their customers, as is illustrated in Figure 11.1.

The critical issue is, therefore: How can a luxury brand acquire brand advocacy? Our take is simple: *You need to add a customer experience that exceeds expectations and previous benchmark experiences.* Each customer keeps in mind similar experiences—very often outside luxury itself—that act as experience benchmarks. Think of a perfect customer experience at Apple, where the brand will offer to seamlessly transfer the contents of your present computer onto your new Mac through its One to One service. This will be your experience benchmark. (See Case Study: Weston—Great Service.)

This remains valid whatever sales model is employed. If a brand is considering a personal sales model it should define what the customer's expectations are before the customer ever enters the store, and be ready to beat them, hopefully setting a new benchmark experience level.

---

[9]"Advocacy Drives Growth," Paul Marsden, Alain Samson, and Neville Upton, LSE, September 2005.

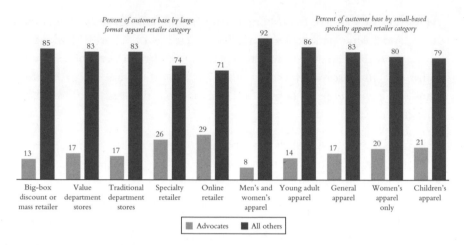

Figure 11.1   Most Apparel Retailers Struggle to Build Strong Positive Relationships with Their Customers
SOURCE: "2007 Customer Focused Apparel Retailer Studies," IBM Institute for Business Value.

This has major consequences that luxury brands need to face up to. For example, a brand with different stores with different traffic levels will have implemented different sales models to accommodate the different situations (the luxury sales model in its flagship store and the personal sales model in its secondary store). It will have to face an excruciating problem: Do we deliver the same level of experience everywhere? Do we develop different experiences even though the customer may be the same?

A typical case is Louis Vuitton, a brand that, given the stores' traffic, faces this issue daily. A first answer was given by Bernard Arnault, who told analysts at LVMH's 2009 results presentation: "When people walk into a Louis Vuitton store, they should get the best service in the world." Yves Carcelle, the Louis Vuitton chairman, added: "We dedicate a lot of our energies to making sure we give our customers a more refined experience."

This goes to show how major luxury brands are shifting their focus to service—and not only for their VIPs!

Whereas luxury brands are only just starting to consider building such experiences, luxury hospitality has a proven track record—because they have always had to focus on their customers' expectations and not on the brand promise.

The worst experience that a guest usually has in a hotel is checking in: Waiting in line after a tiring journey can be nerve-racking. Four Seasons has embedded a unique client experience for some of its best clients: When you alight from your car a person will take you directly to your room and you will have a personalized check-in there.

Ritz-Carlton provides another example of such a success. Based on their motto,[10] they have developed a unique method of inputting data on their CRM so that, if you request a flat pillow because of backache, you will find a flat pillow awaiting you in the next Ritz-Carlton Hotel you go to. Or, when you come back to the same hotel, you will find the same familiar babysitter available for your children.

Step 3: Delivering a Unique Brand Experience and Its Major Internal Consequences

The experience will only come alive successfully if all touch points are in line and all staff, be it sales, marketing, or senior management, is properly briefed and—more importantly—convinced and motivated. The experience needs to be lived throughout the whole company. This will have five important consequences for luxury brands:

1. The brand's organization should be rethought in a customer-focused manner. Particular attention should be given to IT systems and transversal elements of projects. This means that such a customer-oriented culture should be embedded in *all* future hiring (not only in the retail staff).
2. Training will have to include brand culture, values, and service orientation elements—not just policies and procedures.
3. Hiring is required for new competencies such as retail performance directors, CRM directors, loyalty program directors, and customer service directors.

---

[10]"We are Ladies and Gentlemen serving Ladies and Gentlemen—The Ritz-Carlton Hotel is a place where the genuine care and comfort of our guests is our highest mission. We pledge to provide the finest personal service and facilities for our guests, who will always enjoy a warm, relaxed yet refined ambience. The Ritz-Carlton experience enlivens the senses, instills well-being, and fulfills even the unexpressed wishes and needs of our guests."

4. Evaluation of the retail staff will need to include new criteria: service orientation, brand culture awareness, and brand ambassador competencies.

5. Compensation systems will have to reward values-based behaviors, in order to reinforce customer focus and the delivery of unique customer experiences (see Case Study: The Compensation System Issue).

Case Study: The Compensation System Issue

As we discussed in Chapter 10, compensation systems vary from brand to brand and from country to country. Based on real-life examples, let us examine some situations that are directly impacted by compensation systems.

Case A: A sales assistant receives either a monthly sales commission or is competing in an internal "basket" variable system, where the person who reaches the highest "basket" in a given period gets a bonus. Enter a (frustrated) customer with an after-sales issue—which will obviously not become a sale. More often than not, the after-sales process being long (for administrative reasons: Do you have your invoice? Where did you buy this item? Can we examine the problem?), the sales assistant will not be motivated to make sure the customer leaves satisfied.

Case B: Many luxury brands develop recognition programs (employee of the month programs, for instance) that lead to antagonistic behavior among sales assistants instead of collaborative behavior. However, dealing with a customer, especially a dissatisfied one, quite often requires the collaboration of different employees in the store. Sales assistants should therefore be encouraged to develop cooperation. For instance, innovation contests can be used that will help optimize the customer's brand experience. One excellent example here is the "Make Nordstrom Special" contests that help to reinforce the corporate values and deliver excellent customer service.[11]

---

[11]Robert Spector and Patrick McCarthy. *The Nordstrom Way to Customer Service Excellence* (Hoboken, NJ: John Wiley & Sons, 2005).

Case Study: What American Customers Expect from Luxury Brands

Numerous studies have been conducted concerning expectations from luxury customers in different locations worldwide. Here are the major results from customers in the United States—and our recommendations.

Luxury Brands in Department Stores

A 2006 study by Alix Partners is presented in the *WWD* issue of July 13, 2006. Customers were asked to rank a series of shopping expectations on a scale of 1 to 5 for five stores: Saks Fifth Avenue, Neiman Marcus, Nordstrom, Lord & Taylor, and Bloomingdale's. Here are their Top 10 expectations, which should be at the center of the basic contract a luxury brand has to have with its customers.

1. Courteous, respectful employees.
   These attributes, however basic, are considered by the customer to be at the heart of the luxury experience.
2. Quick, hassle-free merchandise returns.
   Customer service departments are often understaffed, resulting in long waiting times. This study shows that clients often feel uncomfortable or even under suspicion, in response to the many questions asked by the staff.
3. Staff expertly addresses customer needs.
   How to serve the customer is paramount: Being called at home when an ordered product arrives, or perhaps a note sent for a birthday, are elements expected by luxury customers.
4. Staff treats customers like they're valued.
5. Staff proficiently wraps purchases.
6. Short wait for purchases.
   Luxury customers want their purchases to be made quickly and easily and will not wait more than a few minutes.
7. Well-groomed staff.
8. Visually appealing store.
9. Employee dress complements store.
10. Information is easily attainable by telephone.
    This emphasizes human contact by telephone.

(continued)

A recent (2010) study by The Luxury Institute, "Leading Edge Insights into the World of the Wealthy," states: "Another finding of the report was that the mystery shoppers preferred the customer service and aesthetics in brands' retail locations over the experiences in department stores selling that specific brand's products. Mystery shoppers found the company stores to be better maintained, with a more welcoming environment, than the brand's area within a department store."

Our Comment and Recommendations

Luxury brands organize and control both their own stores and the corners they have in department stores. It seems, therefore, that they give much more attention to what happens in their own stores, which is something of a mistake: Customers navigate from one brand touch point to another, and expect similar experiences at all touch points. The question luxury brands should ask themselves is: What brings a customer to the department store corner and what brings him or her to the retail store? The differences should lead them to better serve these customers.

Case Study: Weston—Great Service

Attracted by one of the items in the window, I pushed open the door of the J.M. Weston boutique on Boulevard des Capucines in Paris. As soon as I entered I knew this was a good idea: I experienced a rare demonstration of service—a half-hour of pure delight.

It was a Saturday morning and the (small) boutique was full: a dozen people, men in their forties, well-dressed but in a wide range of styles (jeans to casual chic). I walked around casually, looking at the styles. A man came up to me and I told him that one of the styles had caught my attention; he followed me outside, identified it, and led me to a vacant seat. Soon a salesgirl came up to me and there was my first surprise: She was already aware of the style I was interested in—the information had been accurately transmitted. Second surprise, she offered to measure both my feet, explaining that our feet are often not exactly the same size, and the information is needed to choose the best size for me. She then came back with two sizes, saying that I could choose one according to the comfort I sought. She then explained that the width she was showing me is adapted to the morphology of my foot and the construction of the shoe was Michel Perry's contribution, as the brand's new designer. Third surprise: While she took my shoes off, she offered to have them polished by the shoe-shiner installed at the entrance of the shop. Wonderful! I would leave with brilliant shoes, even if I bought nothing. She then spoke to me about my shoe brand (Paul Smith), telling me they have very beautiful designs, good quality, and that she keeps track of what they do. (Even if this wasn't true it made me feel good; just a few words that acknowledged the wisdom of my choice.) She then guided me to a full-length mirror (many luxury brands that sell shoes do not have mirrors such as this). I made my choice, then asked to try on another style, which arrived in the correct size and width. I was willing to buy both. After asking whether I would like to add my personal information to their database, she brought me a form to fill in and a pen on a wooden presentation tray. She offered me a drink, asked me to wait a moment and returned—fourth surprise—with the invoice (in my name) and the credit card machine on the presentation tray. Why wait in line to check out when you might as well pay here, comfortably seated? I left the boutique, delighted.

What can we learn from this unique experience?

The attention flowed smoothly; each moment was prepared for, my expectations as a male customer anticipated.

The experience was totally unlike "classic" selling, with a non commercial aspect (the shoeshine) and the "disappearance" of the cash counter (didn't we already see this in the Apple store?).

A desire to return. A benchmark has been set for my future experiences.

Step 4: Building a Brand Contract and Using Four Tools for Retail Optimization

We suggest, based on our experience in various other industries, that luxury retailers focus on four major tools:

> *In this world there are two tragedies. One is not getting what one wants, and the other is getting it. The last is much the worst.*
>
> —Oscar Wilde

1. *Defining a Brand Contract:* As Hugues Cailleux and Charles Mignot state,[12] "The first step of successful CRM is to define the brand's 'basic contract.' Luxury brands must determine their own, non-negotiable visions of quality, innovation, service and attention. Every single (potential or actual) customer must benefit from this basic contract as soon as he or she enters the boutique. Why? First, this is the basic issue of etiquette. Second, no one can predict a customer's profile, expectations and lifelong value. The 'basic contract' will show customers that they are already part of the family—even before they buy." One such brand whose vision is clearly defined is Hermès: Confronted with the idea that Hermès was a brand, former CEO Jean Louis Dumas-Hermès told one of the authors: "We are not a brand, we are a signature . . . you see my name is on every product we sell. It is as if, every time we sell a product, we signed a contract with the customer that buys it."

2. *Client segmentation:* All customers are not alike and the level of sales to a given person is not the unique criterion to be used. Let us have a look at how Lego develops its relationship with its customers—and its business. The brand has segmented its customer base by level of implication and involvement with the brand. Five groups are defined: covered households, active households (who bought in the past 12 months), the connected community (engaged beyond the brick, visiting the web site, coming to the official Lego stores), the 1:1 community (those who trust the

---

[12] "Is CRM for Luxury Brands?" *Journal of Brand Management,* 2008.

brand with their personal data), and the lead users. When an active household connects to the brand, average Lego spending almost triples and when it becomes a 1:1 household, it increases by five.

A client segmentation that is tailor-made for the brand is the best starting point: There can be no ready-made answer; each brand has to develop its own. We highly recommend that it be based on in-depth interviews of customers to gather a unique understanding of their relationship to the brand.

3. *CRM and database management:* Building a complete qualified database is critical. Take Clarins: It is one of the only beauty luxury brands to have developed a sophisticated CRM strategy. "We get all the feedback from our customers on all our products by mail, phone, fax or email. . . . We centralize data in a unique marketing system, to analyze the impact of the same product in different European countries and make more efficient customer segmentation," says François Boiteux, organization and systems director at Clarins. This unique client database (of female customers) was subsequently used to launch the men's line: In June 2002, a first mailing was sent to the brand's female customers, asking them to send information about the "men in their lives" and complete a short questionnaire. The result? 17,000 contact details collected. This strategy allowed Clarins, within seven months, to establish a database of 24,000 male clients and become market number two within a year!

4. The Lego case also teaches us *the importance of measurement.* They have implemented the very metrics suggested by Bain in 2003. They calculate loyalty metrics and referral economics, measure promoters versus detractors, and focus on four major factors: product experience (immediate post purchase), online experience, store experience, and customer service experience. Measure, measure, measure. Unfortunately, most luxury brands use mystery shopping as their unique measurement tool. This is but the initial step: The customer experience, the engagement, the interaction, the response to communication, all should be measured on a regular basis, using a multidimensional technique, as Lego proves.

Step 5: Defining Customer Journeys and Identifying the Critical Touch Points

To achieve this, a complete customer-focused approach has to be developed, encompassing the before and after in-store experience, which is the traditional focus of luxury brands.

Luxury brands should work on identifying the customer journey: Customers start on a journey, looking for a product or a brand, and embark on numerous moves through different media and in different locations before they buy (or not). This takes them through different touch points with the brand, some of them being less than unfavorable. Luxury brands need to be aware that their customer may encounter negative experiences on their journey before or after the sales. To illustrate:

- A customer in a jewelry store hesitates and the salesperson does not clinch the sale. The customer leaves the next morning for his home city in another country. In most cases, the salesperson will *not* have given the customer the business card of his or her counterpart in the brand's store in that city, because "I will not be commissioned!" It is a lost sale and a negative experience for the customer.
- After-sales can be a trying experience. The CEO of a very important luxury brand said to one of the authors: "It is not normal that when you bring a watch for repairs, you have to wait for a month before you get it back." Tiffany, to counter this issue, has set up a central repair center near La Guardia Airport in the United States—the product to be repaired is sent there overnight by UPS and returned to the customer within 48 hours.

Our experience is that customer journeys will vary according to the customer segment.

The client experience needs to be supported through *all* touch points: in the store; online, when the customer researches; online, when the customer meets the brand on its website; through all communications; at client events; during each possible interaction and through all service instances (warranty, cleaning, repair, etc.).

Step 6: Customer Experience Design for Luxury Brands

It is critical for luxury brands to reengage with their customers by designing integrated customer journeys that encompass all distribution channels and all touch points between the brands and its customers. We have devised a unique method that is described next.

A 5-Phase Method

1. *Knowing your customers*: A precondition to improving the customer experience for any brand is a thorough understanding of consumers. Qualitative interviews with customers have to be conducted by a trained psychologist to gather deep consumer insights and understand consumer motivations, expectations, and behavior. These customer insights can then be consolidated into "Personas" to cluster and represent different customer segments. They also build the basis for the redesign of the customer journeys.

2. *Building internal cooperation and sharing knowledge*: Multiple workshops with cross-departmental participants including sales, marketing, CRM, product management, and country management should be conducted. This enables conversations and knowledge exchange between managers and employees of different departments of the organization who very often do not find a way to communicate directly. This is the basis used to build a Customer Experience Project Team.

3. *Building ideal customer journeys*: The Project Team should then create customer journeys for different customer segments through experiential prototyping; abstract ideas are turned into low-fidelity prototypes, which can be experienced and evaluated by potential customers and communicated to management.

4. *Scenario building*: In addition to concrete improvements of existing touch points, the project team should develop different scenarios for the long-term vision of the products and the brand with the aim of setting the stage for unique and radically improved customer experiences. These high-level scenarios are then broken down into concrete actions and individual projects that can be implemented immediately.

5. *Action Plan*: All findings, discussions, prototypes, and scenarios are then consolidated into an executable project plan with activities for immediate implementation.

The Benefits of This Method

This unique methodology allows a brand to turn customer insights and expert knowledge within the organization into concrete ideas and prototypes to solve underlying problems. (See Figure 11.2.) This method[13] delivers the following benefits:

Customer Experience Focus

- *Deep Consumer Insights*: The qualitative customer interviews done by a psychologist uncover very distinct customer segments based on customer motivation and behavior.
- *Integrated Customer Journey*: The integration of different sales channels into an integrated customer journey helps to identify realistic opportunities to collaborate between different sales channels and strengthen the relationship between consumers and the brand.
- *Creative Reframing and Brand Vision*: Questioning and reframing existing assumptions challenges the status quo of the daily business and leads to completely new ideas and visions for the brand.

Experience Design Method

- *Inclusive*: The integration of different departments in interactive idea generation and prototyping workshops allows all participants to share ideas while stimulating conversations between different departments that are not possible in daily business.
- *Concrete*: Instead of discussing market share numbers, high-level consumer trends, or abstract ideas, the workshops lead to tangible prototypes to solve real problems in different sales channels. These prototypes make it possible to experience, evaluate, and communicate ideas and solutions.

---

[13]M. Gutsatz and B. Schindlholzer, "Customer Experience Design for Luxury Brands," The Scriptorium Company, White Paper, 2011.

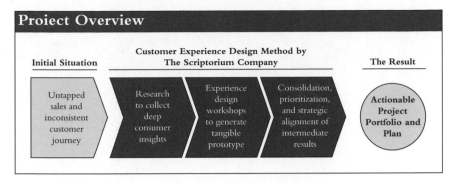

Figure 11.2   A Customer Experience Design Method

Conclusion

Why bother? One of the authors, attending a Walpole Conference in London a few years back, overheard a fascinating conversation: Coach executive: "We have a database of more than a million customers and we develop new products using data-mining."

British luxury brand executive: "If I were you I would not be so proud to have a *million* customers in that database. I would be proud if I had ten thousand."

Two worlds facing each other: Which one do you belong to?

Chapter 12

Advertising and Communication

To communicate a brand's value correctly, "consistency as a story" is more important than visually beautiful advertisements.

—*Kyojiro Hata*

Advertising and communications for a brand are easy to understand and have been studied carefully in various marketing and advertising textbooks. But what is different about advertising and communication for a single retail store? Are the objectives and the tools similar? Definitely not. For a lone retail store, advertising and communications have much more limited objectives.

First and foremost, it must *build traffic*. The whole idea, irrespective of the strength of the brand and the attractiveness of the location of the store, is to make sure people come to the store, enter, and

229

can be convinced of the value of the merchandise. It is often said that mail–order advertising effectiveness is very easy to measure: Just count the number of completed order forms or requests for information. It should be the same for a luxury retail store advertisement: Did the campaign increase the number of people entering the store? This can be easy to measure and over time, through trial and error, it should be possible to hone the campaign to achieve the best results.

But another objective *is to communicate an intention and a benefit.* The *intention* is to tell the targeted consumer that he or she is the only one to whom this message is addressed: This customer should be convinced that the store cares about him or her as an individual. The *benefit* is the recognition that this customer is very important to the store and that store management values very much his or her loyalty.

Explained this way, it is clear that luxury retail advertising and communication must be very operational. In the first section, we will look at general communication principles. In the second section, we will examine customer response management.

Advertising Communication

This section does not analyze the traditional advertising approach, as our focus is really the point of sale. As an introduction, we will discuss the concept of micromarketing, then the way to target customers, concluding with a study of the different uses of advertising media vehicles.

The Concept of Micromarketing

This term was coined by Emanuele Sacerdote in specific reference to a retail store situation. The idea was to develop a complete marketing process that was entirely geared toward an individual retail store, based on consumer behavior and elements of the traditional marketing mix. His idea was to start a new way of thinking about the single-store retail scenario.

The Different Steps in the Purchasing Process In his analysis, Emanuele Sacerdote[1] speaks about four different consumer steps:

1. *The preacquisition phase:* In this period, the target consumer is very far away from the point of sale. He or she should be convinced of

---

[1] *Source:* Emanuele Sacerdote: "Le strategie di micro-marketing," in *La strategie retail nella mode e nel lusso* (Milan: Franco Angeli, 2007).

the strong identity of the brand and become familiar with it. The higher the awareness, the easier the convincing. He or she should be given the address of the point of sale and should be given a good, rational reason to drop by.

2. *The point of sale:* When the consumer is at the point of sale, he or she should immediately recognize the concept of the store and its strength. He or she should be in an environment that is pleasant and intriguing. He or she should feel at home and wish to stay and visit, as if at a location already familiar to him or her. This phase should obviously reinforce the identity of the brand and its attractiveness.

3. *The acquisition:* This acquisition will be the result of the presence in the store of adequate products at the right prices and in line with the general environment of the brand. It will also be the result of staff effectiveness in understanding the needs of the customer and communicating the advantages and desirability of the product.

4. *The post acquisition phase:* As the customer has made a purchase, his or her basic data has been registered and he or she is part of a club of privileged friends of the brand. He or she becomes part of the family and will be asked questions about products, the brand, and the store. This entry into the family of loyal customers is not an easy step for newcomers. At this very early stage, a lot of convincing still must be done on the values of the brand and its attractiveness. This may not be the ideal time to reward this new customer, but this is certainly the time to give positive reinforcement and a very special new comer's approbation and treatment.

The Retail Marketing Mix According to Sacerdote, the retail marketing mix is only limited by the variables controlled by the store manager:

The show window is the first element of this retail marketing mix. It is the first direct communication tool of the store. It should be luxurious, in line with the brand identity, and intriguing enough to entice people to enter the store. The products presented should be striking, but also accessible and attractive. A show window is obviously a strong brand identity statement, but should also be able to communicate a form of complicity with the would-be customer.

The product is the store's reason for being. Products should be presented with the maximum variety of colors and shapes. People should be able to touch them, unless one wants to create an impression of scarcity. Right at the store entrance, customers should be able to understand the way everything is presented and be able to see and understand the general concept of the store merchandising.

The above-the-line advertising is the set of all media available to store managers: radio, billboards, newspapers, or any others. The objective again is to communicate the existence and the address of the store and to make it a future target for a consumer visit. As said earlier, the objective of this tool is to create a direct response: increase the number of people entering the store.

The below-the-line advertising consists of all the activities that organize a direct contact between the consumer and the store: mailing of catalogs, letters of invitation to a specific product presentation, congratulations on a birthday with special purchase conditions in the store, or invitations to previews of bargain sales. All these vehicles should have a quality in line with the brand standing and reflect the merchandise assortment available in the store.

The staff is also part of this retail marketing mix. It organizes the sales and communicates the brand identity. A salesperson in a Versace store should be very different from a salesperson for a Nina Ricci store or a Chanel one. Salespeople should also be appropriate to the basic ages and demographics of the main target customer.

As we look at this retail marketing mix and compare it with the traditional marketing mix, we can see that two elements are missing: the physical distribution, as the store is a given, and the price, as it is part of the product and its merchandising strategy. But the idea is to show that the five elements described should be coordinated and balanced to make the store effective and convincing for target customers.

Old or New Stores? Old and new stores require different sets of communication priorities. For a new store, the basic message to convey is that there is a new address, a new location, a new concept, and something that is worth visiting. A major opening event would have the objective of making sure the press mentions this new location and explains why it is interesting and different. For a new store, a special budget should be allocated to ensure that the new address appears in as many shopping guides as possible for both tourists and local residents.

For an old store, the idea is to speak of enlargement, new decoration, new merchandise, and new presentation, so that people think it is worth a new visit.

Targeting Consumers

Which consumer should be the target of a retail advertising and communication program? Let's first look at the different groups of consumers and discuss the paradox of efficiency.

Defining the Consumer With specific information about its clients, the store manager can define different groups of customers. For luxury, the concept of loyalty (someone who makes all their purchases in a single store) is fanciful, since the same person will buy a Prada handbag, a Dior dress, and Ferragamo shoes. Instead, top consumers may be defined as those buying, for example, four times a year at full price. The second group would be those who buy at least twice at full price, and the third group consisting of those who buy at least twice a year during bargain sales and maybe once at full price during a given year. An occasional buyer is someone who has bought at least once in the past two years.

In Table 12.1 we have classified the different types of consumers by frequency of purchase. The top regular customers, as they visit

Table 12.1   Customer Base Targeting

	Part of the Population	% of Sales Tickets	% of Sales
Top regular customers	1%	30%	40%
Second regular customers	2%	25%	25%
Bargain sale customers	1%	15%	10%
Occasional customers	10%	30%	15%
Noncustomers	85%	—	—
Total	100%	100%	100%

SOURCE: Taken from Andrew Wileman and Michael Jarry, *Retail Power Plays* (London: Macmillan, 1997).

the store at least four times a year plus maybe also in bargain periods, represent 30 percent of the sales receipts and 40 percent of sales. The second tier regular customers number twice as many but they come twice as seldom to the store, and therefore they represent almost the same level of sales receipts and 25 percent of the sales. The bargain sale customers visit the store almost as much as the second tier regular customers, but they concentrate their purchases on bargain sales. They represent 10 percent of sales in this example. The occasional consumers, because of their large number (71 percent of the customer base) still represent 30 percent of the consumer base as they come on average once every two years.

The Paradox of Retail Efficiency One would tend to think that non users would be the best target to increase sales. It is true that if we convince half of them to visit the store and buy once a year, we would double the number of sales. Also, if we could convince occasional customers to come to the store more often, we could also increase our sales level significantly.

But what we call the paradox of retail efficiency is the fact that the most effective way to increase sales is to convince regular customers to come more often. This very small number, 1 percent in Table 12.1, is the key to easy sales increases.

Andrew Wileman and Michael Jary mention a statement by McDonald's in 1995 that 77 percent of its sales were derived from "super heavy users" (adding the joke: "probably in both possible senses") being males, aged 18 to 34, who eat at McDonald's between three and five times a week. This is an amazing figure, which probably holds true in luxury retail. If we gather the top regular customers and the second tier regular customers, we arrive at 75 percent of total sales. The paradox of retail efficiency is clearly at work in this field.

Media Advertising

Advertising should probably be concentrated toward the regular customers, or at least toward people who belong to similar sociodemographic groups. Let's first look at the purpose of advertising for retail, then look at meaningful types of advertising schedules.

The Purpose of Retail Advertising For a brand, the purpose of advertising is very clear: Its objectives are to increase awareness and to develop a positive attitude and preference for that given brand. For a retail store, or a retail chain, the objectives are much more specific, leading to different types:

Promotional advertising has only one objective: to increase store traffic. The point is to explain the products and services and present their prices. The purpose couldn't be more straightforward. But sometimes retailers find this objective too limited and want to do more. In the early 1990s, a relatively unknown Italian brand called Fontana di Trebbia was sold in two Hong Kong luxury stores. Apart from Hong Kong, the brand had only one store in the world: in Milan, in the best location, close to via Monte Napoleone, but slightly out of the way. In Hong Kong, this brand was advertised with brand identity campaigns in very upscale magazines. This was probably a mistake. It would have been more effective to concentrate all advertising efforts on promotional advertising to make sure Hong Kong consumers and tourists knew where the stores were located, what they had to sell, and, every other month, promote a very special product at an interesting but still upscale price.

Institutional advertising could be another advertising purpose. Again, the idea is not to speak about the brand as in institution, but to promote what is different about the store: When was it opened? Why is it located in such-and-such a place? How large is it and why? What kind of assortment does it have? The objective is not directly to build store traffic but to promote the store as an institution: Why is the Chanel store in Paris, rue Cambon, so special? Because it was opened more than 60 years ago by Miss Coco Chanel. Why is the new Ralph Lauren store in Paris, boulevard Saint Germain, so special? Because it is huge, it presents a full assortment of merchandise, and because it has a restaurant which, from the very start, in June 2010, was fully booked for more than two months.

If the store is nothing special per se, the advertising can concentrate on early receipt of merchandise, special invitations to fashion shows, or special events. The idea is not to build immediate traffic, but to make sure everybody from the target audience would know where the store is located and why it is so different.

Promotional and institutional advertising is when the objective is to do both at the same time: promote the stores as an institution, but also build traffic.

Complementing the brand image advertising may be an objective for very strong brands with heavy brand advertising budgets. The purpose is not to replicate the brand advertising but to piggyback on it and come with a very upscale and sophisticated institutional campaign, which builds on the brand communication, is very similar in look, atmosphere, and design, but has an objective that is much more limited to the institutionalization of a given store or a group of stores.

The message here is that brand image is not enough to bring customers to the stores. There are creative ways to make sure everybody knows about a given retail location among the target consumer group.

Media Selection One effective way to communicate is by sending mail to selected target consumers. The document should be in good taste, specific enough, luxurious enough to be perceived by the recipients as a reward for their brand patronage, but it should not be overpowering. This would be part of the below-the-line advertising mentioned earlier as an element of the retailing marketing mix.

For the above-the-line advertising, different media vehicles are available:

- *Magazines* are the traditional luxury medium and also can be used for retail advertising. But lead times are long and the planning of a special event must be done well ahead of the actual date. Also, the advertising execution should be subtle and different from the traditional brand image advertising. A very useful tool is the "city magazine." In many cities like New York or Chicago, but also Shanghai or Beijing, you will find a magazine that bears the name of the city and acts as a news medium for fashion and culture. Such magazines lend themselves well to retail advertisement.
- *Newspapers* are the traditional retail medium. They provide the required level of frequency and are where consumers look for special events. The difficulty is to create the advertisement in such a way that it looks sophisticated and in line with the upscale identity of the brand.

The same newspaper can also differ according to the subscribers' addresses: This may be very useful for customer targeting.

- *Outdoor advertising*, when it is sophisticated enough (e.g., the JC Decaux transparency panels or airport light boxes) is considered to have an immediate impact on store traffic, but this medium lends itself more to brand image messages than to very specific communication objectives. In a given city it can have a very strong impact.
- *The radio* is also a very operational and action-oriented medium, but it provides a large reach not suited to communicating to a small segment of sophisticated customers.

Types of Advertising Spending Schedules *Reach versus frequency*: When deciding on an advertising investment, it is necessary to decide whether the priority is to reach as many consumers as possible or to reach a small target with as much frequency as possible. Given the fact that any retail advertising investment, even in the case of institutional advertising, should be action-oriented, the thrust of the campaign should look at frequency: A single advertising wave, once a year, would be ineffective. Advertisements should be targeted to a limited audience and should appear often to provide renewed opportunities to think about the store.

The opportunities to communicate: In a yearly retail advertising plan, it is necessary to list the different events that can provide special opportunities to communicate. Some examples are:

- The renovation of the store.
- The store opening anniversary.
- A special spring or Christmas event.
- The presence in the store of the famous brand designer.
- A trunk show with products that are not part of the regular assortment.
- The opportunity to present a live Paris or Milan fashion show on-screen.
- A special brand anniversary.
- A major brand event happening elsewhere that can be seen online or on-screen.
- The beginning of bargain sales or special pre sales for regular customers.

The event doesn't need to be the event of the century, but it should provide some interest, if not some excitement.

How to Distribute Advertising Spend Throughout the Year As said earlier, for mass-market or general advertising, the investment is generally concentrated in waves. If the budget is limited, marketers may opt for a single wave for the year. Generally, marketing people plan to have two waves; for example, perfume and cosmetics companies concentrate their advertising spending around Mother's Day and Christmas. Some heavy advertisers may use three or four waves per year, but they have to make sure each wave is strong enough to be noticed and registered by the target audience.

For luxury retail, where advertising is generally action-oriented, this system of waves may not be ideal as it does not yield the frequency required all year long. To define the ideal setup, retailers can start with the percentage of yearly sales achieved each month. Table 12.2 shows an example of this approach.

In the first example of pacing (A), the advertising follows basically the percentage of monthly sales, with each month corresponding to 5 percent and an increase in investment for stronger months (May and June) with a concerted effort for Christmas.

In the second pacing example (B), the budget is concentrated on the best selling months and the low sales months have no advertising spending at all.

In the third pacing example (C), concentrated efforts are made during the best months of the year, but with an anticipatory effort made just before the strong sales period starts in order to build consumer interest.

Which is the best system? It depends on the size of the annual budget and how action-oriented one wants to be. If the advertising objective is 100 percent promotional, then schedule A may be the best fit. If the objective is slightly more operational, then schedule C may be more effective.

The Specific Messages In their book, *Brandstand*, Arthur A. Winters, Peggy Fincher Winters, and Carole Paul describe 10 communication strategies that make sense for a retailer. Many deal with brand identity

Table 12.2 Distribution of Advertising Spending by Month (for a Fashion Brand)

	Jan	Feb	March	April	May	June	July	August	Sept	October	Nov	Dec
Percentage of yearly sales	5%	5%	6%	6%	8%	9%	5%	5%	7%	7%	12%	25%
Advertising pacing (A)	5%	5%	5%	5%	10%	10%	5%	5%	7.5%	7.5%	10%	25%
Advertising pacing (B)				15%	15%	15%			12.5%	12.5%	25%	15%
Advertising pacing (C)			15%	15%	10%				20%	15%	15%	10%

(image positioning, attribute branding, benefits branding, etc.), but two are specifically designed for immediate action-oriented strategies: destination and spiral branding.

By *destination*, they mean all activities that are geared to giving the target consumer the desire to visit the store.

They speak in particular of the New York specialty store, Henri Bendel, which was moving from a small location on Fifth Avenue to a much bigger one (four times the size) on 57th Street. They printed a luxurious booklet, using Isak as the illustrator. The booklet was sent to 45,000 people from their mailing list and was affixed inside the *New Yorker* magazine. Then, tiny shopping bags with free samples of products and a card describing other gifts they could receive in the store were given out in New York to people coming into the city from upscale commuter trains. They even made sure that this campaign was reflected in the way the store was decorated.

In 2000, as a result of their consumer research, Saks Fifth Avenue found out that consumers viewed them as "the ideal place to buy designers clothes and special occasion clothing" but did not consider them as an "all occasion store for all times of life and all times of day." They wanted to change this perception so that customers would visit on a regular basis. They decided to run an advertising campaign with the theme "live a little, save a little, enjoy a lot" in many New York magazines, including the *New Yorker*. But they also ran other activities:

- They created a 186-page catalog and mailed it to 450,000 customers.
- They invited 600 privileged customers to a launch party, not in the store but in the Boathouse Pavilion on Central Park.
- They distributed postcards with the advertising campaign and included some in their catalog.
- They created a shopping bag with the campaign image.
- They sent out a direct-mail campaign that provided a 15 percent discount for a full week to a select group of customers.

The campaign was notable not just for its strength but also for the coordination of the different elements of communication.

The second action-oriented strategy discussed in *Brandstand* was *spiral*. By *spiral*, they refer to surrounding target consumers with different communication elements that, like a spiral, all wind up in the store.

They give the example of the Canadian specialty store Holt Renfrew, which supported a strong magazine advertising campaign with several mailers, each with distinctive formats but all referring to the print advertising campaign: One mailer included the poster of the advertisement, in another mailer, a booklet, then a newsletter—each with a strong reference to something happening in the store.

Destination messages or spiral messages—whichever you choose, the crucial thing is to use action-oriented messages that are designed to increase store traffic.

Customer Relationship Management (CRM)

The CRM tool is very well suited to retailing and even though the system was created for a different purpose (to assess the special relationship of manufacturers with their end users), it seems to have developed faster in the retail realm than elsewhere.

The objective of CRM is to get as close as possible to an idyllic state of one-to-one marketing. The idea is to have as much information as possible on each individual customer (sociodemographic variables, purchasing patterns, as well as attitudes and preference toward different brands) so as to be able to develop a marketing program that is almost 100 percent geared to that customer: an adapted communication program focusing on his or her main purchase criteria, with price levels taking into account his or her individual price elasticity, and research into products that correspond to that person's size, look, shape, and color preferences. In a way Mrs. Joyce Ma, the founder of the eponymous multi-brand luxury fashion retail chain in Hong Kong, was simply doing her own CRM when she called her best customers to tell them, "Hello, Mrs. So-and-So, I just received a new Armani dress that I purchased in Milan during the last fashion show just for you. We should make an appointment so that I can show it to you." In her own very commercial way, she was already embarking into individualized CRM activities.

But obviously to systematize this, one must start by building a database and then use this database both on a regular basis and for exceptional items.

Building a Database

Getting the Information It all starts with information about the customer. When a consumer pays by check and shows an identification card, it is easy to take down their name and address. But since most people today pay by credit cards, this information is not necessarily accessible. After the sale, the sales staff or the cashier should therefore say to the customer: "We would like to keep in touch with you and advise you when we have private sales or special events. Would you like to fill in this form so that we can know you better?" The form should not be a plain piece of paper: It should be a small card where people are invited to specifically put their name, address, telephone number, and e-mail address.

What about the person's age? This question should not be asked, but the sales staff can estimate age ranges. In the same way, they should note the appropriate size of the person. Large mail-order houses (also using CRM, of course) even have a way to access a probability of age as a function of the first names. It has been found that someone named Kevin or Bianca in the United Kingdom has a probability of being born around a precise year or a range of years. Of course, for some first names like John or Peter, it does not work, but when it does, computer programs can help.

The second element to the data is purchasing patterns: How often did the person come to the store in the past year—and in the past five years? How many purchases (at full or at bargain prices) have they made? What type of purchase is made in every store of every country? It can also be worth noting whether the product was purchased for the person's own use or to be given as a gift. The sales staff or the cashier can simply key in all this information on the cash register.

Maintaining the Database

Unfortunately, customer data ages very fast. People change addresses, marital status, and purchasing patterns. One person who used to buy four or five times a year may stop buying altogether: Illness, changes in employment, or changes to their social situation can modify this.

Purchasing is easy to register; changes from purchasing patterns in one store to purchases in another may be an indication that a person has changed addresses or jobs.

During a pleasant in-store discussion, it is worth asking the customer: "Do you receive catalogs from time to time from us, and do we have your correct address?" but avoid doing this at the door when the customer is on the way out.

Another way to check addresses is through the telephone book, but many people have restricted numbers and cannot be found.

One certainty is this: If a database is not maintained regularly, after two years it will need a thorough and painful clean up. When a mailing is sent out, it is possible to analyze the percentage of returns (unknown at this address). If it reaches 10 percent, you have a problem.

Using the Database

Adjusting Mailings Different mailings can be adapted to the purchase history of each person as well as their estimated age and style (trendy? conservative?). One could therefore envisage not one catalog, but two or three, with different moods and an adjusted selection of products. There could also be a very luxurious and expensive brochure for top regular customers and a cheaper but still upscale one for other customer groups.

Invitations for events in the store (and for high prestige events outside of the store) will be sent to those customers who are primary targets, as well as to those who have reacted positively to a similar mailing in the past.

The beauty of CRM is that if it is well maintained and if it is flexible and powerful enough, the longer it exists for a retail group, the more effective it becomes.

Identifying Customers in the Store The most rewarding experience upon entering a store or a restaurant is to be called by name: "Good afternoon, Mrs. So-and-So." For restaurants, it is a bit easier, as people make reservations and give their names. Before dinnertime, the manager can review the names of those with reservations to check their preferences and their peculiarities. The welcome will then be more friendly and more specific. This is much more difficult in a retail store, since people only give their names when they pay. Good sales staff should undertake learning one or two hundred of their best customers by name. For the others, as the name will only be known at the cash register, a good database should flash out small details that could be mentioned as the sales staff walks the person back to the door. These parting words should be different from one visit to another and will serve to tell the consumer that his or her patronage is welcomed and recognized.

Unlimited or Restricted Access? A good CRM system should record sales anywhere in the world. This will help the brand assess the volume of purchases done, for example, by Japanese or Chinese consumers in Hong Kong, Paris, Milan, and New York. It therefore becomes possible to evaluate the business volume conducted by Chinese or Japanese residents outside of their home country and observe the total effect of people from these two countries on worldwide sales. It will help identify top Chinese customers who buy more products abroad than in their home country, and make sure their mailing program is adapted to their full purchase performance.

But if this information is useful at headquarters and at the individual country level, should it be available in every store? Operationally, if the CRM system is effective and if the information is not too fuzzy, there is nothing against a full disclosure. Nevertheless, CRM data remains highly confidential information and, since staff often move from one brand to another, there is a need for "Chinese walls" to make sure confidential information on nationality or top customers' sales is restricted to regional marketing people. In each store, the data should probably be restricted to its individual store information.

A good CRM system is a very powerful tool. The stronger it becomes, the more confidential it must be.

The Use of CRM for Special Events

A good CRM system can provide information on the top 200 Japanese customers or the top 200 Italian customers. This is an opportunity to reward and recognize those people with invitations to very special events like fashion shows or special launch ceremonies. They should never be forgotten.

Ultimately advertising and communication should be used to create a system that is as close to a one-to-one relationship as possible with all customers.

Chapter 13

The Future of Luxury Brand Retailing

In 1982, the theory was that the Swiss watchmakers would have to go to the future: We have to innovate! But the future alone is never the whole solution. The future, by itself, is just a concept. The future must always be related to the past.

—*Jean Claude Biver*

Luxury brands are at a crossroads. Over the past 15 years they have based their business model on moving from a 100 percent wholesale model to a mix of wholesale and retail, with company-owned stores seeing their numbers grow with the strength of the brand. The major divide now is not between wholesale and retail, but between strong and weak brands: Strong brands will enter a new market directly with own-store retail operations (either in a joint venture or by themselves), while weak brands still have to develop through wholesale.

This has led luxury brands to master a skill that is totally new to them: retail management. They have developed new competencies in store locations, local legal operations, store merchandising, hiring, and sales staff compensation. Retail is now part of their business model, and it allows most luxury brands to show strong profit margins.

But retail is not yet one of their core competencies.

Luxury brands are driven by acts of creation and they consider their core competencies to be the creative process, production, and communication. When country managers with a retail background are hired by luxury brands, they soon understand that they have been hired for their retail competencies: Identifying new promising store locations, organizing stores, and managing sales staff is how they earn their daily bread.

Now that retail is essential to the luxury business model, brands must start to include it as a core competency, as Louis Vuitton has been doing since their early days, since their business model excludes wholesale completely. What consequences will this have for other luxury brands?

The major change is that luxury brands will have to face up to the fact that the store is where the brand meets its customers. This may seem obvious, but in a creation-driven business, the store is at *the end* of the value chain. This is where we have to separate mature markets from emerging markets: In mature markets (including the domestic market), bringing new customers to the store and building loyalty is the luxury brand's next major challenge. This can only be done through a serious reevaluation of the role and importance of the customer, and by viewing customer relationships as key to the brand's success. This means that retail and the store will be as important as creation and will have to become a core competency of the brand.

In the previous chapters we have identified four retail issues that luxury brands will have to face in the coming years.

Issue No. 1: Building Branded
Customer Relationships

First and foremost, luxury brands will have to reevaluate their relationship with customers. The Chanel customer relationship model will have to be different from the Dior customer relationship model, as much as their products and brand images are different. This is a major challenge. It means that they will have to create branded customer relationship departments, and not just CRM departments. It also means that each brand has to deliver an identifiable brand experience— and that today's luxury customer wishes to have more than a branded product plus a store concept plus be a name in a database. This means a brand contract, brand-specific customer segmentation, and branded customer journeys.

This has strong organizational consequences because silos will have to be broken: Internal teams bringing together design, marketing, sales, customer relationships, and information systems will have to be set up and work together to define the customer relationship strategy.

Issue No. 2: Developing Best-in-Class
Luxury Service

Customer segmentation will become an important component of luxury brands. To achieve this, they should look at how American department stores have been structuring their customer base, offering growing rewards, both in products and in service, to the different segments identified. Given that one of the fundamental drivers of luxury consumption is status, achieving greater status can be a major driver: Brands should learn to offer best-in-class service to all their customer segments, with strong enticement to move up, so as to obtain more service, more recognition, more rewards—in a word, more status. But this must be done in a subtle and refined way.

The hospitality industry is another benchmark luxury brands should use. Ritz-Carlton and Mandarin Oriental are examples they should ponder. Best-in-class service is a mix of two essentials: a strong recognition system of the staff (remember the Ritz-Carlton motto: "We are

Ladies and Gentlemen serving Ladies and Gentlemen") and a unique information system that keeps track of all the clients' wishes.

This will have consequences on hiring, compensation, and career paths, of course.

Issue No. 3: Integrating All Communication and Distribution Channels, Therefore Using the Internet Wisely

Luxury consumers are increasingly younger, especially in the new growth markets like China. (A recent McKinsey study shows that people under 34 represent 28 percent of British luxury consumers and 45 percent of Chinese luxury consumers, 73 percent of which are under 45, compared to just over half in the United States.) This has a major consequence: Their attitude toward shopping is significantly different. They look forward to being engaged by brands. This is no small task: They look for a full-fledged experience that embeds itself into their life. They need to connect with the brand everywhere: There should be no time or space limit and no boundaries between their online and offline contacts with a brand. This means that luxury brands must expand their brand presence to new devices like the mobile phone (and not just iPhone apps!) and tablets, allow full e-commerce, create events with privileged access for select customers (and not just to media and VIPs)—all seamlessly integrated with clicks and bricks: Young luxury consumers look for unique experiences they can share with their community.

The fact is that the retail environment is multi-channel, and each should have its role and function, be it in-store, mobile web (mobile apps for all mobile platforms), stationary web (websites, social media), out-of-home, direct mail, and print. For instance, the mobile web has specific functions such as location awareness, immediacy, personalization, voice capabilities, and social connectivity: It is about action and connection, while the stationary web is about presentation and reflection.

Accepting this reality will have strong organizational consequences.

Issue No. 4: Managing the Talent Pool in Stores

Having retail become a core competency will make talent management critical—and not just at headquarters. Two dimensions will have to be managed simultaneously.

At the corporate level, human resources directors will have to develop store management tools, defining competencies for each position, devising modern compensation systems, and rethinking career tracks. They will have to follow the Louis Vuitton model and should hire business graduates to manage stores as business units.

At the regional level, the talent pool for stores will be broadened and poaching from competitors will not be the only norm anymore. If service is considered a key success factor for the brand, hiring will be done from the hospitality industry, private banking, and wherever service is considered critical. This may lead managers to completely revise their thinking about whom to target, and look, for instance, for sales staff trained at Apple.

Managing the talent pool will also lead some luxury brands to invest in their own retail schools: Over the past 15 years they have hired numerous MBA graduates to fill managerial positions and have been working with major global business schools. Considering retail as a core competency and defining a branded service will have some effect on the uniqueness of the training that sales staff should be given. Some brands will follow examples of internal schools like the Montblanc Academy—a move that can give them not only a real competitive advantage over their competitors, but help them retain their retail staff.

Achieving all this will be a multiyear challenge for most luxury brands and can give a strong competitive edge to smaller brands.

Looking beyond these issues, we suggest three other elements that luxury brands should examine if they wish to go on building their image of exclusivity and the strong emotional bond they have with their customers:

1. Inventing new store formats to develop the emotional bond with the brand
2. The China retail blueprint
3. Inventing twenty-first century retail

Inventing New Store Formats to Develop the Emotional Bond with the Brand

For the past 10 years, luxury brands have been developing branded stores in two main directions:

1. Stores that carry the brand's core offer, mostly in fashion and leather goods
2. Category-oriented stores that carry specific product lines, like Dior jewelry stores

Surprisingly, no brand has really tried as yet to build stores that deliver a complete branded experience, mostly because some of their product lines (like beauty, eyewear, and watches) are distributed through specific distribution channels that require specific know-how. This is now changing: Dior reopened its Asian flagship store in Hong Kong (located at One Peking Road, Tsim Sha Tsui, Kowloon) early in 2011. Inside, customers find all of Dior's product lines: clothes, bags, shoes, baby clothes (Dior Baby), menswear (Dior Homme), watches, and jewelry. Only beauty is missing. The store is set in a 10,000 square foot, three-story building and resembles a modern apartment, decorated with all the Dior codes (the color gray and the cane work used in the stone floor of the bag section, two references to the original Montaigne store) and a fascinating mix of fashion and art. Here, Dior presents itself as a lifestyle brand and follows the tracks of Ralph Lauren.

Simultaneously, some brands are moving out of the one-store format to offer a more diversified approach. This is mostly the case in watches, because even if they are sold in the brand's stores, they are mostly distributed in multi-brand stores, which means through wholesalers. Hermès is an excellent example. Having understood that this environment (often cluttered) did not allow the brand to express its uniqueness, Hermès recently decided to open free-standing Hermès watch stores in Asia, in Singapore, Taipei, and Shanghai, after having tested shop-in-shops in Chinese department stores. The success was immediate: In Singapore, not only did the new store see sales beyond budget, but its opening boosted the watch sales in the neighboring

Hermès store by 25 percent. A branded store allows the brand to deliver its storytelling in a consistent manner and helps build the relationship with the customer in a manner no multi-brand store can.

We see these two examples as forerunners of future retail developments for luxury brands, with one question still open: What about the beauty offer, especially perfumes? Will luxury brands stop considering their beauty offer as nothing but a cash cow and integrate it into their flagship stores?

The China Retail Footprint

In their book, *Luxury China*, Michel Chevalier and Pierre Xiao Lu[1] describe the situation of the luxury market in that country. They present the location of the stores of 12 major brands. The figures are eloquent, both globally, and brand by brand:

- 2008: The 12 brands concerned (Armani, Bulgari, Cartier, Chanel, Coach, Dior, Gucci, Hermès, Louis Vuitton, Prada, Tiffany, and Zegna) totaled 169 stores.
- December 2010: The store count was 315—almost double, in less than three years.

If we include other brands like Burberry, Dunhill, Hugo Boss, or Salvatore Ferragamo, with less selective approaches, four strategies can be identified:

1. Brands spread throughout China (in Tier 1, 2, and 3 cities) with approximately 100 stores and are not always directly operated. This strategy is favored by men's luxury brands that consider the Chinese market as mostly a masculine one. Dunhill and Hugo Boss are examples.
2. Brands with a strong retail presence (50 to 60 stores). These brands also target the men's market (mainly in sportswear and leather

---

[1]Michel Chevalier and Pierre Xiao Lu. *Luxury China: Opportunities and Market Potential* (Hoboken, NJ: John Wiley & Sons, 2010).

accessories, which represent 50 percent and 20 percent of sales) but in a much more controlled manner.[2] Examples include Burberry, Ferragamo, and Bally. With 62 stores in 33 cities, Zegna should also fall under this category. (Zegna has been present in China since 1986 and China represents 25 percent of its sales.)

3. Brands with an average retail presence (30 to 40 stores). This is the strategy adopted by the leading brands that seek to grow, but control their retail footprint. Think Gucci, Louis Vuitton, and Cartier.

4. Brands with a small retail presence (less than 20 stores). These brands have decided on the most exclusive retail strategy consistent with its brand positioning. They include Hermès, Versace, Dior, Prada, Bulgari, and Tiffany. Chanel, with six stores, has also taken this restrictive strategy, even though it is ranked as China's number three most desired luxury brand by Bain.[3]

All brands within their strategy grow mostly at the same pace, with the exception of Ferragamo, which went from 10 to 48 stores (+380 percent). It was a brand with a small to average retail presence in 2006 and decided to accelerate its growth exponentially.

Luxury brands face three related challenges in China:

The service issue: When Chinese customers are asked how luxury brands should improve their performance in China the answer is a loud and clear "service experience" (57 percent say more professional and warm service by salespeople; 56 percent ask for better after-sales service; 43 percent demand an overall enhanced shopping experience).[4] They feel that they pay for the luxury experience and lifestyle the brand should convey.

The talent issue: As we discussed in the preceding chapters, luxury retail management is a talent issue. This is a major hurdle: Luxury brands have problems staffing their stores. If most of the store managers outside Tier 1 cities have never experienced luxury spas or upscale restaurants, the brand image is at stake: All sales staff—not only the store manager—must give customers the essence of luxury service.

---

[2]"Zegna Looks to China," *WWD*, November 2, 2010.
[3]"China Luxury Market Study," Bain, November 2010.
[4]Bain, 2010.

The brand value issue: "For those eager to expand in China, it is critical to take note that success in the Chinese market requires far more than opening many retail outlets. Product, presentation, packaging, promotion, distribution, merchandising, and advertising should all contribute toward a simple, unified purpose: delivering genuine brand value to customers."[5] This means that, once more, talent is required: Brand management is a complex discipline that needs people who are aware that the brand image has to be delivered consistently and that all details are important.

As a consequence, we believe that some luxury brands are overextending themselves in China: Too many stores opened too quickly, resulting in smaller sales per square foot, poor service, and dissatisfied customers.

Inventing Twenty-First Century Retail

PSFK, a trend-watching and innovation company, publishes reports that are enlightening as to future trends in specific domains. Their January 2011 "Future of Retail" is a great synthesis of where retail is headed. Luxury brands should be aware of this because their customers use other retail experiences as benchmarks.

PSFK has identified retail trends[6] that we present here, and the future consequences for luxury brands.

- "Increased access to the mobile web is freeing the retail experience from the confines of the physical and traditional online environment, allowing shopping to take place virtually anywhere. . . . [but] Physical stores still provide the best means to communicate with customers and offer a brand experience."
  Consequence: The store, although essential in the relationship to the brand, will only be one of the numerous touch points a luxury brand has to manage. E-commerce will develop both on the web and through mobile devices, even if ultimately the customer will

---

[5]KPMG, "Luxury Brands in China," 2007.
[6]PSFK, "The Future of Retail," 2011.

go back to the store to experience the brand. We are moving from a "the store or nothing" attitude to a "the store and all its satellites" attitude.

- "Creating a flexible in-store environment through design, product offerings and promotions, ensures that each visit will feel like a brand new experience."
  Consequence: Luxury brands have learned that they need to drive customers into the store with new collections on a regular basis. This has led them to move from the traditional two collections a year model to a multi-collection model. This should be strengthened by a similar approach in design, service, and events. Each visit to a store should be viewed as a new experience.

- "Leveraging collaborations based on aspects such as locale or cultural touchstones, maintains a brand's relevancy in the eyes of the customer."
  Consequence: Luxury brands have long adhered to a one-size-fits-all model. The issue they now face is: How can we maintain our unique global image while simultaneously integrating regional idiosyncrasies? Do we only do this by using Asian models (as in beauty) or with specific product lines? What about regional service levels? Is the perception of quality the same worldwide?

- "Whether physically or through connected technologies, shopping is still best experienced socially."
  Consequence: Luxury brands are learning about one-to-one customer relationships. Here is a difficult one: How can they identify friends who shop together, or groups who share their passion for the brand? Shopping is social; customer relationships should have a social dimension also. Remember (see Chapter 9) that two women together spend 60 percent more time in a store than a woman alone.

- "In a connected world where access to information is fluid and transparency is the expectation, brands must actively take part in the conversation; otherwise their customers will do so without them."
  Consequence: This is where the top-down, very aristocratic, control-oriented culture of luxury brands is challenged. How can they build a conversation without losing their essence? How can they empower their customers?

- "The introduction of connected technologies into retail environments is changing the ways that stores are able to provide customer service."

Consequence: Connected technologies are nothing but (useful) tools. This means luxury brands must start by defining their customer relationship strategy and then integrate all communication and distribution channels, using these tools whenever necessary.

We hope that this book will provide luxury executives, managers, and retail staff with answers to their questions and that it will help the luxury industry embed retail into its critical core competencies. Retail is detail: Luxury brands should never forget that this is an endless journey. They should strive for excellence in retail as they achieve excellence in design and creation. As former Gucci CEO Domenico De Sole once said, "You can have the best strategy in the world, the difference between the excellent and the incompetent is execution, execution, execution."

APPENDIX

Managing a Store Toolbox

1. Presentation of a Standard Retail Organization
2. Managing Retail Recruitment
3. Defining Staff In-Store Responsibilities
4. Job Descriptions and Competencies
    a. Cluster Manager
    b. Store Manager
    c. Assistant Store Manager
    d. Sales Consultant
5. Defining Career Opportunities and Employee Development
6. Setting Sales Targets
7. Designing a Fair Retail Compensation System
8. Example of Grooming Standards
9. Business Ethics

Tool No. 1: A Standard Retail Organization

All companies and brands will have their own specific organization—which very often will depend on the size of their operations. As soon as a significant number of stores need to be managed in a given region, at least three levels of responsibilities need to be organized (see Figure A.1):

1. At headquarters: a retail operations director
2. If the company is structured by country: a country manager
3. If the company is structured by store clusters: a cluster manager (the cluster being a certain number of stores that are his or her responsibility)

Then within a store, the organization will depend on the size of the store (see Figure A.2):

- For a small store (a staff of less than 10 to 15): Three positions are standard—store manager, assistant store manager, sales consultant (senior and junior may be designated).

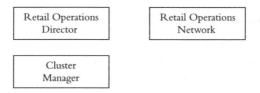

Figure A.1   The Three-Level Retail Organization

Figure A.2   The Four-Level Store Organization

- For a large store (30 or more employees): The store manager will be supported by a certain number of assistant store managers aligned by function (special orders, stock, administration, service, cash desk, merchandising) or by product line (menswear/women's clothing, accessories). The bigger the store, the more numerous the product lines and their managers.

Tool No. 2: Managing Retail Recruitment[1]

1. The Behavioral Approach

It is difficult to select and hire people who, on a daily basis, must engender a broad range of professional attributes such as:

- Welcoming and appreciative customer needs and desires
- Explaining to the clientele the craftsmanship experience
- Dealing with client complaints and after-sales issues
- Negotiating pricing and services, when necessary

All of these attributes are about education, appropriate behavior, and personal competencies; they can be evaluated with effective interviews including a behavioral approach. This involves behavioral questions, such as those aimed at understanding what the candidate has done in a real situation, which may illustrate that he or she has the right competencies required for the retail job.

The behavioral approach requires significant preparation, including:

- A detailed plan for each candidate meeting, specifying each competency to be investigated as well as the questions intended to measure them.
- Questions that are focused on behavior, which should be followed up with significant probing to understand what the candidate's exact role was, and the consequences of his or her actions.

---

[1] These tools are best understood when viewed in conjuction with a forthcoming book that analyzes the complete human resources issues in the luxury industry by Gilles Auguste and Michel Gutsatz, *Leading and Mangaging a Luxury Brand—A Talent Management Perspective*.

Competency	Questions Asked
Retail knowledge and experience	▪ Describe a situation in which you invest your time to know new collection/creation products? How did you proceed? What did you learn? ▪ How have you maintained your knowledge of key competitors? What do you do with this information?
Performance competencies	▪ Describe the most successful commercial "deal" you've negotiated. What did you do to achieve it? ▪ When has your network of contacts really paid off for you? How did you learn from it? ▪ Describe a situation in which you personally have been involved in managing a customer's complaints. What actions did you take? How did you learn from it?
Personal competencies	▪ Describe a situation for which you made an extraordinary effort to meet a deadline. What were the results? ▪ How do you manage to recharge yourself?
Management competencies	▪ Describe a time you led a boutique team to be more effective. What did you do? ▪ How did the team and the retail organization benefit from your actions?

Figure A.3　Examples of Behavioral Questions

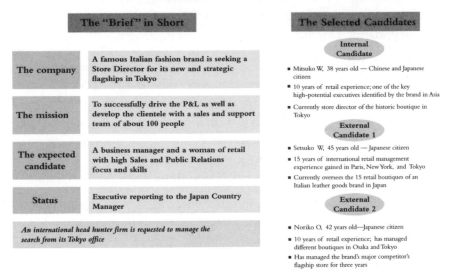

Figure A.4　The Brief and the Selected Candidates

2. Examples of Behavioral Questions to Be Asked

We identified key questions relevant to a large number of retail positions and a series of technical qualifications. Figure A.3 shows examples of those questions—focused on behavior—not opinions or generalities.

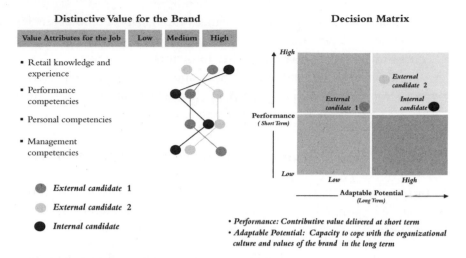

Figure A.5   Evaluation and Recommendations

3. Case Study: Recruiting a Store Director

Featured elements: the brief and the selected candidates (see Figure A.4).

Material provided by the headhunter: *Evaluation and Recommendations* (see Figure A.5).

Analysis and Comments   The key point of recruiting for this position concerns behavior that should be checked, using two major criteria:

1. Short-term candidate performance: delivering significant added value on commercial performance, team management, and daily operations.
2. The potential ability of the candidate, on a long-term basis, to cope with the routine and procedures, corporate culture, and informal management systems of this Italian company

In this case study the material provided by the headhunter leads us to the following comments:

- *Internal Candidate:* Despite the fact that she has less experience, her "High Potential" status within the Italian company and a positive evaluation regarding the key recruitment criteria, enable her to be a serious outsider for the job.

- *Candidate 1:* Both her performance and personal competencies seem lower than those of other candidates; these factors could constitute a risk to integrating her into an Italian company.
- *Candidate 2:* Her retail operational and management experience are an asset to lead the flagship; her current position at an Italian direct competitor gives her a definitive advantage.

Tool No. 3: Defining Staff In-Store Responsibilities

In order to ensure maximum efficiency and productivity in the stores, all in-store responsibilities are assigned to specific staff members. When assigning tasks, it is important to take the following steps:

- Introduce the idea of dividing tasks among the staff during a store meeting, if possible, to build awareness of how individuals contribute to a team effort.
- Involve the staff members in the decision-making process. They will be more committed to the task if they choose it.
- Delegate the tasks appropriately, depending on the skills and knowledge of the individual staff members, and adapting to their needs by spending more or less time to explain and demonstrate the task to them.
- Use the following chart to track staff responsibilities.
- Follow up on a regular basis to check completion and provide feedback.
- Rotate responsibilities regularly to keep commitment alive.

Tool No. 4: Job Descriptions

Introduction

It is critical for a brand to have a very detailed job description for each position.

A job description is based on six fundamental elements:

1. Purpose of the position
2. Duties and responsibilities
3. Performance evaluation criteria
4. Required profile in terms of experience and skills

Example of Staff Responsibilities		
Department	**Name**	**Definition of Responsibilities**
Category A		Classify/organize the product
		Conduct quality checks
		Prepare goods for the sales floor
		Check for labels
		Ensure all products are displayed in the store
Category B		Know the stock situation (best sellers, etc.)
		Prepare returns and transfers
		Prepare sale periods and special events
		Follow visual merchandising/sale/ window guidelines
Stock keeping		Check stock regularly
		Place orders
		Organize stock
		Send product to the repair partner
After sales and repairs		Receive product/call customer
		Organize stock
Visual merchandising		Follow the guidelines
		Always be aware of the store's aspect
		Implement window changes
		Train team
Stock movements		Check and register the movement of goods
		Prepare inventories
		Ensure stockroom organization procedures are implemented
Cash desk		Control bank operations
		Send documents to the accounting department

5. Functional links and positioning within the organizational chart

6. Career path prospects

A job description should always be accompanied by:

- A list of the *competencies* required to hold the position
- An *evaluation grid of candidates,* to be used during the hiring process.
- An evaluation grid, to be used during the *annual evaluation process.*

We present here four significant retail job descriptions, two of them being quite detailed:

1. Cluster manager

2. Store manager (detailed)

3. Assistant store manager

4. Sales consultant (detailed)

We also provide further information related to the two job descriptions that are more detailed: the store manager and the sales consultant. One of the store manager's major responsibilities is that of coach: We therefore detail how he or she can be excellent at being a coach for his or her team. For the sales consultant, we detail an assessment grid, which should be used by the store manager during the annual evaluation process.

Cluster Manager

Reports to: Retail Operations Director

Purpose of the Position Ensures the implementation of the sales strategy and merchandising policy in all stores in his or her area. Is an ambassador for the brand.

Duties and responsibilities

- Commercial sales monitoring and operational steering of stores within his or her region (five maximum)
- Ascending and descending communications relay
- Supervision and management of teams within his or her region
- Oversee the application of the retail strategy
- Provide authority delegation for retail management
- Occasional sales and administrative support

Evaluation criteria
- Commercial sales results
- Commercial sales dynamics
- Behavior and quality of management
- Team management (turnover, motivation, training, etc.)
- Respect for the brand strategy and policies

Store Manager

Reports to: Cluster Manager

Purpose of the Position To develop total satisfaction for the clientele and optimum profitability for his or her store by implementing the brand strategy.

Duties and responsibilities
Development of customer satisfaction and representation of the brand inside and outside the store
- Responsible for the quality of customer service (in the store, on the telephone, or by letter)
- Responsible for the upkeep and maintenance of the store
- Ambassador for the brand within his or her close environment, responsible for the store's external relations:
  - In its competitive environment
  - With traditional partners (hotels, restaurants, etc.)
  - With local officials (local authorities, journalists)
- Responsible for developing the clientele and local prospecting

Development of the store's turnover while respecting the retail strategy
- Involvement in the design of action plans for his or her store along with the cluster manager
  - Strengths/weaknesses, risks/opportunities reports
- Implementation of store's action plan: steering and monitoring results
  - Determination of store objectives (quantitative and qualitative)
  - Division into short-, medium-, and long-term actions (3, 6, and 12 months)

- Monitoring of performance indicators (KPIs such as average transaction, conversion rate, units sold, number of transactions, number of after sales service interventions, percent of clients acquired, percent of loyalty)
- Weekly/monthly report on the period's activity and the competition, with comments and analysis
- Customer campaigns: targets and resources (catalog, events, gifts, services, etc.)
- Staff actions: training, motivation, challenge, personalized objectives, and so forth
- Store actions: renovation, maintenance, equipment, signs, windows, and so forth

Management of store team
- Involvement in recruitment of sales personnel
- On-site integration and training of new sales personnel
- Compliance with grooming standards (wearing of uniform, makeup, hair and accessories, etc.)
- Individual objectives
  - Fix individual annual and monthly turnover objectives linked to KPIs
  - Fix individual qualitative objectives
  - Periodical individual appraisals (every 4 to 6 months)
  - Proposal of end-of-season bonuses
- Management and motivation
  - Weekly, monthly, and annual team meetings
  - Leadership and on-the-job training
  - Evaluation of training requirements (linguistics, sales technologies, products, service, etc.)
  - Record individual expectations in terms of mobility or professional promotion
  - Conflict resolution
- Administration
  - Delegation of tasks and assurance of versatility among sales personnel
  - Authorization in cases where gifts or other commercial sales gestures are requested, within the policy defined by the management
  - Scheduling for weekly hours
  - Budgetary commitments

A Store Manager's Competencies		
	Experience	**Skills**
Indispensable	Sales or Management	Charisma/leadership
		Coaching skills
		Teaching skills
		Precision and organizational skills
		Detail oriented
		Mastery of service skills
		Available when needed, eager to help
		Listening
		Integrity
		Confidentiality
		Quality presentation/image representative of luxury
		Vocabulary and elocution skills
		Fluent English
Preferable	Luxury	Advanced communication skills
		Sales/administration versatility
		Loyalty with respect to his or her hierarchy
		Resistance to stress
		Dynamism
	As consultant managing a store	Initiative above expectations
		Knowledge of the market and the world of luxury
		Commercial sales skills
		Eye for marketing
		Management skills
		Basic IT knowledge
Unacceptable		Strong individualism
		Lack of managerial skills
		Impatience for promotion

Example of a Store Manager Candidate Evaluation Grid	
Competency	**Rating**
Delivers Customer Service in Line with a Luxury Brand	
Builds Client Relationships	
Delivers Product Knowledge	
Is Detail-Oriented	
Interacts in English	
Interacts in Another Foreign Language	
Manages the Business	
Develops the Brand Locally	
Is Organized and Able to Coordinate	
Listens Actively	
Works Proactively and Takes Initiative	
Leads People	
Coaches People	
Is Fluent in Fashion and Trend Styles	
Overall Presentation	

Management of store operations

- Stock
  - Replenishment
  - Feedback with regard to theoretical stock (regular and year-end inventories)
  - Maintenance of top sellers: request more stock if necessary
  - Sell off discontinued lines
- Accounting
  - Compliance with legal, tax, and customs regulations and procedures
  - Cash register receipts
  - Bank transfers where necessary
- Health, safety, and security regulations
  - Compliance with procedures
  - Permanent oversight
- Profitability (in areas of responsibility where he or she can exercise control): management of allowances, general expenses, third-party commissions, gifts, bonuses, and payment terms

The Store Manager as a Coach One of the critical roles a store manager has to play is that of team leader: She or he is the store team's coach. This requires specific competencies and skills that we describe here.

Step 1: Listen and Observe All too often managers are unable to give effective feedback to their employees because they do not take sufficient time to observe their performance. Take the time to watch and listen to your employees sell! It will be a worthwhile investment. Take note of your observations. This will give you specific points in order to coach each sales consultant on his or her individual development needs.

Step 2: Give Balanced and Specific Feedback Once you have filled out the checklist, you are ready to give feedback. Be specific by giving examples of what you observed. It is important to give balanced feedback in order to keep your employees motivated and eager to learn more:

> Stop: Use "Stop" feedback when an employee is behaving in a way that is not in line with brand standards (e.g., "Please do not continue chatting with your peers when a customer enters your area of the store").
>
> Start: Use "Start" feedback when an employee is not demonstrating a behavior that is requested in brand standards (e.g., "I really would like you to begin handing out your business card to every customer you assist in the store").
>
> Continue: Use "Continue" feedback when an employee is demonstrating the appropriate behavior described in brand standards (e.g., "I heard you use open-ended questions with that customer in order to better determine his needs. Thanks to this you were able to quickly assist the customer and sell him two additional items even though he was in a hurry to catch a plane. Keep up the good work!").

It is important to recognize a job well done. If an employee does not feel recognized, he or she will not be motivated to repeat the desired behavior. Furthermore, *all employees* should receive all three types of feedback regularly regardless of their level of performance: It is always possible to find at least one positive point and one point needing improvement in everyone. This will keep an employee who is being told he or she has a lot to improve on motivated to keep trying, and also keep the employee being told that he or she is performing well, motivated to keep getting even better.

Remember, feedback must also be given in a timely manner or it loses its impact.

Step 3: Ensure Your Employee Practices While You Observe This is the step most often forgotten by managers. Giving feedback is great, but not sufficient to change a behavior. The employee must practice, and the manager must coach the employee throughout the practice. Below are three easy ways to coach while the employee practices to enhance his or her performance:

1. Live situation: Continue to observe and give feedback to the employee as he or she interacts with customers throughout the day.
2. Partnering (in a live situation): When time permits, spend time actually selling with your sales consultants. Lead by example. Show them how to perform the steps they are having difficulties with and then ask them to practice the same steps on a different customer. Continue to observe and give feedback throughout the time spent with the employee. Partnering with your sales consultants and leading by example will help you gain your sales consultants' respect and they will then be more open to receiving your feedback.
3. Role-playing: When customers are scarce, it's a good time to coach. At these times, role-plays can be most effective. Take on the role of the customer while your employee practices his role of the sales consultant. Change roles to demonstrate the desired behavior. Provide feedback throughout the process.

Assistant Store Manager

Reports to: Store Manager

Purpose of the Position Assist the store manager in the development of total satisfaction among customers and the optimum profitability of the store.

For this purpose, his or her presence is required whenever the Manager is absent.

Duties
Assist the manager in:
- Turnover
- Team training
- Operation of the store
- Image
- Steering, coaching
- Achievement of his or her commercial sales objectives

Evaluation criteria
Accomplishment of store objectives based on the KPIs:
- Volume
- Margins
- Conversion rates
- Budget (in controllable expenses)
- Customer portfolios:
  - General condition (rate of information, size, etc.)
  - % of clients acquired, % of loyalty, % of attrition
  - Inventory, shrink results, and so on
- Achievement of the individual targets for each sales consultant in the store
- Team progression:
  - Turnover
  - Promotion, and so forth
- Respect for the brand image

Sales Consultant

Reports to: Store Manager or Assistant Store Manager

Purpose of the Position Deliver a unique shopping experience to the clientele in line with the brand strategy, in order to maximize sales and establish long-term customer relationships

Duties and responsibilities

Achieve his or her individual objectives and contribute to the achievement of store objectives

- Key Performance Indicators (KPI)
- Customer portfolio (if customer base established):
  - Client acquisition, loyalty
  - Quality and quantity of information gathered
- Support for other sales consultants
- Support for administrative teams, if they exist (cashing out, stock, etc.)

Permanent application of brand service standards

- Sales and service guidelines
- Quality of greeting and service
- Personal appearance
- Appearance of the store and products presented (windows and counters)
- Knowledge of the brand, products, and policies:
  - Safety guidelines
  - Procedures, administrative rules for authorization
  - Information systems

Participate in the daily running of the store

- Store cleaning and upkeep
  - Cleanliness of the store
  - Quality of the windows, counters, and furniture
  - Cleanliness of the products
  - Versatility for cash register and stock tasks
- Active participation:
  - At team meetings (suggestions, proposals, etc.)
  - In periodical challenges, events, and meetings
  - At customer incidents (new products, defects observed, etc.)
  - In regular and year-end inventories
- Any duty entrusted at a scheduled time or periodically by the store manager, such as:
  - Setup and maintenance of windows and counters
  - Replenishment and maintenance of products presented
  - Complying with training schedules
  - Complying with attendance schedules
  - New product information, and so on

A Sales Consultant's Competencies		
	Experience	**Skills**
Indispensable	Sales	Commercial sales skills
	If beginner: "average cycle" level of studies (two to three years minimum)	Open-minded and curious
		Detail oriented
		Resilience
		Presentation and expression qualities
		Interpersonal and listening skills
		Service oriented
		Patience/availability when needed
		Integrity/confidentiality
		Versatility
		Team spirit and teamwork
Preferable	Luxury/fashion	Fluent English
	sales experience in store	Flexibility above expectations
		Enthusiasm
		Dynamism
		Interest in the products
		Identification and loyalty to the brand
		Mastery of one or more foreign languages
		Initiative above expectations
		Knowledge of market and world of fashion
		Taste for a career track within the network (geographical and functional)
Unacceptable		Inability to communicate or interpersonal difficulties
		Resistant, rebellious, or individualistic mentality
		Instability

Sales Consultant Assessment Form						
Function	**Sales Consultant**					
Professional Competencies	Explanations	1 = Outstanding 2 = Above Standard 3 = Good—At Standard 4 = Below Standard 5 = Unacceptable Performance				
Delivers Customer Service in Line with a Luxury Brand	*Successfully applies the brand's client experience guidelines*	1	2	3	4	5
Builds Client Relationships	*Developing a client base—shows interest and succeeds in developing repeat business with client base—transforms customers into clients*	1	2	3	4	5
Delivers Product Knowledge	*Has extensive knowledge of the collection; develops arguments in selling the products in all categories*	1	2	3	4	5
Is Detail Oriented	*Gives attention to those details that develop the feeling of luxury in the store and in the client relationship*	1	2	3	4	5
Sells in English	*For non-English mother-tongue employees*	1	2	3	4	5
Sells in Another Foreign Language		1	2	3	4	5
Personal Competencies						
Listens Actively		1	2	3	4	5
Works Proactively and Takes Initiative		1	2	3	4	5
Is a Team Player	*Supports overall team goals*	1	2	3	4	5
Is Fluent in Fashion and Trends	*Takes interest in fashion; reads fashion magazines . . .*	1	2	3	4	5
Personal Presentation	*Embodies and implements the brand grooming and presentation standards*	1	2	3	4	5
Communication Skills	*Self-expression—speaking style in relating with customers*	1	2	3	4	5
Self-Assurance	*Is convincing in his or her relationship with others*	1	2	3	4	5

Tool No. 5: Career Opportunities

Introduction

Developing career opportunities within the retail organization is critical for the success of store management—and to minimize turnover. These career tracks should span three organizational departments to allow sufficient flexibility: store operations, retail operations, and merchandising (see Figure A.6).

The Retail Career Tracks

There are two levels for sales consultants: junior sales consultant and senior sales consultant.

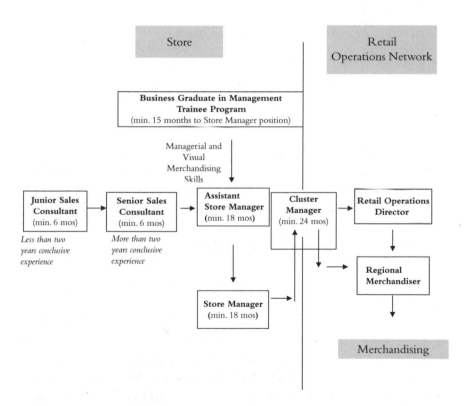

Figure A.6   Retail Careers

Assistant store managers can be:

- Senior sales consultants with extensive sales expertise as well as management and visual merchandising competencies.
- Business graduates who show good management and visual merchandising competencies and wish to make a career in retail.
- After having proven their capacity to manage a team and develop the store's performance, they will move on to store manager responsibilities.

Store managers will have the possibility of:

- Managing a standard store and then a flagship store
- Becoming a cluster manager after a proven track record as store manager

Cluster managers will have three possibilities:

- Retail operations director
- Career path into merchandising
- Career path into training

Managing a Retail Career

To facilitate career conversations, we suggest a model we have developed that builds on the work of Dave Ulrich and Norm Smallwood in *The Leadership Code* (Harvard Business Press, 2008) that describes four stages in a professional's development.

This model helps HR people facilitate development opportunities for individuals in the organization as well as identify organization-level development gaps in the talent pipeline. (See Figure A.7 for a graphic representation of these stages.)

The career development model helps the professional define his or her career aspirations and understand what is required for high performance at the current job level. It articulates how the stages and the track differ in the tasks that the professionals are expected to perform, in the types of relationships they form, and in the psychological adjustments they must make.

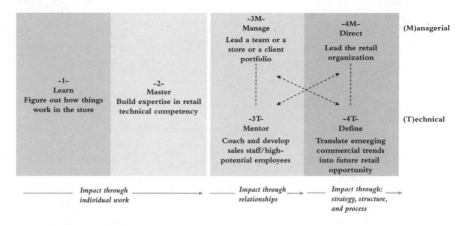

Figure A.7   The Four Retail Stages Model of Development

- To learn, depending on others, how things work in the boutique.
- To master, contributing independently, retail technical knowledge competencies.
- To manage, contributing through others, a team, a store, or a client portfolio.
- To lead, throughout organizational leadership, the retail future development.

Upon the career stages model, we build a specific retail career development framework. It integrates:

- The available retail job categories that currently exist in the luxury organizations.
- The opportunities/possible scenarios people who want to join the retail career may have. (See Figure A.8 for a graphic representation of these stages.)

In addition to these models, and in order to be comprehensive, we have provided examples of a retail career scenario that shows the different stages and opportunities to be handled if one wishes—starting as sales staff—to grow within the boutique staff. (See Figures A.9 and A.10 for a graphic representation of these career scenarios.)

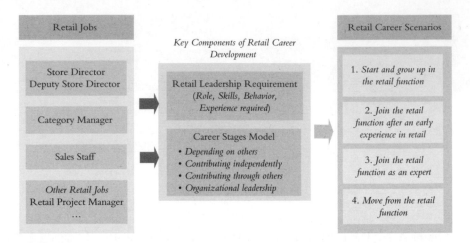

Figure A.8   The Retail Career Development Framework

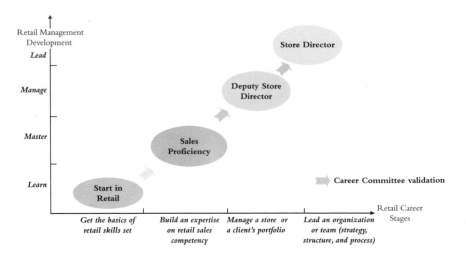

Figure A.9   Retail Career Scenario: Start and Grow Up in the Retail Function

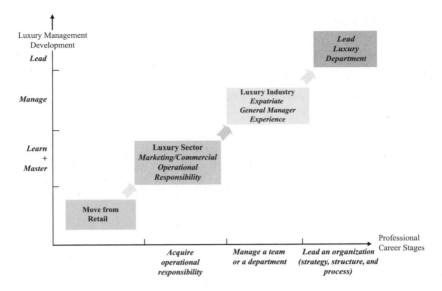

Figure A.10   Retail Career Scenario: Move from the Retail Function

Tool No. 6: Setting Sales Targets

In order to manage sales performance and ensure it is inline with budgets, sales targets are set in a consistent manner at all levels of the retail organization. This sets standards of performance and improves performance results at all levels.

1. Once yearly budgets are set, they are cascaded and communicated down to the store manager level.
2. Sales targets are set monthly for cluster managers and store managers, and are to be reviewed monthly (the first month's sales target should correspond to the first month's sales budget).
3. Sales targets for sales consultants are set monthly, weekly, and daily, and are to be reviewed weekly. Managers should use the following forms for this purpose:
   • Staff Daily/Weekly Performance Forms
   • Store Daily Target Forms
4. Sales consultants can also track their own sales and analyze their proactive sales by using the forms in their client books:

- Daily Sales Tracking Sheet
- Monthly Sales Tracking Sheet

5. Targets and action plans are reviewed monthly (weekly for sales consultants) and feedback is provided.
6. Sales results are tracked and comments are noted in the sales comments diary.

Tool No. 7: Designing a Fair Retail Compensation System

Three key principles must be kept in mind:

1. Redefining total rewards.

    The intent is that the brand's retail organization acknowledges the importance of reward programs in achieving business goals and understands that it encompasses a significant part of the overall value proposition that the employer offers to the employee. It should be a total package that includes:
    - Compensation, including base pay, short-term incentives, and long-term incentives
    - Benefits, including health, retirement, and pension
    - Careers, including training and development, lateral moves, stretch assignments, and career incentives; in short, the future value of staying with an organization

    The total reward package is a key tool for influencing employee behavior and attitudes, especially when a shift in business strategy requires behavior to change.

2. Balancing three perspectives.

    Balance requires attention to three distinct yet interrelated perspectives: the employer's, the employee's, and the cost perspective (see Figure A.11).

3. Measuring return on investment.

    A retail organization should answer critical questions that will help direct labor investments to maximize value.

Build a Fair and Clear Compensation System When designing effective reward systems for retail, the HR department and the executive committee should focus on four key principles.

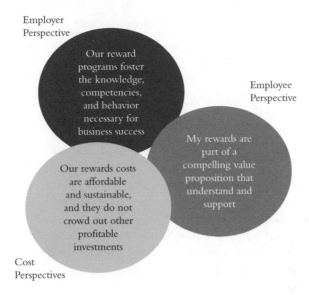

Employer
Perspective

Our reward
programs foster
the knowledge,
competencies,
and behavior
necessary for
business success

Employee
Perspective

My rewards are
part of a
compelling value
proposition that
understand and
support

Our rewards costs
are affordable
and sustainable,
and they do not
crowd out other
profitable
investments

Cost
Perspectives

Figure A.11 Balancing Employer, Employee, and Cost Perspectives

Key Principle 1: Align all components of the compensation system with top-line organizational objectives (see Figure A.12).

- Increase the amount of base pay by ending individual financial incentives (that go by the name "*eat what you kill*") since they push sales consultants to close transactions at any cost while treating team members and marginal clients in a destructive way (this should be adapted to acknowledge regional practices).
- Treat short-term incentives differently by relating them to the key drivers of the retail business, such as employee performance, critical behavior, customer data collection, and customer data use.
- Promote team incentives related to the daily management of store operations in order to motivate individuals to collaborate rather than to compete, and measure collective performance.
- Adjust base pay and incentives in each of the retail stages of development.
- Provide reward and recognition solutions such as participation in highly visible projects, participation in a mentoring program, attending a prestigious event.

Key Principle 2: Balance the way to reward performance according to market and business timing (see Figures A.13 and A.14).

Critical Questions	Suggested KPI for Retail
What attributes, experience, and behavior does the retail actually reward?	*Retail technical skills: "critical behaviors" for clientele; "customer data use," sales performance: "high ticket sales," negotiation skills*
What job progressions and assignments lead clearly to successful employee performance?	*Retail stages of development: "fast tracker," apprenticeship*
What are the business consequences of these employee performance gains?	*Talent departure ratio, employee engagement climate, employee climate perception, customer satisfaction*
Which parts of the rewards package do retail employees truly value, as shown by their actions rather than their words?	*Brand awareness importance, craftsmanship experience, valuable new client sales, team versus individual incentives*
Which retail employee segments contribute the most to business value, and how?	*Store director, sales expert, other*

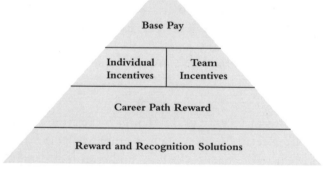

Figure A.12　Five Components of the Retail Compensation Package

Key Principle 3: Conduct positive quarterly, mid-year, and end-of-year reviews to keep people on the business track. This is traditionally done in all organizations, but not necessarily for sales consultants. We contend it should be done for them too (see the Sales Consultant Assessment Form in Toolbox No. 4).

Key Principle 4: Benchmark your compensation system against best-in-class companies that address the same clientele (luxury competitors, private banking, for example).

This example of engineering a retail career package illustrates how to integrate the four key principles and how to find the right balance between each and every element.

1. The *risk of discontinuity* between the candidate and the brand regarding pay and incentives along the career path. A misunderstanding on this matter could represent a serious problem for the company and result in a significant financial loss.
2. The *retail objectives* are those defined in the career development stages. It is important to check and to validate each job progression with the help of a career committee.
3. The *career opportunities* concern job progression, specific training development, and other relevant rewards that maintain employees' motivation, keep them on the business track and help them prepare for the future.
4. The *compensation system components* represent the job career progression, balancing the importance of the base pay, the individual and team performances, and the contribution of the management role.

Tool No. 8: Grooming Guidelines for Women

Introduction

Every employee's appearance and grooming contributes to a brand's distinctive style. Therefore, appearance and grooming standards, as

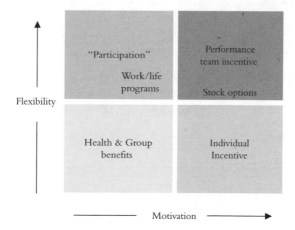

Figure A.13   Mapping of Some Components: Flexibility × Motivation

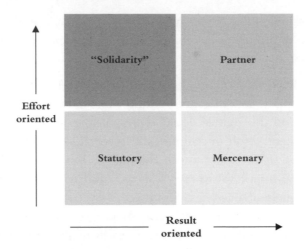

Figure A.14   Four Ways to Reward Performance

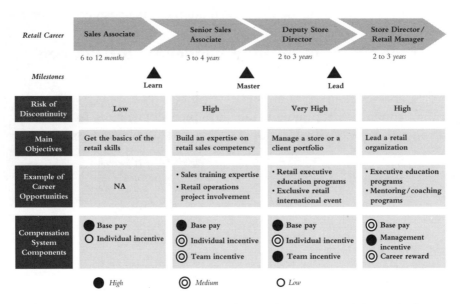

Figure A.15   Integrating the Four Key Principles into a Retail Career Package

well as uniforms, have been developed so that clients will be aware of this style.

Each brand will have its own grooming guidelines: These are defined so as to be consistent with the brand values. Adherence by the sales staff to standards of grooming and dress reflects their attitude toward both clients and merchandise.

The following grooming standards are a possible example:

Hair
- Wear hair in neat, classic styles, not blown out or teased
- No hairpieces or wigs
- Hair accessories to be limited to neutral barrettes and bands
- No scrunchies, headbands, banana clips, or brightly colored barrettes or bands
- No unnatural hair color

Makeup
- Foundation:
  - Minimal, in natural skin tones
- Eyes:
  - Eye shadow in neutral, understated tones
  - Minimal eyeliner and mascara
  - No heavily penciled eyebrows
- Lips:
  - Understated lip color
  - No contrasting lip liner
- Nails:
  - Clear or skin-toned nail polish, one color only
  - Nails no longer than 5 mm.
  - No appliqués or jewelry

Accessories
- Earrings:
  - Small, stud styles only
  - No drop or hoop hearings
- Necklace:
  - Small, single-drop styles on very thin, single-strand chains
  - Single-strand pearl necklaces
  - No medallions or distracting necklaces

- Pierced ears to be limited to one piercing per earlobe
- No brooches or pins
- Rings and bracelets should not distract from the merchandise being handled
- Tattoos are to be avoided
- Piercings of any kind other than in earlobes should not be visible

Note:
- All employees should practice daily personal hygiene.
- Comments on an employee's personal appearance, grooming, and hygiene should be avoided except in appropriate, private consultations with a supervisor.
- Employees are reminded that directives on wardrobe and grooming are not personal and are given to maintain the quality of the company's visual standards.

Tool No. 9: Global Business Ethics

Purpose of Global Business Ethics

The current development of corporate social responsibility standards and reports has been anticipated by numerous luxury brands: They have developed business ethics regulations to ensure that all company employees are committed to the highest standards of ethical and legal conduct wherever they do business. This applies to all employees of a luxury brand, including sales staff.

Such procedures are developed to exclude risks for the corporation resulting from nonethical behavior. A global ethics committee is often set up to enforce such rules.

An Example It is the role of all employees at any level to ensure that business is conducted in the appropriate way, and that non ethical behavior is reported to their manager and to the global business ethics committee (GBEC).

Scope of the Procedure The following issues will be handled by this procedure:

- Purchasing of goods or services
- Handling "conflicts of interest"
- Dealing with gifts, presents, or compensation from competitors or suppliers (current and potential).
- Dealing with governmental officials requesting gifts/presents/ money from company.
- Awareness of working conditions not meeting legal requirements.
- Awareness of dubious financial transactions.
- Dealing with hostile attempts from competitors to get information on company.
- What to do if an employee detects this kind of unethical behavior from a colleague or a superior.

Procedure
Purchasing of goods/services

While buying goods or services from possible suppliers, any employee, entitled to make agreements with suppliers (see legal authorizations), will always ensure to work in an independent and neutral position toward all suppliers.

He/she will always check at least two offers from possible suppliers before taking any decision on the purchase. Both offers should be stored in a Purchase File.

In case a unique supplier is available, the employee will contact a member of the GBE Committee. The GBEC will decide and sign for their decision to buy a good/service from this unique supplier.

Handling "conflicts of interest"

If an employee (or his family or close friends) directly or indirectly own a substantial interest (that is, more than 5 percent of the company's assets) in a company doing (or seeking to do) business with the company, this should be reported up front in writing to the GBE Committee.

Only once the GBEC and the involved line manager have evaluated the situation can a decision be made concerning the cooperation with this company.

Dealing with gifts, presents, or compensation from competitors or suppliers (current or potential)

If an employee, or any family member or close personal friend, is offered gifts, presents, or compensation from any company or person that does (or seeks to do) business with the brand, this should be reported immediately to the Department Head or Regional CEO and the GBE Committee.

Any employee receiving gifts or entertainment worth over . . . from any single person or business that does (or seeks to do) business with the company, or is in competition with the company, should be immediately reported to the Department Head or Regional CEO and the GBE Committee.

The definition of "gift" will depend on the current business practices in each region (e.g., current standards in Japan are different from those of the United States). In case of discussion the members of the GBE Committee will jointly decide.

Employees who are invited for professional reasons by suppliers/ customers or stakeholders of the company, can accept being hosted in a hotel at "reasonable" expenses, in order to guarantee their "neutral attitude." This is common business practice.

Material advantages of a value higher than . . . are not acceptable.

Examples:
- Product presentations by suppliers, during one week, partner included, in a luxury hotel
- Vacation/long weekends offered by suppliers
- Cash money hidden in a gift
- Car offered to the partner of the employee for private use
- Credit cards/gasoline cards offered
- Study costs paid to children of an employee
- Annual membership in a club paid by a supplier, and so forth

Dealing with questions from governmental officials requesting gift/presents/money from the company

Any question coming from any governmental official to any employee should be notified to the members of the GBE Committee. In accordance with our own standards, and the regional business standards, the GBE Committee will take an appropriate decision on the issue.

Awareness of working conditions not meeting legal requirements

Any employee who discovers labor situations not meeting legal requirements or that can be considered as unethical or harassment of any kind, must inform all members of the GBE Committee.

Appropriate actions will be taken by the GBE Committee to eliminate these situations.

Awareness of doubtful financial transactions

Any awareness of any doubtful financial transaction issued internally in the company by an employee, who could hurt the corporation's interests, should be reported immediately to the GBE Committee.

Dealing with hostile attempts from competitors to get information on the company

If a third party (supplier/competitor, etc.) tries to get confidential information in an unethical way from an employee at any level, the GBE Committee should be informed immediately in order to take the appropriate actions to prevent this information leaving the company.

What is to be done if an employee detects this kind of unethical behavior from a colleague or a superior?

If an employee, at any level in the organization, has proof of an unethical behavior of a colleague or a superior, the person should inform all GBE Committee members, to ensure confidentiality.

The GBE Committee will protect the informing employee's privacy while handling the case and will decide on appropriate corrective actions.

Fernie, J., C. M. Moore, and A. Lawrie. "A Tale of Two Cities: An Examination of Fashion Designer Retailing within London and New York." *Journal of Product & Brand Management* 7, no. 5 (1998).

Fionda, A. M., and C. M. Moore. "The Anatomy of the Luxury Fashion Brand." *Brand Management* 16, no. 5/6 (2009).

Frankel, A. *Punching In.* Collins, 2007.

Gist, R. E. *Retailing Concept and Decision.* New York: John Wiley & Sons, 1968.

Gutsatz, M. "Luxe Populi / Developing Luxury Brands." July 2002 (unpublished).

Harvard Design School Guide to Shopping. Taschen: Köln, 2001.

Hichman, D., and E. Marze. *The Affluent Consumer: Marketing and Selling the Luxury Style.* New York: Praeger, 2006.

Hsieh, T. *Delivering Happiness: A Path to Profits, Passion, and Purpose.* New York: Business Plus, 2010.

Jones, Lang Lasalle. Real Estate Transparency index, 2009.

Keller, Ed. "Word of Mouth Marketing." ARF, September 2007.

Koolhaas, Rem. *Projects for Prada, Part 1.* Milan: Fondazione Prada.

Kozinets, Rem. "E-Tribalized Marketing? The Strategic Implications of Virtual Communities of Consumption." *European Management Journal* (June 1999).

Leadbetter, J. *Sales and Service Excellence: How to Stand Out from the Crowd.* Management Books, 2000, 2011.

Lent, R., and G. Tour. *Selling Luxury.* Hoboken, NJ: John Wiley & Sons, 2009.

Levy, Michael, and Barton Weitz. *Retailing Management.* New York: McGraw-Hill Irwin, 2004.

Luxury Digital IQ Report. L2, 2010.

McKinsey & Company. "The Promise of Multi-Channel Retailing." 2010.

Michman, R. D., and E. M. Mazze. *The Affluent Consumer: Marketing and Selling the Luxury Lifestyle.* Westport, CT: Praeger, 2006.

Moore, C., et al. "Flagship Stores as a Market Entry Method: The Perspective of Luxury Fashion Retailing." *European Journal of Marketing* 44, no. 1/2 (2010).

Nayar, V. *Employees First—Customers Second.* Harvard Business Press, 2010.

Oechsli, M. *The Art of Selling the Affluent: How to Attract, Service and Retain Wealthy Customers and Clients for Life.* Hoboken, NJ: John Wiley & Sons, 2004.

Okonwo, U. *Luxury on Line.* New York: Palgrave Macmillan, 2008.

Palmer, A. "Customer Experience Management: A Critical Review of an Emerging Idea." *Journal of Services Marketing* 24, no. 3 (2010): 196–208.

Reichheld, F. F. "The One Number You Need to Grow." *Harvard Business Review* (December 2003).

Rosenthal, Peter, and Lars David Koller. *Faszination, Visual Merchandising.* Deutscher Fachverlag, 2002.

Sacerdote, E. *La strategia retail nella mode e nel lusso.* Milan: Franco Angeli, 2007.

Shaw, C. *The DNA of Customer Experience.* Palgrave Macmillan, 2007.

Spector, R., and P. McCarthy. *The Nordstrom Way to Customer Service Excellence.* Hoboken, NJ: John Wiley & Sons, 2005.

Stanley, T. J. *Selling to the Affluent.* New York: McGraw-Hill, 1991.

Taubman, Alfred. *Threshold Resistance: The Extraordinary Career of a Luxury Retailing Pioneer.* New York: HarperCollins, 2007.

Thomas, D. *Deluxe: How Luxury Lost Its Luster.* New York: Penguin Press, 2007.

Twitchell, J. B. *Living It Up: America's Love Affair with Luxury.* New York: Columbia University Press, 2002.

Uncles, M. D., G. R. Dowling, and K. Hammond. "Customer Loyalty and Customer Loyalty Programs." *Journal of Consumer Marketing* 20, no. 4 (2003).

Underhill, Paco. *Why We Buy: The Science of Shopping.* New York: Simon & Schuster, 1999.

Value Retail News, November 2009.

Wetpaint & Altimeter Group, "The World's Most Valuable Brands: Who's Most Engaged?" July 2009.

Willeman, A., and M. Jary. *Retail Power Plays.* New York: New York University Press, 1997.

Winters, Arthur A., Peggy Fincher Winters, and Carole Paul. *Brandstand: Strategies for Retail Brand Building.* New York: Visual Reference Publications, 2003.

About the Authors

Michel Chevalier is an expert in luxury brand management and in retailing.

He has worked in the United States, Japan, China, Latin America, and several countries in Europe. He was Executive Vice President of Bluebell Asia Ltd., a group that then directly operated 180 retail stores in Asia. He also managed the Paco Rabanne perfumes and the Paco Rabanne fashion companies.

He is now a consultant with EIM in Paris and a visiting professor of Luxury Marketing and Retailing at HEC and University Paris Dauphine in Paris. He also teaches at Instituto de Empresa in Madrid, Universita Cattolica di Milano, and Lorange Institute in Zurich.

A graduate of HEC, Michel Chevalier holds an MBA and a DBA from Harvard Business School.

He is the author of *Luxury Brand Management* with coauthor Gérald Mazzalovo and *Luxury China* with coauthor Pierre-Xiao Lu, both published by John Wiley & Sons.

Michel Gutsatz is an international expert in luxury brand management, based in Paris.

Founder of The Scriptorium Company, a Brand Strategy Agency, he advises investment funds, luxury brands, and retailers in Europe, China, and the United States. He is a renowned speaker at international conferences on branding, luxury, and beauty.

He is currently Director of MBAs at Euromed Management and a visiting professor, teaching brand management and luxury retailing, at major international business schools.

Prior to that, Michel was managing director of an image strategy agency and human resources and internal communication director of the Bally Group in Switzerland.

Michel also created and developed the MBA in International Luxury Brand Management at ESSEC Business School, through partnerships with L'Oréal, LVMH, The Estée Lauder Companies, Cartier, Montblanc, Escada, Ermenegildo Zegna, and Firmenich.

Michel holds a PhD in Economics.

His blog BrandWatch at www.michelgutsatz.com is now a reference in brand strategy.

Index